DISCARDED

D1220708

Contents

Illustrations

Preface

How should a cross-cultural study of modernity proceed? The history of colonialism has made "modernity" a global phenomenon. But what exactly is meant by that statement? Does it imply that modernity arose as a discrete set of practices in the West and then was simply mimicked in the rest of the world? Does it mean that certain places remain that still need to arrive at this selfsame identity—or, to the contrary, that the globe has congealed into transnational homogeneity? Finally, should we think of modernity as indigenous practices established within discrete cultures with their own histories?

These questions arose for me in the context of two and a half years of anthropological fieldwork in China from the mid-1980s to the early 1990s. I had gone to study post-Mao transformations in social life, with a particular interest in their effects on women. As is often the case, I found something I had not quite been looking for but that, in the end, made sense out of what I was seeking. This was the pervasive concern with modernity. "Modernity" was something that many people from all walks of life felt passionately moved to talk about and debate. This radical moment of transition away from Maoist socialism opened up a public space for people to create new visions about what they wanted for China's future. In discussions that ranged from highly academic exchanges to idle chatting on the streets, the people I met held forth with their strong views on "modernization," "development," "the West," "backwardness," and "progress." Intellectual friends argued about free-market economics with me, while others commented on where they thought China stood on the road toward wealth and power. I remember vividly the day an elderly shoe repairman, who had set up his small workbench right out on the street, insisted on expressing his views to me on these matters while he repaired the leather strap on my bag. It was then that I began to pay more attention to what people meant by "modernity."

These engaged discussions have led me to propose a cross-cultural approach to modernity that, as against the aforementioned notions, treats it as a located cultural imaginary, arising from and perpetuating relations of difference across an East-West divide. I am most interested in the "other" modernities necessarily produced by those who have been the objects of the world history of the West. These other modernities are neither merely local enactments nor simply examples of a universal model. They are forced cross-cultural translations of various projects of science and management called modernity. For some years now, I have followed with interest a newly invigorated anthropology of modernity. I have been struck by two implicit assumptions: that modernity arises autonomously within nation-states and that modernity leads to the same practices and effects everywhere one finds it. In highlighting the cultural locations in modernity as variously imagined, I hope to make it possible to rethink these assumptions.

This study asks several basic questions: How does the passion to pursue modernity continue to invigorate cultural imaginations in places such as China, a country that has been the object of colonial knowledge but is also a subject of a strong socialist state? How might one grasp both the mimicry involved in modern projects and the heterogeneity that results from that mimicry? What of the specificities of cultural histories made within the normalizing differences of East versus West? What are the contours of power, agency, and subjectivity in imaginaries of modernity?

In addressing some of these questions, I intend to draw attention to several aspects of modernity that seem to have been overlooked of late. These include its discursive construction within unequal intersections of global imaginations, the way modernity points to a space of deferred desires, modernity's centrality in constituting otherness, the heterogeneity of projects carried out in its name, and the gaps and disjunctures that unsettle its "realness." The promise in these areas of inquiry lies in their potential for opening out the fissures and unearthing the power enacted in the name of modernity. Such exploration requires a nuanced theory of culture, one that neither makes of culture a fixed substance nor throws out the concept altogether. This project is imperative in light of the nexus of entangled transformations of the local and the global in the late twentieth century. We must learn to think creatively about how to challenge neoliberal ideologies—one might say enchantments—of the free-market economy of late-twentieth-century capitalism. East Asia and postsocialist countries figure centrally in these transitions. One version of this enchantment, shared by the likes of Samuel Huntington (1996) and the Singapore government, is that an Asian civilizational way of thinking is responsible for capitalist successes in Asia. On the other side, of course, remains the older, rationalist vision that capitalism is fundamentally a system that operates along narrow economic lines, inevitably pulling postsocialist countries into its purview. In place of these assumptions that reinvigorate images of cultural homogeneity or thrust meaningful struggles to the sidelines of social life, we need an approach to culture that traces how it gets invoked and toward what ends, while also analyzing its lived realities where meaningful struggles over a sustained and fulfilling life are recognized as existing at the heart of these local/global processes.

In this ethnographic study, I explore the overlapping projects of modernity that the Chinese state has pursued since the socialist revolution. I conducted my fieldwork in the city of Hangzhou from September 1984 to August 1986 and visited the same people again in the winter of 1991. Stories that people told me of their lives after the 1949 revolution led me to realize the critical role that history and memory play in these projects. Forgetting and remembering the socialist past unsettled the postsocialist allegories of modernity. I thus tack back and forth between past cultural imaginings and their contested reconstruction in the present. While I generally agree with Foucault that invocations of modernity signal a radical break with previous forms of power, I nonetheless found that when memories are involved, the rupture is not as clean as Foucault theorized. My concern is, then, with the complexities of agency, history, and subjectivity in overlapping worlds of power and knowledge produced in the name of modernity.

Given the role that women have played in colonial knowledge of the other, it should be no surprise that matters pertaining to gender have been central to the Chinese state's successive imaginaries of modernity. Gender conceptions, relations, and practices thus receive a great deal of my attention, and they illuminate the forgetting and remembering that continue to intertwine socialism with postsocialism. Certainly my argument should not be mistaken for the idea that China has still not arrived at the selfsame modernity as the West. Rather, I want to break open this site of modernity to understand not only how it continues to normalize neocolonial relations of difference but also how modernity's disjunctures provide room for challenging its power.

The book is divided into three sections. In the first, "Re-Collecting History," I explore the multiple meanings of "women's liberation" that were part of the early project of socialist modernity. These meanings also have multiple resonances over time. For members of the oldest cohort, the memories of the their past turn into nostalgia when set against their marginalization in the present. The double-edged nature of their stories helps me illuminate and redefine cross-cultural feminisms as well as the writing of history in anthropology. The second section, "Unsettling Memories," opens with a story of one woman who was beaten during the Cultural Revolution. Her story unsettles hegemonic narratives intended to provide a sense of resolution about experiences in the Cultural Revolution. I continue by arguing that the project of modernity relevant to that period, a continuous and revolutionary challenge to authority, lives on in the practices of those who came of age with the Cultural Revolution even as they reject the specific politics of Maoism. This cohort continues to engage with and unsettle authoritative knowledge. In the final section, "Space and Subjectivity," I turn to the young women who have been most fully formed within current post-Mao visions of reaching modernity, tracing state practices that encourage them to achieve a "natural" feminine identity. These young women both adhere to and exceed normative gender constraints. Throughout, I portray the resourceful imaginations of women who, as subaltern workers, helped me understand the complex unpredictabilities and creative openings in a world saturated with power.

A word about names. I have changed the names and a few details about the lives of the people I discuss. In doing so, I have been most concerned to protect them from official harassment. However, I have also followed the practice of naming people in relational terms. I use *shifu*, meaning "master worker," after the last name as a term for senior workers. I use *xiao* and *lao*, meaning "little" and "old," respectively, in front of last names as terms of familiarity people used to place themselves in relationship to me. *Zhuren* and *Changzhang* are official titles, placed after last names, meaning "director" and "factory director," respectively.

The length of time it has taken me to finish this book means that the trail of acknowledgments could wrap itself around the globe. The Committee on Scholarly Communication with China and a faculty grant from the Massachusetts Institute of Technology made possible my field research in China. The writing was supported by a postdoctoral fellowship from the Center for Chinese Studies at the University of California, Berkeley; a fellowship from the American Council for Learned Societies; a quarter sabbatical at the Humanities Research Institute, University of California, Irvine; and teaching relief at my home institution at the University of California, Santa Cruz. I am grateful to all of these sources for their generous support.

I thank numerous friends, teachers, and colleagues who contributed to the intellectual development reflected in this book. Jerome Grieder and Eric Widmer first stimulated my interest in Chinese history as an undergraduate. The generosity and guidance of Sylvia Yanagisako, Jane Collier, Donald Donham, and G. William Skinner encouraged me to explore the diversity of knowledge that goes under the rubric of anthropology. Chen Li, president emeritus of Hangzhou University, gave me mentorship I hardly deserved and sustained my project in China. I am deeply grateful to many who have read my work or discussed it with me. Kerry Walk served as my writing angel. Without her, my pen might never have stayed on the paper. Graciela Trevisan tried to lend me her ability to discern the magical and absurd qualities of social life. Dorinne Kondo, my writing partner, gave unfailingly her emotional shoulder and her intellectual sensitivity. Her comradely encouragement spurred me on. I owe a great deal to Jacqueline Brown, Gail Hershatter, Anna Tsing, and Sylvia Yanagisako, whose creative, critical, and close engagement with my project has improved it immeasurably. Ann Anagnost, Dorinne Kondo, and Angela Zito gave the manuscript a thorough scrutiny. I thank them for their numerous insightful suggestions for revision. The participants in the Colonialism and Modernity in East Asia Seminar at the Humanities Research Institute—Yoko Arisaka, Chungmoo Choi, James Fujii, Takashi Fujitani, Gail Hershatter, Theodore Huters, Amie Parry, Shu-mei Shih, Miriam Silverberg, and Lisa Yoneyama—offered the kind of intellectual companionship that makes writing pleasurable. I thank others who offered stimulating comments on individual chapters or who engaged in conversations with me about the themes in the book: Kathleen Biddick, Dai Jinhua, Hu Ying, Sandra Joshel, Rachel Lanzerotti, Lydia Liu, and Erica Marcus. The writing benefited from the dynamic intellectual atmosphere that my colleagues and students at the University of California, Santa Cruz, have provided. I would also like to thank Sheila Levine and Laura Driussi, my editors at the University of California Press, for their unfailing support and patience. Alice Falk performed the Herculean task of copyediting; my stubbornness alone is responsible for any awkwardness remaining in the prose. I owe my deepest debts to the people among whom I lived in China, whose names I have withheld; to my partner Graciela, who sustained me throughout; and to my parents, Jacqueline Rofel Berger and Herschel Rofel, who taught me to refuse the dangerous enticements of American solipsism. I regret that my father passed away long before he could see the path on which I have embarked.

Introduction

MODERNITY AND ITS DISCREPANT DESIRES

The deadly cold of winter had descended on Hangzhou. The sky was a wan yellow on the days it did not rain, and the biting air infiltrated every pore of my skin. The numbing weather, however, did nothing to deter the intensity of human activity that filled the streets I bicycled through on my way to and from the Zhenfu Silk Weaving Factory. It was the winter of 1986 and over the past year and a half, the Chinese government had cautiously instituted a set of policies in urban areas, known as economic reform. They were part of the "Four Modernizations"[1] through which the state hoped to pull China out of the Maoist era and into a position of leadership in the new world order. I lived in the university end of town, just north of the famous West Lake, whose serene beauty had inspired much of classical Chinese painting and now attracted a steady stream of tourists, both domestic and foreign. Elegant parasol trees imported earlier in the century from France shaded the spacious streets at this end of town. Behind them, at a distance from the road, stood new high-rise apartment buildings with the latest amenities. Married professors and cadres associated with the two major universities resided in them. Farther down, parklike estates rimmed the lake's perimeter. They had once belonged to the elite, before the socialist revolution. Since the revolution, army cadres and their families had moved in. It was said (discreetly) that Lin Biao, the man designated to succeed Mao but accused of plotting against him during the Cultural Revolution, had once occupied the mansion on the south side of the lake that currently served as a three-star hotel for foreigners.

Each morning, I left this area of town behind, riding my bicycle out the sequestered gate of the university guest house for foreigners, through the bus-tling "free market" that was edging out the languishing state-run market ad-jacent to it. The free market was filled with people from the countryside selling live fish and chickens, mounds of tangerines and apples, and an assortment of beancurd products and vegetables. I rode on down the street past tentative neon signs of newly emerging cafes that stayed open late into the night. Skirting the east side of the lake, I made my way through the downtown area, alive with numerous small shops overflowing with consumer goods; the free market in clothing, where mainly young men sold the latest fashions; and elaborate hotels for foreigners, which most Chinese were forbidden to enter. Joining the wheel-to-wheel bicycle traffic of people on their way to work, I wended my way over to the east end of town, to the long-established working-class neighborhood where the silk factories are located.

The east end of town was a maze of narrow, dense streets. Bicyclists and buses jostled with laborers pulling or pedaling carts filled with everything from concrete slabs to new refrigerators and even elderly parents. Zhenfu was located inconspicuously among winding side alleys filled with the one-story, often one-room homes so characteristic of this neighborhood, with their sloping gray-tiled roofs and whitewashed plaster over brick. In this area of town, I could lose myself in the crush of people and almost forget I was a foreigner. Life spilled out of cramped homes onto the street. Women on their day off or already retired in-variably sat out on the sidewalk to air the family commode, hang the wash, or knit, while older men played a leisurely game of chess or leaned against the house to sleep under the sun. Later in the afternoon, schoolchildren pulled their desks out on the sidewalk to catch the last rays of light. But in the mornings, workers crowded around the corner food stalls, gulping down beancurd soup and deep-fried crullers before heading off to work.

The Zhenfu Silk Weaving Factory stood imposingly at the end of one such alley. Occupying the space of several square city blocks, it was walled off from the neighborhood. Yet the low family dwellings, many of which had served as household workshops before the revolution, still hugged the wall, as if not want-ing those inside to forget their history. Even before I reached its magisterial gate, the ubiquitous and never-ending hum of the looms and spinning machines an-nounced Zhenfu's location. Young women and men crowded the entrance, hur-riedly dismounting from their bicycles to begin their morning shift. Just beyond the entrance, above their heads, a huge red banner proclaimed: "I love Zhenfu and devote myself to the Four Modernizations."

This book addresses the cultural politics of modernity in the late twentieth century. It suggests how modernity is imagined, pursued, and experienced not in the Euro-American centers that have conventionally been designated as the preeminent origins of modernity but rather in those places marked by a deferred relationship to modernity. My argument goes against the grain of much recent anthropology of modernity: I propose that modernity persists as an imaginary and continuously shifting site of global/local claims, commitments, and knowledge, forged within uneven dialogues about the place of those who move in and out of categories of otherness. By opening out the imaginary space of modernity we pay attention to its gaps, fissures, and instabilities, those moments when "others" unsettle forms of domination enacted in the name of modernity.[2] This space is filled with culturally positioned projects formed within intersecting global imaginations.

To understand the passion with which modernity is pursued by people who have been made to live in a decentered relationship to Europe and the United States—and, in the case of China, also to Japan—we must recognize specific histories of colonialism and socialism, as well as the contours of late-twentieth-century global political and cultural economies. Ethnography captures these specificities. The significance placed on ethnographic specificity does not merely reflect a disciplinary conceit. It also makes possible a challenge to current theories both of modernity and of global capitalism.

What follows thus engages in ethnographic theorizing about the imaginary of modernity in China in the postsocialist era, as the country makes an uneven and highly contestatory transition to capitalism. From the mid-1980s through the mid-1990s, people in China witnessed a moment of vivid social transformation, in which both the future and the past were matters of explicit debate and sources of highly articulate hopes, desires, and frustrations. I highlight this social process from the perspective of those made into subalterns in China in relation to the pursuit of modernity. "Subaltern" here refers to a category of subjectivity that represents the underside of power. I also recognize that those who identify with or participate in the discursive space constructed as subaltern do so through and not outside of relations of power.[3] These people actively engage their subalternity by challenging and reinterpreting, even as they embrace and are shaped by, the post-Mao vision of modernity. In so doing they fracture, at times inadvertently, the apparently seamless "real" of modernity.

Arguments about femininity and masculinity, and their articulation with diverse social practices, have figured centrally in post-Mao modernity. Gender thus necessarily comes to the fore of my analysis: rather than being one factor to be considered in or added to discourses of modernity, it is formative of relations of power in visions of what constitutes modernity. By "gender," I mean contingent, nonfoundational differentiations of femininity and masculinity that are mapped onto social relations and bodies, defining the nexus of power/knowledge that permeates social life. Gender categories are not unified or stable but subject to negotiation, conflict, and change. I thus treat gender as compelled through, rather than parallel with, other forms of difference, including class, race, and age—or, more precisely, the formation of cohorts based on successive political mobilizations.

In post-Mao China, three distinctive cohorts of women workers encountered one another as they each developed what Paul Gilroy (1993), after W. E. B. Du Bois, has called a "double consciousness" of being in but not of modernity. In disparate ways marked by history, these cohorts maneuvered to position themselves in relation to several overlapping processes in the post-Mao vision of modernity. They experienced disjunctures in their genealogies and memories about political convictions, as the contours of state power changed and China entered into networks of transnational capital. The overlapping meanings of "political convictions" are suggestive, because they point to a dynamic approach to modernity. All of these meanings—beliefs in politics and economics, the discursive production of believing subjects, and the sentencing and judgment people undergo for those beliefs—taken together, allude to ruptures within socialist and postsocialist versions of modernity.[4] Accordingly, in this book I consider disjunctures that reveal what we might think of as allegories of modernity. I pursue the ways that the active creation of cultural forms is possible even under states with well-developed mechanisms for social control.

Since at least the time of the Southern Song dynasty in the twelfth and thirteenth centuries when it served as the imperial capital, Hangzhou has been a primary center of silk production. During the imperium, the elite reserved for themselves the privilege of wearing silk. Silk thus furnished a vital sign of Chinese culture or, more accurately, of imperial civilization. From the late nineteenth century on, silk pulled Hangzhou into a global cultural and political economy, as the material became one of China's major exports. Today, China exports 90 percent of the world's output of raw silk and 40 percent of its silk fabrics (China Daily, *25 March 1985). Zhenfu is one of Hangzhou's major export factories. Over twenty-five hundred workers labor there.*

Zhenfu's Number 3 silk-weaving shop was kept dim so that weavers could discern mistakes in the fine mesh of the weave. Shades covered the tall windows of the cavernous room to block the glare of the sun. Only one bright bulb hung precariously over each of the several hundred looms. These iron jacquard looms were oddly beautiful, as the rows of bulbs threw off a shimmery light onto the thousands of translucent silk yarns in the warp. Their beauty was enhanced by the intricately patterned silk quilt covers emerging from within the looms; used throughout China in marriage dowries, these quilts featured their gay greens and reds of double phoenixes symbolizing a long life for the couple.

But the deafening cacophony of shuttles pounding furiously back and forth across these machines spoke loudly of production quotas, pulling the women and few men who worked in the shop to cleave to their assigned four looms — recently doubled from two — ever watchful for breaks in the delicate silk. Mistakes were the border between workers and machine, where the past of old looms and the present of workers jarred into strained efficiency, and the meaning of productivity became caught in the fissures of post-Mao economic reform. Most weavers hovered over their looms even during mealtimes, so they might meet their daily quotas. I followed Qiu Shifu, the assistant shift leader, as she painstakingly mended the tears in the warp or pulled out faulty weaving.

Amid the hard work, there were subtle refusals. The younger women weavers wandered briefly away from their looms to visit one another, while the young men, inveterate chain smokers, took regular cigarette breaks in the tiny office off the shop floor. One machine repairer liked to flirt with the young women weavers, as did the floor sweeper, who tried to get them to go dancing in the evenings at the newly opened clubs.

Tourists regularly passed through a neighboring silk factory to gaze at the "process of silk making" ("here the cocoons are sorted, there the yarn is spun out of the cocoon, here the cloth is woven"), a reification of the production process mirrored in the commodity fetishism in the attached silk shop, where tourists hoped to buy Chinese authenticity at third world prices. Workers appeared to be there as adjuncts to help the process along and to supply a more "human" touch to the tourists' silk. Zhenfu, in contrast, was not a living museum of cultural artifacts.

In Zhenfu's weft preparation shop, Xiao Ma, the energetic young shift leader, led me on her brisk inspection rounds. In the prep shop, the noisy hum was less jarring but no less incessant. Row upon row of ring frames and spindles spun ceaselessly and twisted endlessly as women walked back and forth to check for broken silk yarns. Women-machines spun, combined, twisted, and rewound the weft thread in preparation for weaving. In the winter, a thick blanket covered the shop door to insulate the shop, which was slightly heated to keep the silk threads from suffering the biting winter chill. Just inside the door, a torn red poster with faint Cultural Revolution slogans hung neglected and ignored. Overshadowing it was a gigantic production board suspended on the back wall of the shop floor where Mao Zedong's larger-than-life portrait had once stood.

When Xiao Ma wasn't making her rounds, I sat at the table off the shop floor where some of the women, especially those who had entered the factory together during the Cultural Revolution, came to chat during overly long rests. Or I might make my way upstairs to help Xiao Bao, the assistant shift leader who had also come of age during the Cultural Revolution, while away the slow hours. At other times, I walked through the tall forest of machines and searched out the older women, who more discreetly suspended their work activities while remaining near their assigned positions. Still, the steady hum of the machines never ended. Even when Xiao Ma rang the lunch or dinner bell and the shop emptied out, the spools and ring frames continued to spin until the thread ran out. But by that time, the half hour for the meal was usually over.

My interest in the disjunctures of modernity arose during my two and a half years of fieldwork in the mid-1980s and early 1990s among women workers in the silk industry of China's eastern coastal city of Hangzhou, in Zhejiang province. During those years, I found it almost impossible to generalize about the effects of China's latest modernization program on "women" as if they were a homogeneous group.[5] Instead, I found that women who had come of age as workers during different political movements since the socialist revolution held a strong sense of identity as political generations, loosely marked by age, who self-consciously distinguished themselves from one another in terms of their identities as women and their relationships to labor, as well as in their interpretations of how gender and class relations inform China's future. To phrase it in poststructuralist terms, the various social projects trafficking under the sign of advancing modern socialism constituted anew the social categories of "women" and "workers"; thus, those who became subjects through these categories at different historical conjunctures did not necessarily identify with each other.

Indeed, the very idea of generational differences emerges in China simultaneously with the pursuit of modernity. Since the beginning of the twentieth century, the notion that groups of people related horizontally to one another in terms of demarcated periods of linear history has accompanied a quite different cultural notion of vertical ties through kinship. That these groups can be attributed shared experiences and characteristics makes sense only when the modernist idea of progress— of always overcoming and surpassing that which came before—appears and takes hold.

The politics of memory serve as a critical site for creating these differences among women. They bring to the fore the conflicts between forgetting and remembering, as these are entangled in state projects. Post-Mao narratives of modernity explicitly decentered workers, who became icons of all that went wrong with Maoist socialism. Women workers, however, did not negotiate their increasing marginalization uniformly. Their dynamic memories of their shifting relationship to the state and to powerful rhetorics of socialism led to divergent struggles over the meaning of their changing experiences of subalternity. Their commentary and back talk, which tugged at their strongly held desires for China to be modern, led me to question the idea that modernity endures as a unified project that produces a homogeneous form of subjectivity.

The ways that the two oldest cohorts—those who came of age in the first flush of revolutionary activity in the 1950s and those who formed their identity in the violent upheavals of the Cultural Revolution—remembered how they became self-conscious political subjects unsettled the process of naturalizing power in the name of a post-Mao modernity. The youngest cohort, fully formed within the post-Mao era, implicitly challenged the identities of the others, which had made labor and political authority such central sites for configuring gender. This younger generation both embraced the post-Mao imaginary, which naturalizes femininity and masculinity, and at times exceeded its official grasp.

The ruptures in China's successive imaginaries of modernity mark a desire, begun within a history of semicolonialism and repeatedly deferred, to position China as a nation-state that has fully arrived in the selfsame identity as former western colonizers. Indeed, the answer to why the project of modernity presents itself as so compelling in China, why it has been pursued so persistently, lies in the specter of China's exclusion, which serves to construct a Eurocentric universalist modernity. The strength of socialism in China derived, in part, from this history of semicolonialism and the search to make China a vigorous nation-state. This deferred desire lives on, now motivating postsocialist pursuits of wealth and power. It continues to exist in the global transformations resulting from transnational capital, even as so-called Asian capitalism takes center stage. A recurrent historical amnesia in the United States about China's semicolonial past obscures an acknowledgment of this dynamic. By contrast, in China one can hear its echoes not simply in official discourse, with its ongoing critique of the West, but in stories told by those who might in other regards be quite critical of the state.

The Liu family took me into their home at an early moment when my naïveté about political life in China was shattered, leading to a crisis about whom to trust and how to proceed. We were first introduced through Australian students who had come to study under the grandfather, a renowned acupuncturist. He and Liu Bomu, the grandmother, as well as their son and daughter-in-law, accepted what seemed at the time potentially enormous risks to open their home to me whenever I needed succor, warmth, advice, or just a delicious meal. Our friendship was outside of anything related to my formal research project and thus avoided the complications of official concern, usually expressed through individual work units, about intimate interactions with foreigners. No one in the family held any love for the party. From the socialist revolution through the Cultural Revolution they had been targets of criticism and rectification, because of their elite family background and their class status as intellectuals. Now they alternately praised Deng Xiaoping's policy of reform, which involved courting intellectuals, and castigated "those uneducated, uncouth party cadres" for retarding China's progress.

Liu Bomu was a superb storyteller. I was an enthralled audience to her dramatic tales of her experiences as a doctor, or her painful stories of giving birth to thirteen children and losing seven, or her angry reminiscences about the Anti-Japanese War (World War II). One day I asked Liu Bomu to tell me her life's story. I thought it would be wonderful to record, I said. She immediately set her lips tight with disapproval. Her refusal was in the form of another story, though not the one I had asked for: she spoke of two men from America. They were wandering around the back alleys of Hangzhou with their cameras, peering into the most downtrodden, most poverty-stricken scenes in town. What were they going to do with these pictures? she asked rhetorically. I took her story as a warning about the politics of cross-cultural representations and the ways in which China has been made to serve as one of the central markers of those who have not quite reached modernity.

Precisely because they have been the objects of a world history that has enabled the West to distinguish itself as that history's principal subject, people in China and other non-western countries enact modernity in a form that must overcome this historical difference. Their exclusion from modernity can be discerned not merely in past orientalist texts but in current European philosophy (Derrida 1974; Kristeva 1974). I thus begin with an awareness that what gets called modernity in China is neither a purely localized matter nor a mere instantiation of a universal discourse. It exists instead, as I argue below, as a repeatedly deferred enactment marked by discrepant desires that continually replace one another in an effort to achieve material and moral parity with the West. These deferrals reflect cross-cultural translations that Chinese elites and government leaders undertake as "China" continues to represent, for universalizing projects—and theories—of modernity, the formative "outside." The differences, too, mark gaps in the domination of modernity, manifesting its instabilities and thereby providing room to challenge, exceed, and inflect its seeming transparency.

In this approach, I both join and challenge a recently emerging anthropology of modernity.[6] This important and rich literature has developed from critiques of colonial anthropology and its teleological comparisons between the modern West and its nonmodern others. It rejects a still prevalent western mode of imaging that "explains" the inability of third world peoples to invent local futures by citing radical cultural difference. These anthropologists instead have turned a critical eye on the authority of collective projects undertaken in the name of modernity; their new scholarship sees modernity and its troubling effects proliferating everywhere.

What is now meant by this term? Critical theories of modernity highlight the articulation of epistemology, power, and subjectivity. They urge us to reexamine some of modernity's most cherished ideals of freedom and equality. They also convey an implicit assumption that modernity constitutes a unified set of practices, in part because it takes place amid an implosive "global ecumene" (Hannerz 1989; Marcus 1992). Transnationalism thus appears to make modernity a way of experiencing the world as homogenous. As recently employed, the term modernity encompasses the invention of humanism, the secularization of society, and the emergence of technical reason. It is taken to mean a belief in the triumvirate of truth, reason, and progress, whose singular subject for grasping the world in these terms is Man—a subject free of located interests with a will and agency that originates from within himself. In short, it is identified with the European Enlightenment project. Modernity manifests itself in metanarratives such as neoliberalism—and also Marxism—whose emancipatory historiographies assume a telos of a utopia free of power. One finds its positivistic, instrumental, and universalizing morality materialized in bureaucratic mechanisms, capitalist production, and mass media. Modernity further assumes a noncontinuous break with what it constructs as the irrationalities of tradition.

Much of this new anthropology of modernity has been inspired by the writings of Michel Foucault (1979, 1980).[7] For Foucault, modernity ushers in a novel regime of disciplinarity. Far from offering a mode of greater individual freedom and progress, this regime signals an ever more thorough form of domination. Modern disciplinary power distinguishes itself by its political technologies of individuation, subject formation, and biopower. These subtle, nonspectacular technologies produce sovereign subjects who assume responsibility for "self-discipline" through the discursive practices of various institutions (e.g., penal, medical, industrial, educational, psychological), as well as the disciplines of the human sciences. At another register, biopower operates through governance of the social body, in regulating the population's physical and spiritual health, its life and growth. Disciplinary technologies both underlie and are furthered by the triumphs of capitalism. The centrality of the human sciences in disciplinarity reveals how knowledge and truth do not stand on the other side of power, opposed to it. Rather, modern power works its way through the construction of knowledge. Moreover, power exists not merely "out there" in macroinstitutions but in the very formation of bodies and desires, abrogating the distinction between subjectivity and institutions. Modern disciplinary power, then, operates most effectively when self-interested, individuated subjects believe they are most free, and thus it confounds the emancipatory premises of modernity. Put another way, actions we take in the name of individual freedom are figured by and within, rather than externally to, regimes of power.[8]

The anthropology of modernity written in this vein, while it successfully moves us beyond colonial forms of knowledge, inadvertently configures a new set of troubling assumptions. Most prominently, the modernity that emerges appears to be a unified discourse originating autochthonously from within Europe, which is then extracted from that history and given universal application.[9] Spatially, such theories project an even global integration; temporally, they imply progress toward a stage of complete identity that, once achieved, retains a certain ontological stability.[10] This anthropology presumes that the processes of modernity elsewhere have been identical to those in the West, rather than viewing those processes as the effects of a complex cultural production forged within tangled relationships of (neo)colonialism and uneven transnationalism. Paradoxically, then, it reinvigorates a cultural geography of discrete holistic cultures within which modernity appears to develop immanently. If we are to succeed in challenging the dominations of modernity (including universalizing theories about it), we will need a quite different theory of culture, one that does not eviscerate the specificities of cultural practices emergent within histories of intersecting global imaginings.[11]

Such a cultural theory would attend to discursive spaces created within the simultaneous emergence of "local" histories and "global" forms of power. It would notice the unequal relations of power and knowledge across regional, national, and transnational contexts and would highlight processes of contested meanings in specific locations. It would attend to how the moves to domination carried out under the sign of modernity are unstable. It would pay more heed to the porous boundaries that keep discourses of modernity from being a seamless whole. This theory would highlight the challenges wrought by the processes of "othering" that accompany the reiterative regulations (Butler 1993) of modernity and the modern production of subalterns and their submerged presence, which registers potential dissension. One can recognize that a powerful discourse on modernity has emanated from Europe and North America. Nevertheless, we must remain wary of creating unified, solipsistic readings out of local Euro-American practices or allowing those to overpower interpretations developed elsewhere.

Without losing the insights of Foucault, I wish to open up this theoretical critique by displacing some of the troubling assumptions that the anthropology of modernity has thus far produced. If one relocates modernity by viewing it from the perspective of those marginalized or excluded from the universalizing center, then it becomes a mutable project developed in unequal cross-cultural dialogues and contentions. Paul Gilroy (1993), for example, articulates this challenge when he argues that modernity has been generated within the antagonistic relationships of the imperial world, integral to which is "the fatal junction" of slavery, racial domination, and racialized reason. In contrast, then, to much of the recent anthropology of modernity, I here emphasize two interrelated points: modernity's persistent history of normalizing colonial and now transnational relations of cultural difference, as well as the locatedness of the cultural imaginaries that engage modernity. This conjoined perspective renders more visible the active processes by which projects of power and knowledge crafted in the name of modernity are simultaneously naturalized and exposed as contingent, at once maintained and altered. These endeavors both encompass and abandon the subalterns they create, leaving them to maneuver along the boundaries of inclusion and exclusion. If modernity is that imagined nexus linking a series of projects of science and management, then one must trace the translation process of these projects as they travel through history and across the East-West divide.

Modernity enfolds and explodes by means of global capitalist forms of domination in conjunction with state techniques for normalizing its citizens. Along with these specific practices, modernity exists as a narrated imaginary: it is a story people tell themselves about themselves in relation to others. Modernity persists as a powerful narrative because nation-states organize the body politic around it (Dirks 1990). As a story, it can illuminate matters and shape subjectivities—but it can also fool and mislead us. Even in those moments when nation-states declare themselves most faithful to an assumed universal modernity, specific histories turn it into another form. For like all tales, its meaning acquires different valences with its various narrations. Modernity as a goal generates consequential struggles because people living in heterogeneous circumstances have been pulled into a "worlding" (Said 1983) of the term. Dreams, rhetorics, and power ricochet off its local/global dynamics. Modernity exists, then, alternately as discursive practice, allegory, trope.[12] One critical terrain for such stories is offered by culture, and tales of how it smoothes the way for modernity or blocks its potential are themselves modernist tropes. Culture thus appears as a substantive agent in the world. But there is another way to think of the cultural: not so much as substance but as process, always emergent, always relational, permeated with power, existing through subtle and overt contests over meanings both practical and imaginary, shaping the desires that infuse modernity.

Therefore, my analysis in this book centers on stories—narratives that contribute to the construction of social life. At first I took people's stories for granted, treating them as transparent descriptions. In doing so, however, I immediately faced the unsatisfying ethnographic generalization that in the moments of telling their life stories, Chinese people could, at times, sound oddly querulous, emphasizing failure or lack. Such assumptions of cultural difference only serve to reinforce rather than subvert the colonial project.[13] Moreover, these complaints jostled with apparently contradictory stories—shared by the same people at different times—that signaled pleasure or a nicely sardonic sense of humor. Only gradually, through critiques of ethnographic writing, increased attention to narrative within anthropology, and my own growing understanding of the relationship between politics and speech acts, did I begin to see people's narratives as one of the means through which modern socialist subjects had been constituted in China. Listening to and analyzing these stories, paying attention to both the form and content, to rhetoric, mode, context, and tone, allowed me to appreciate the differing political and cultural contentions that competing projects fostered in the name of modernity. Such attention also pushed me to reenvision culture as such, for these stories spoke of the cultural poetics of political desire. They made culture into a provisional space for imagining one's location in the world; a culture became a space full of stops and starts, contradictions and claims—and always infused with power.

As a result of communist organizing in China, telling one's life story turned into a self-conscious political act with concrete, material ramifications. A particular form the party fostered, known as "speaking bitterness," framed stories at the moment of liberation but also, as I argue here, continued in informal mode up through economic reform.[14] Narratives, then, evince the culturally specific means by which people represent and therefore experience the worlds in which they live. Yet narratives also provide the moments of challenging those world orders. As Kathleen Stewart (1996) argues, narration opens up gaps in the order of things and the meanings of signs. My emphasis is not on the poetics of narrative but on the manifold ways that power works through narratives that bind together the practical and the imaginary.

Modernity, then, is conveyed in inconstant projects of governmentality, education, and scientific management: restless, discontinuous cultural interactions that create impure, syncretic subjects.[15] Its core entails the transverse dynamics of cultural differentiation and multiply positioned subjects. The multiplicities of what counts as modernity exist in the unforeseen outcomes of domination, the diverse cultural struggles to deploy its power, and the couplings of intersecting histories that reroute it.[16] These processes forestall ideological closure on modernity. This, I believe, is what Homi Bhabha (1994a) means when he speaks of the "belatedness" of modernity. Bhabha highlights the deeply contradictory processes by which those oppressed by colonialism carry, in its aftermath, the sign of a "time-lag" of cultural difference. As subordinated people strive for modernity, which promises to overcome their belatedness, they create disjunctures in the "present" of modernity. Modernity is thus fissured with paradox and incompleteness, not simply because all categories implode on their own unstable differences but because of distinctive social histories within a global imperialism.

What is called for here is not another universal theory of modernity but specific cultural histories that make for necessarily "other" modernities. On this account, even Bhabha's concept of belatedness could be historicized. A brief and admittedly overly schematic set of comparisons might prove useful.[17] Through its colonial experience, "South Asia" came to represent the ancient wisdom available to Europe. Its position is always already that which comes before Europe, anOther Greece. The notion of belatedness helps explain the history of these depictions. "Africa," in contrast, represents to Europeans and Americans not ancient wisdom but the "natural" within human behavior that needs to be civilized to create modern subjectivity. Africa is the site of the magical fetish that can be tapped to stimulate the modern economy or the modern psyche. It is the spark of sexual and material desire that enlivens modernity even as it is controlled by it.[18] Belatedness is less useful here than perhaps a concept of reification, implosion, or grooming, where grooming is a site of civilizing the body's actions and appearance. China offers yet another position of otherness, representing less the repository of Europe's ancient wisdom or the heart of Europe's darkness than the constitutive "outside" of western civilization. China shapes modernity by representing to Europe everything modernity is not, rather than supplying the raw material of the past or the nature from which modernity is formed. Given this history, projects in China to reach modernity might best be thought of in the theoretical terms of mediation, (im)purification, and lack.

Perhaps a set of contrasting examples would be useful to illuminate the argument about modernity presented here. Bruno Latour, in his recent polemic about the social study of science (1993), has forcefully argued that the sign of modernity under which "we" have lived is an imaginary one, insofar as it manages only partially to frame our existence. For Latour, modernity rests not so much on the birth of humanism as on a fundamental division that separates knowledge of the nonhuman realm, or nature, from the human realm of society, culture, and language. This "purification" of realms—what "we" usually take to mean modernity—in turn obscures the "translations" or mediations that actually occur among nature, power, and culture.[19] Indeed, modern political critiques are founded on the ability to separate out what belongs to science or things-in-themselves or "reality" and what belongs to the functioning of language or symbols or the unconscious.[20] Only so long as we imagine that these sets of practices do not coexist—even as the proliferation of hybrids relies on the pretense of purified realms—can we continue to act as if we were modern. "By playing three times in a row on the same alternation between transcendence and immanence, the moderns can mobilize Nature, objectify the social, and feel the spiritual presence of God, even while firmly maintaining that Nature escapes us, that Society is our own work, and that God no longer intervenes" (Latour 1993:34).[21] Latour concludes that we have never been modern in the sense of living according to the pure separation of realms. Modernity is rather an imaginary order that we are now able to discern because it has exhausted itself.

Although Latour insightfully renders the paradoxes of the modern imaginary, his assumption of an unmarked "we" as the coherent subject of modernity, coupled with an embarrassing anthropological distinction between premodern and modern peoples, must be set aside.[22] Much postcolonial writing has been dedicated to troubling just such forms of

Eurocentric identification. Particularly relevant here is Dipesh Chakrabarty's argument (1992) that modernity operates by way of exclusions and by the constitution of difference that together generate the Euro-American sense of a unified subjectivity. We need, then, to heed Chakrabarty's demand for a history of modernity that will "provincialize" Europe.[23]

His challenge embodies neither a reductionist rejection of modernity and the violence attending its universalization nor an effort to retain cultural relativism. Rather, Chakrabarty wishes to hold simultaneously to two ends of an analytical pole: by one, examining the process by which Europe's modernity has been made to look obvious in its application far beyond its originary ground; by the other, investigating the ambivalences, contradictions, tragedies, and ironies attendant on a third world nationalist embrace of this narrative. The first studies a global history of European imperialism that continues to make non-western worlds rehearse a transition narrative of modernity in which they figure as "lack." As Chakrabarty emphasizes, it also highlights the "imaginary hyperrealness" of Europe that nonetheless has a phenomenal existence in metanarratives and everyday relationships of power. The second traces the articulations configured in modernities that do not simply replicate Eurocentric teleologies even as non-western nationalists struggle to make their country's modernity stand on its own as a metanarrative of non-western history.[24] To take Chakrabarty one step further, one must also place postcolonial critiques within their specific historical contexts.[25] That no one country ever completely colonized China and that the socialist revolution rejected western domination even as it proceeded to invoke the Enlightenment assumptions embedded in socialism mean that China's grappling with western hegemony has taken a different form than, for example, India's.

Though being modern is an imagined status, it is not a mere mythical representation. People deeply feel modernity in their experiences precisely because techniques of normalization are secured in its name. Just as social theorists have come to accept that the nation-state is an imagined community that leads citizens to kill in its honor, so, too, modernity leads government leaders, development agents, intellectual elites, subaltern workers and peasants, and women—those who represent political power as well as those who are the objects of its operations—to act in the name of the desires it engenders. The cultural representations that make these actions and desires appear to be the only possible ones are precisely what should alert us to the allegorical rather than literal quality of modernity.

Modernity, then, is a struggle that takes place in specific locations and a process that knits together local/global configurations. Here, the "local" becomes not simply a site but an angle of vision. One can discern the relationships, from this angle, among city, provincial, national, and transnational networks. As an ethnographic study, my project locates practices of modernity at the local level, in the practices of everyday life.

In the several months that I spent at Zhenfu Silk Weaving Factory, moving around from weaving to prep to inspection shop, it dawned on me only gradually how relationships among workers—their informal friendship "cliques" and ways of helping one another—might be based on politically induced generational differences. The sinological descriptions of contemporary China tend to point to sociopolitical networks, or guanxi, *and political behavior, or* biaoxian, *as explanations for social hierarchies and antagonisms in China; but these seemed inadequate to account for workers' divergent remarks on what they hoped or feared would happen to them following the vast upheavals signaled by economic reform. Women workers who had come of age just after the socialist revolution reminisced with me about their boldness in that earlier time, when the socialist discourses of liberation inspired them to reimagine their identities as women. Or, more tellingly, they recounted the way they felt freed from the necessity of embodying femininity and acting as women, at least for a time. They strained to bring the past into the present, as their narratives of overcoming "bitterness" wavered on the border between historical tale and current nostalgia for a moment in which the formation of their political agency allowed them to envision themselves as national heroes.*

Women who had come of age in the often violent struggles of the Cultural Revolution over the meaning of "proletarian power"[26] placed their sense of political conviction and female identity less in heroic labor and more in a politics of challenging authority. That daily acts of challenge made life meaningful to

them was evident in more than their words. Their memories of political convic-
tion were also being lived in the seemingly banal activities of threading spools
or mending broken yarn. Older women workers' performance of their identity
on the shop floor was an enactment of heroic socialist diligence, an implicit
reminder to the state not to forsake them after they had "eaten all that bitterness"
of hard work in its name. But Cultural Revolution workers made their exag-
gerated gestures of refusal to remain positioned on the shop floor speak worlds
about proletarian defiance of state power. Their memories adroitly disrupted the
postsocialist politics of knowledge that made of workers a barely visible presence
in paeans to modernity. They made manifest the symbolic violence in the im-
agery of a natural economic order through which the power of postsocialist
modernity is exercised.

Coming of age under this symbolic violence, the youngest women workers
held another form of gendered "interests," as hyperfemininity became the sym-
bolic ground of a new liberation from socialism. Their embodied desires were
crafted through official and popular representations celebrating the "recovery"
of the natural genders buried beneath a supposedly asexual socialism. They were
diligent enough in their work, but they were far more excited about figuring out
how to "become" women. Their distance from the women senior to them was
palpable, as each group talked past the other. Older women workers, in the minds
of the youngest women, seemed like ancient socialist figures who bent to the will
of the state, while the women of the Cultural Revolution just appeared to be bad
eggs. They had little interest in either of these two cohorts' projects of political
agency. Thus, they implicitly laid open the arbitrariness of the category "labor"
as a foundation for liberation or identity, even as they carried forth new forms
of power that operated through regimes of femininity.

Recent discussions of modernity have shed a great deal of light on the
importance to modernity of global relations of difference, but they have
ignored the centrality of gender in shaping the forms by which and force
with which desires for modernity take hold. In this book I contend that
gender serves as one of the central modalities through which modernity
is imagined and desired. Gender differentiation—the knowledges, relations, meanings, and identities of masculinity and femininity—operates at the heart of modernity's power. Discourses on women's place in

colonized societies among both colonizers and elite colonized men; the use of women to represent by turns "tradition," the essence of culture, the constitutional "lack" in third world countries' ability to modernize, or resistance to the West; the "feminization" of non-western cultures; the construction of a hypermasculinity through which the West imagines its power; and, more recently, the focus of development aid on women, the transnational constitution of gender in multinational factories, and the sexualization of local/global interactions—these multiple processes demonstrate ways in which gender is invoked to naturalize power.

In making this claim, I do not mean to carve gender out as a separate domain or discourse. As feminist theorists have demonstrated, the historical and cultural contingencies of gender are best understood as imbricated in multiple relations of power (see Alexander and Mohanty 1997; Anzaldúa 1987; J. Brown forthcoming; Ebron 1997; Grewal and Kaplan 1994; Haraway 1997; John 1996; Kondo 1997; Mani 1987; Spivak 1987, 1990; Tsing 1993; E. F. White 1990). The technologies of power are not distinct and autonomous elements that then intertwine with one another. Rather, they produce, organize, and take shape through one another.[27] Thus, the cultural materialization of (neo)colonial relations, racial difference, state power, and nationalism—all structural and discursive components of modernity—have operated through specific normalizations of masculinity and femininity.[28] Gender, then, is not just "about" women and men, but is about the state, the nation, socialism, and capitalism. While I am here concerned with the constitution of gendered subjectivities, I also accentuate the institutionalization of forms of gender knowledge that shape desires for modernity, relations to work, and China's place within global networks of capital.[29]

Classical anthropological approaches that create separate "cultures" and study women's status within them remain inadequate to the task at hand. Chinese women have long figured in transcultural conversations as a primary sign of China's "difference" from the West. In the early part of this century, western missionaries, colonial administrators, foreign entrepreneurs, and the predominantly male Chinese educated elite made women the grounds for reinterpreting Chinese tradition and measuring China's ability to become modern (though often deploying them for different ends).[30] China's socialist patriarchs came of age during this period, known in China as semicolonialism. It should be no surprise, then, that the socialist state's political imaginary centered on the question of "women's liberation." The assertions, denials, and critiques of whether women were indeed "liberated" by the socialist revolution continue a multivocal, politically charged exchange about metanarratives of modernity. Much feminist inquiry, both in the United States and in China, has directed itself to this question.[31] My work initially grew out of these discussions. The challenges that women workers as well as feminist theorists in China posed to me have led me to change its focus and to ask instead how the socialist state crafted a discourse of women's liberation that reconfigured the meaning of labor and hence the subjectivity of women.

If modernity is constituted through gender and is reimagined differently in diverse periods, then these layered temporalities in modernity also shape the heterogeneity of Chinese women. The three political cohorts of women workers who worked alongside one another in the 1980s and early 1990s had characteristic ways of embracing, evading, contesting, and crafting their subaltern existence. Often, they posed themselves in opposition to one another. Each of these cohorts came of age as workers during distinctive and dramatic political movements under socialism, experiencing disparate versions of what might constitute modernity for China.[32] They formed visibly divided political generations, whose differential responses to the post-Mao vision of modernity implicitly formed a debate about the meanings of "woman" as well as "worker." The self-definitions of these women as political actors were forged in terms of cohort identity. I hasten to add that these cohorts were in themselves by no means uniform. While members of each cohort were pulled into a dominant project that shaped their identities as women, the cohorts in turn were far from unified as a group in negotiating their respective gender projects. Within each cohort, there were also women who, because of diverse class or marital circumstances, found themselves marginalized with respect to dominant gender discourses. I thus trace the differences within as well as among cohorts. Their insistent heterogeneity brushes against the grain of a Marxism that posits immanence of consciousness in the materiality of production. The multiple discursive fields of gender, class, and political movement produce—rather than reflect—workers' consciousness.

Since the early 1980s, cohort analysis has been one important means through which anthropology has addressed complex social relations and advanced a nonhomogeneous view of culture. Moreover, unlike life cycle approaches, it highlights the dynamics of temporality and history. Whether the focus has been coming to manhood and head-hunting at different junctures of war and colonialism in the Philippines (Rosaldo 1980), the symbolic construction of kinship and "tradition" among first- and second-generation Japanese Americans (Yanagisako 1985), or the abortion debates in the United States and the historical transformations in the tensions surrounding issues pertaining to reproduction (Ginsburg 1989), these studies have recognized that coming of age at particular moments creates telling fault lines through which meaning is transformed.

I build on these insights. Yet rather than analyze a singular moment of formation, I emphasize the *reformation* of cohorts as they live through diverse historical periods. The cliques women workers formed among themselves, along with attitudes ranging from polite distance to open hostility that these cliques displayed toward one another, the differences in their critiques of post-Mao modernity, and the specificities in their performance of those critiques all point toward cohort distinctions. But these were not biological cohorts. They were groups who had developed a sense of identification in coming of age through particular political movements and state regimes—the early years of Liberation,[33] the Cultural Revolution, and the post-Mao era. These historical moments also differed in popular culture, urbanization, marriage and kinship patterns, and work trajectories.

Writing of these subaltern experiences in a socialist nation-state presents a challenge quite distinct from that of exposing the liberal suppositions of capitalist democracies. The United States continues its one-note cold war chant about the Chinese state, using it in barely concealed self-congratulatory attempts to screen its own anxious uncertainty about what "America" stands for. The Chinese state, we are told over and over again in ponderous political science tracts, media briefs, and presidential homilies to free trade (though not when weapons are concerned), acts in a simply repressive manner, using political power to create a unified and uniform social polity. Here, in these transnational competitions of global strength, we surely find the magic of state fetishism—that "aura of might"—about which Taussig (1997) so compellingly warns us. To open out this fetishism, I work from the opposite assumption: that domination in China materializes itself as distinct in kind but not in degree from domination in the West.

One could take the matter of bodies and their interest to the state, for example, as I do in chapter 7. The disturbing politics of reproduction and sexuality in the United States expose not a lesser amount of domination but the specific modes by which bodies and power come to augment one another. The Chinese state—itself not a uniform entity—and the U.S. government both extend their reach far into the intimacies of daily life, but the former does so through the fiction of socialist order while the latter does so through the fiction of legal legitimacy and a nonpoliticized civil society. Moreover, state power in China, as in the United States, operates not merely repressively but productively, creating a differentiated population and a forceful vision of social reality. Only by upending taken-for-granted truths about the way state power operates will we ever challenge new forms of transnational domination.

My research on gender, labor, and modernity drew me to a wide range of silk factories—some large, state-owned factories; others neighborhood collective factories; and still others small, privately owned, family-run factories in the countryside surrounding Hangzhou. In one state-owned factory, Fudan, not far from Zhenfu factory, I was presented with an administrative cadre who knew a great deal about the period just after the 1949 socialist revolution. I was interested in how gender differentiation in the industry had changed after socialism. Wang Shouchu had been an accountant for many of the small household silk workshops that produced most of Hangzhou's silk prior to state control of the industry. These household workshops were headed by male weavers; wives and daughters spun the thread. In 1956, the Labor Union chose Wang Shouchu to go around and convince these individual households to form small cooperatives. I asked

how he had managed such a seemingly Herculean task. "It wasn't easy work,"
he quickly acknowledged, "to get them to turn over their productive materials
to the state. At the very beginning of Liberation, they didn't understand what
was the proletariat, or communism or such things. They'd never heard of it. We
didn't know either." "How did you figure out what to say to them?" I asked.
"When we started," he replied, "we didn't understand what communism was,
except from announcements. All we knew was 'The Soviet Union's today is our
tomorrow.' So we told them what the future might be like. It was hard work,
with a lot of conflicts. The older ones didn't want to hear it. They would curse
you." "When did you begin to understand?" I asked. "I don't think I've really
ever understood. Aren't we in the midst of reform now?"

For China, the pursuit of modernity did not begin in the 1980s. This
quest has coursed through its history throughout the late nineteenth and
twentieth centuries, as China first grappled with the semicolonialism
that parceled out the country among competing imperial powers and
then established a socialist nation-state.[34] The socialist revolution and its
current repudiation in the post-Mao era, however, has positioned this
quest in a new way.

To exist in the modern world—and here the tautology proves meaningful—non-western nations must substantiate their modernity. China
has had to contend with the orientalist representation of its being inherently weak because of the overarching and stultifying tenor of its "culture." The idea of a holistic, patterned, and functionally complete "Confucian culture" or "Confucian tradition" was invented in China in the
early twentieth century simultaneously with China's transition from empire to nation-state (Huters 1996; L. Liu 1995).[35] "Confucianism" served
as the obverse term, the displaced site on which the intellectual elite
struggled to enact modernity. Demonstrations by students, intellectuals,
entrepreneurs, and laborers against World War I's Versailles treaty,
which legitimated China's fragmentation, soon led to a vibrant cultural
revolution to overthrow forms of newly discovered Confucian tradition
and its modes of authority as found in language, family life, social mores,
and politics. (T. Chow 1960; Lin 1979).

As Cathryn Clayton (1995) has argued, by defining the nation in terms of a narrative of modernity, successive generations of nationalists have constructed the compelling "other" of tradition against which they strive to distinguish themselves and the nation.[36] The semicolonialism of China, however, made this process distinct from, for example, that in India. The absence of full colonization under a single power meant that no one of the competing imperialist powers felt compelled to fully decipher and order what it meant to be Chinese or, conversely, to create a class of "mimic men" (Bhabha 1994b) who would become consummate colonial subjects. Paradoxically, the specificity of this colonial situation threw China back on itself more intensely, displacing the dilemmas and desires of modernity more thoroughly onto Chinese culture (Hershatter 1997; Huters 1996; Shih 1998).

The socialist revolution in China took definition and direction in this context.[37] Socialism enabled China to position itself not behind but in advance of a decaying Europe, in a global vanguard of radical revolutions (Dirlik 1989). Far from desiring to abandon modernity, however, the socialist movement fought in the name of the critical underside of modernity—modernist Marxism. Its leaders declared that China was able to reach modernity through a radical reconceptualization of time that could mobilize the country to slough off its newly discovered cultural stultification, labeled "feudal tradition" by Chinese socialists. They fomented a revolution and installed a state in the name of their desire to claim the progressive narrative of modernity.

This revolution can hardly be separated from changing political conceptions of nationhood. Its political discourse was informed by a broad, earlier transformation in how to conceive of the polity. In their efforts to mold China into a modern nation-state, socialist as well as nonsocialist reformers radically reimagined the political community (Duara 1995; Friedman 1994; Hoston 1994). They replaced an imperial polity, imagined as a homologous series of relations in which kinship mirrored the emperor's relations with his subjects, with a nation-state imaginary in which "politics," "culture," "economy," "society," "family," and "religion" became separate domains, structured horizontally rather than hierarchically.[38] Communist organizers in the countryside, for example, expended a great deal of effort to break down kinship loyalties in favor of horizontal identification along the class lines that they discursively and institutionally established (Chan, Madsen, and Unger 1992; Hinton 1966). The anti-imperial nationalism of the Chinese Communist Party differed from the nationalism of other Chinese elites in that the party interpreted exploitation by European powers rather than simply the "Chineseness" of China as the cause of China's lack of modernity.[39]

The newly imagined nation-state facilitated the appearance of new forms of social identity. The end (in 1905) of the Confucian examination system that had wedded learned elite men to political service, the institutionalization of schooling, the rise of industrial enterprises in coastal cities, and the burgeoning of commerce linking China to a global economy shaped by colonial capitalism also contributed to this process. "Intellectuals" became those who were autonomous creators of culture. They occupied political positions in the name of the nation but not necessarily in service to state rule, even as they harked back to the past to justify their right to lead (Grieder 1981). The category "women," at least among the educated urban elite, became an essential gender identification separable from kinship relations (Barlow 1991a; L. Liu 1991; Meng and Dai 1990). "Laborers" appeared as part of a newly conceived "populace" whom intellectuals hoped to enlighten and on whose behalf they strove to speak (Dirlik 1989). Indeed, among radicals, "laboring" became a fundamental social virtue and one of the foremost criteria of citizenship in the envisioned new society (Hershatter 1986; Honig 1986; Perry 1993). As the "common people" emerged as an identifiable social category, socialists grappled with how to endow this entity with effective and intentional agency to make revolution while at the same time bringing it within the purview of new forms of political authority (Anagnost 1997; Apter 1995; Dirlik 1989; Saich and van de Ven 1995).

Much of the power of the Chinese Communist Party, and later the party-state, rested in its ability to create and sustain a new mythos of the polity, a new moral discourse of the nation, and a new hegemonic interpretation of experience. These elements constituted mutable interpretations of modernity. The new political mythos framed a story of a double loss and overcoming: the displacement of subalterns from their rightful place as inheritors of the fruits of their own labor and the loss of the nation to foreign powers. This double marginalization could only be overcome, at least in the Maoist view, by continuous revolution. The ideological disputes that characterize the Maoist period from the 1949 revolution to the end of the Cultural Revolution in 1976 reveal the projects of modernity to be split between building national unity within the newly conceived social agent of "the masses," thus constituting "the masses" as a unified polity, and developing the nation along Marxist dialectics of class struggle, thus positing conflict along social lines of difference as the teleological path to progress. These catachreses, or paradoxes in how to conceive of the nation (and here I deliberately stretch the rhetorical term), disclose the compelling character of modernity as allegory even as socialist forms of power and subjectivity are produced in its name: class differentiation as opposed to national unity; nationalism as overcoming the intransigence of the past versus nationalism as confronting history enacted in the present; power as pervasive and unifying versus power as operating along a dialectic; subaltern agency set against new forms of political authority; the continuous effort to contain revolutionary agency within the discursive frameworks established by the state; and the tension in the historiography of the Chinese nation between finding external imperialism at the root of China's dilemmas and blaming internal problems of social exploitation and "Chinese culture."

Socialist power operates by positing within workers and peasants a subaltern consciousness that the state then authorizes and represents. For Chinese Marxists, subaltern agency was the major means of constituting modernity. To materialize it, they turned to various methods: language and literacy campaigns, active performances of life narratives in terms of newly received class categories, a semiotics of political spectacle staged in struggle sessions against those designated as class enemies, and a moral discourse of virtue about class oppression. Storytelling, especially narrating one's life history, was thus a political activity with serious consequences for one's relationship to state power. The state infused the most mundane of events and activities with ethical, political, and symbolic gravitas. As David Apter has put it, "Action becomes exemplary. Everyone is an example of *something*" (1995:202). Ideological discipline and a moral/political system of rewards and punishments stimulated divisions along class lines (Billeter 1985). To speak as a subaltern meant intimately intertwining one's life with the fate of the nation in reaching for modernity.

These political performances and the "consciousness" that resulted from them were enormously empowering for those designated to speak as subalterns. Many of them eagerly embraced a language of oppression that made possible a better future for them. The story of their lives that the party offered mobilized in some of them an impassioned desire to bring about radical change. Some of them became members of the new political elite. Nonetheless, this hegemony, while exceedingly effective, has never been complete. The state has needed to forcibly reiterate both the content and form of subaltern subjectivity through numerous political campaigns that have had to address the complexity of the lives of those designated as subalterns. For example, although the socialist state under Maoism spoke in the name of the subaltern as the source of its political authority, class labels and class divisions were always contested; successive political campaigns to redraw the categories culminated in the most widespread and violent of them, which brought down Maoist socialism: the Cultural Revolution (1966–76).

Official discourse in the post-Mao era represents social life as empirically verifiable through neutral procedures of observation and measurement that are beyond politics. This objectification of social life has made the post-Mao regime of modernity appear to be the only imaginable one, and the emphasis on objectivity is also one means of distinguishing that regime from Maoist forms of politics. It is meant to reassure the populace that no form of political interference, whether class struggle politics, party concern with morality, or cadre abuse, hinders those who seek to create wealth through means formerly castigated as capitalist. "Seek truth from facts" was a catchy slogan that captured this idea, implying that a "pragmatic" road to wealth could be distinguished from an ideological one. In the mid-1980s, one came up against this slogan everywhere: pasted on factory walls, as the headline of newspaper articles, and in repetitive official speeches. For some, "seek truth from facts" held out hope that they could find a satisfying future based on their individual efforts, efforts not stymied by arbitrary politics.

But one could also find it used in parodic mimicry, implicitly producing a
slippage in the kind of objectivity being invoked.

Liu Bomu's daughter-in-law Xie Hongxian was an acupuncturist, like her
parents-in-law and husband. She specialized in herbal medicines for women. A
hardworking mother of two, Xie Hongxian was caught between wanting to
advance her career, now that intellectuals were being courted, and believing that
women should make a proper home for their husbands and children. Though
they all lived in the same dwelling that the grandfather had bought in the early
1950s—a traditional three-sided home built around a courtyard—Xie Hong-
xian and her husband had recently separated off their household from the grand-
parents by setting up their own stove to take their meals apart. Respecting the
proper hierarchies in the family, I spent much of my initial time at their home
with the men—the grandfather and his favorite second son, Hongxian's hus-
band. I would take my meals with the grandparents, joined by their grandson.
But gradually, I was able to drift back into the quarters of Hongxian's family,
which occupied one side of the house. At first diffident and respectful of proper
etiquette with a foreign guest, Hongxian gradually began to exchange confi-
dences with me about the troubles of being a woman. Eventually, whenever I
joined them instead of the grandparents, Hongxian included me in her household
chores. I kept her company and she also gave me advice about proper woman-
hood. One day as we prepared a meal, we disagreed about a small matter con-
cerning the vegetables. To support her opinion, Hongxian drew herself up and,
looking serious like a cadre, intoned: "Seek truth from facts." Then she burst
out laughing.

The current post-Mao era, beginning with the death of Mao Zedong in
1976 and then the official termination of the Cultural Revolution shortly
thereafter, is marked by the decided rejection of everything Maoism represented. The change includes the introduction of a market economy that
has inserted China into global networks of capital and labor, as well as
the reconfiguration of relations between "state" and "society." New allegories of modernity continue to signal the deferred desire for the
wealth and power that will finally banish the lingering past of colonial
difference and punctuate China's arrival as a self-referential nation-
state.[40] This post-Mao revolution is known as "economic reform"

because of its overriding emphasis on economic development. But "development," as Arturo Escobar (1995) has noted, operates to create imaginaries that make the "economic" inextricable from political discourse about the kinds of subjects and social relations deemed appropriate to carry development forward. For this reason, I take a different approach than do those who treat power in China as a measurable quantity. Some would argue that the political gaze of Maoist socialism that reached into the inner recesses of personal life has been lifted. To the extent it still retains its force, this argument goes, one finds it in repressive measures that hinder political democracy or, alternatively, the "freedom" of the market.

That may be. But I find it more useful to analyze not the amount of power but its direction and quality: how state power has shifted its gaze and mode of operation. Placing gender at the center of analysis makes such an approach possible, for one finds then a renewed focus of power, but with distinctive pressures and novel areas of application. This kind of power operates through multiple arenas, in which the state does not so much oppose market forces that might represent freedom to some as intersect with them in overlapping networks of inducement and constraint, thus creating the kind of postsocialist modernity for which so many yearn. Such power rests on the policing of certain borders of difference, namely those of socialism/capitalism, Maoist socialism/post-Mao socialism, East/West, and femininity/masculinity.

In this respect, my study challenges a widespread conception of postsocialist countries and gender. Scholars and popular media alike, in formerly socialist nations as well as in the United States, have joined in representing postsocialism as the opportunity for natural genders to assert themselves. Socialism, it is now said, masculinized women and emasculated men. Clearly, this kind of essentializing gender analysis will not do if we are to understand how femininity and masculinity and the social arrangements that make them materially effective are contingent on specific configurations of power/knowledge.[41]

Political discourse in the post-Mao regime operates most powerfully on the terrain of representations about the "natures" of women and men. While Maoism invoked the mutability of the social as the foundation of the subaltern agency necessary to enact modernity, post-Mao political culture makes the immutability of the natural serve as a nonsubaltern foundation for a similar purpose. In this postsocialist allegory, Maoist women's liberation is portrayed as a transgression of innate femininity that repressed gendered human nature. Maoist repression, so the story goes, deferred China's embrace of modernity by impeding Chinese people's ability to express their essential humanity, which lay beneath the cultural politics of socialism. The view that political culture impeded China's ability to reach modernity is thus wedded to the retelling of history, so that a history of emancipation from Maoism can remake the legitimacy of the state.

The shaping of new gender identities in terms of human natures overlaps the naturalization of other arenas of social life. Postsocialist discourse echoes post-GATT capitalist economics in portraying the laws of economic development as having "natural" rhythms and mechanisms that operate best if left unimpeded to go their own way.[42] Economic reform has thus been intended in part to create a separation between "politics" and "economics." Similarly, the state announced the separation of power from everyday life when it ended class labels (even as new forms of class inequality arose). In their place, official, scholarly, and popular discourses individuate and essentialize bodies, households, "private life," and unequal talents and statuses. The new forms of power in post-Mao China operate precisely in those realms it has made liberatory, because it makes them appear as if they are separate from power.

There was much excitement among members of a diverse cross section of society over the possibilities in the post-Mao imaginary of modernity. Many were drawn by the desire to put Maoism behind them. Still, the assumption of their new identities was neither automatic nor without debate. Older women workers tended to engage these transformations through a politics of memory centering on their earlier heroism as women workers. The retelling and thus remaking of history, for them, was a crucial site for negotiating new forms of power. Those who defined themselves as the Cultural Revolution generation had an implicit politics of space through which they carried out more overt challenges to authority. Though all of the people I here write about accepted the official repudiation of the Cultural Revolution, this cohort of workers nonetheless displayed in their stance toward authority a residual embodiment of that period. Those in the youngest cohort of workers, who have come of age since the end of Maoism, found neither labor nor the politics of authority meaningful to their identities. Rather, they turned to a politics of the body in which they embraced ideas about innate femininity, marriage, and motherhood that explicitly reject the practices of womanhood they saw in the two older cohorts.

These differences in gender identities were not merely implicit; they were the stuff of much commentary, as women of each cohort constituted their gender by way of contrast with women in the other cohorts. Again, the contours of these gender projects shape the boundaries between cohorts, but no essential homogeneity within cohorts is implied. Taken together, the overlapping differences between and within cohorts lead to questions of what counts as knowledge of gender, how is it produced and by whom, and how this knowledge authorizes, incites, and excludes specific subject-positions. In tracing these lines of commentary, I argue that women maneuvered not outside of or against power, but within and through it.

One day at Zhenfu a group of women gathered around a new calendar that the provincial silk bureau had put out to advertise the allure of silk. Each office was encouraged to hang it. The calendar featured white western women scantily clad in tight-fitting silk dresses, some with feather boas wrapped all too suggestively around their necks. Western consumption of silk had multiple meanings for Zhenfu's workers: western fashion signified the heights of modernity and they were eager to learn more about it; the emphasis on exports of Chinese silk — traditionally a central symbol of Chinese culture — to feed western desires meant a volatile dependence on the West that made some angry even as it gave others hope of soaring profits; and what many viewed as fetishistic western tastes made silk work a much more high-pressure endeavor as the "quality controls" meant to satisfy these demands intensified the measures determining rewards and punishments.

Several of the women in the group turned to me awkwardly. Without wanting to offend or appear unworldly, they clearly thought the photos a bit ridic-

ulous but weren't sure how to interpret them. They had already pegged me as someone who was "plain and simple" in her dress—a euphemism that some used in disappointment that I couldn't teach them more and others used in praise of what they saw as lingering signs of possible class identification. "Was this winter or summer dress?" they wanted to know. "Summer," I said uncertainly. "Well," they ventured, "what do you think of these photos?" I assured them that no one I knew dressed like that. They then dissolved into loud exclamations at the peculiarity of at least some westerners.

How can one be both local and global at the same time? As anthropology ushers in new objects of knowledge, such as diasporic subjects, mass media spectators, and hybrid identities, it is critical to trace how these representations, like earlier colonial representations, also exist within changing networks of power. We cannot afford to assume that these novel phenomena are the answer to power. Discussions of modernity, the end of socialism, global capitalism, and the nation-state, for example, must attend to the politics of representation both within and beyond ethnographic texts. Too often, one finds overemphasis on one or the other, as if the dynamics of capitalism could be grasped apart from the dynamic construction of knowledge about it, or as if attention to narrative form alone can resolve the dilemmas of cultural power.[43] This cautionary note is especially relevant as we focus on social transformations and political movements, rather than consigning them to the background of studies of enduring cultural logics (including "a" logic of modernity). The passions of political commitment make a careful regard for the relationship between representation and practice all the more urgent.

Poststructuralist approaches to power eschew dichotomies of domination versus freedom, consent versus repression as the way to understand the effective operation of power. The aim is to search instead for the complexity of how power produces subjects who speak in its name. Talal Asad (1993) cogently reminds us that the metaphysical concept of consciousness hinders our understanding of how social agents can modify the world even as they are subjects of systematic structures of knowledge that do not originate with them. Nonetheless, people exist within multiple and shifting fields of power, and unexpected challenges arise in the gaps and ambiguities. Anthropology must not discard a commitment to cultural heterogeneity even as it wishes to understand processes that some label "globalization." One must try to theorize interstices where power loses its grip and to expose its ironies and inability to wholly define us. Moreover, anthropology reminds those engaged in poststructuralist debates not to assume that such categories as "modernity," "the subject," or "women"—to take just a few that are relevant to my own work—are universal.

These questions of power are inseparable from the critique of western representations of the other, a critique that challenges anthropologists to position ourselves in relation to the subjects we create in our ethnographies. Positioning is part of the story of the negotiation of power and knowledge. Decisions about modes of writing and cultural representation are of a piece with discussions about agency and contests over cultural meaning. In this regard, my project is especially inspired by feminist revisions of ethnography.[44] Such revisions are informed by wider feminist discussions about the situatedness of knowledge (Haraway 1991), the gendered negotiations of meaning and power, and the differences among women that make of identity a multiple and often self-contradictory phenomenon. The ethnographic story is also a story of who writes histories of others, at what moment in time, in which institutional settings, out of which political convictions or implicit assumptions, and for which audiences. Most important, it clarifies the responsibility of ethnographers—and their readers—to account for the shifting ground of power and meaning on which various interlocutors strain to understand one another. Because feminism is an avowedly political project, it encourages placing oneself in the text as one way to explore the constraints and possibilities of cross-cultural political alliances. Thus, among the audiences for this book I hope to count those feminists—in China, as well as from China and now in the United States—with whom I have explored this challenging terrain.

I was fortunate, in the spring of 1986, to be invited to the wedding of a friend's brother. My friend taught at the local university, but his family lived in the town of Huzhou to the north of Hangzhou, several hours away by bus. Huzhou is also a center of silk production, and my friend's brother, fiancée, and their friends all worked in silk factories. My friend thought it might be good for me to go.

The wedding festivities were boisterous, the three days of feasting sumptuous. During the first evening, the young friends of the couple regaled them with songs, many of them suggestive and ribald. One young man stood up and sang in a beautiful tenor voice a song he had learned in elementary school. But after the first verse, the others inexplicably cut him off. An uncomfortable silence filled the room for a moment as he was quickly hushed. The next morning, at breakfast, the groom's parents apologized profusely to me for the previous evening. Making matters worse, I asked them to explain, for the song had been sung in Huzhou dialect, which I had not understood. I had merely appreciated the beauty of the voice. It turned out to be an anti-American song about the Korean War. But now we are friends, the American people and the Chinese people, they hurriedly exclaimed.

Never for a moment could I forget, not just that I was an American in China but that to many people there I represented the potential power to place them in the world through my textual production of China. Many of those I knew in China understood much better than I did when I first arrived the ways in which narratives situated in an unequal world can shape the face of global politics. The Chinese state, of course, has presented foreign scholars with the most thoroughgoing reminders of this concern. In both subtle and direct fashion, party cadres in various capacities, from the foreign affairs office of the local university all the way up to the central Beijing government, have tried to make the Chinese state a co-creator, as it were, of foreigners' stories about them.

Access to those I interviewed as well as to a variety of documents initially depended on formal bureaucratic permissions. There were restrictions, often ambiguous, on what foreigners could and could not do and on where we could and could not go. Western scholars chafe under these regulations, a chafing in which the will to knowledge and the desire for genuine understanding are difficult to disentangle. My own networks of social connections, known as *guanxi*, and personal friendships, which came to include many of these same party cadres, eventually replaced the need to go through formal state channels for my research. And the disorderliness of power ultimately created a crucible within which telling relationships were formed. Still, I never lost my sense of how seriously the Chinese state weighs westerners' words and of the force with which that realization struck me. Regardless of what one thinks about the state's practice, we would do well to remember that it exists within a context that includes recurrent memories of a colonial past, the barely fading traces of over thirty years of virulent anticommunist U.S. rhetoric about "Red China," and China's desire to become a nondependent, formidable player within global networks of political and cultural economies.

The anthropological endeavor in China becomes all the more difficult and misleading if this context is ignored. Yet, it is hampered even further if one assumes that the party-state in China exists as a monolithic entity that acts in a unified fashion or that ideological processes are a simple matter of state control peculiar to communism. Anyone who has lived or worked in China, whether Chinese or foreign, recognizes the multifaceted character of state power and the simultaneously centralized and decentered nature of state politics. For, as I have argued, state power operates not just through its institutions but also in the way it creates itself as an imagined entity. My ability to enter Zhenfu factory and to become a regular presence there—and the fact that both the officials who gave permission and I considered it a special privilege rather than an inalienable right—reflects the ambiguities and complexities of how "the state" functions in China. The power of the party reaches down into each factory and each workshop within each factory. Zhenfu was no exception in its network of party organs that went from the highest levels of its management to the smallest subgroups within each work shift. Doing fieldwork there meant a daily engagement with party concerns. These included the deeply felt nationalist sentiments I have already mentioned as well as a lingering anxiety (particularly among the older generation) left over from the violent vicissitudes of the Cultural Revolution—that openly sharing information with an American foreigner might lead to punishment.

Nevertheless, Zhenfu's party cadres had specific and local ways of interpreting state power that often conflicted with others who also represented the state. Much later, for example, I learned they had defended my presence in their midst to one provincial office that had caught wind of my project only after the fact. People at Zhenfu and elsewhere in Hangzhou spent many months assessing my commitment to China's well-being and my ability to be circumspect about our personal interactions. Having apparently decided that I was fairly trustworthy—indeed, their most pleasurable joke was to tell me I sounded just like the party in my criticisms of the United States—and having turned me into someone who was less than an outsider—by placing me in fictive kin relations—they began to share more of their complaints about the state, as well as their hopes for the future. But the sense of an ambiguous pride in China was never far from the surface.

It is important, however, not to typify the ethnographic encounter as one between the western self and the non-western other. Rather, we should be destabilizing the taken-for-granted quality of these encounters. While I certainly stood out as a western white woman in China, I was never in a position to normalize myself as a typical westerner. I cannot tell stories of how I pointed to a spouse and child to reassure my hosts that my sexuality was safely contained. Instead, I lived with a different set of curiosities and learned perhaps about different kinds of constraints. I hope that I lent some strength to the imagination of women in China who likewise hope for nonconventional lives.

Part One Re-Collecting History

Everybody who tells a story tells it differently, just to remind us that everybody sees it differently. Some people
say there are true things to be found, some people say all
kinds of things can be proved. I don't believe them. The
only thing for certain is how complicated it all is, like
string full of knots. It's all there but hard to find the
beginning and impossible to fathom the end. The best
you can do is admire the cat's cradle, and maybe knot
it up a bit more.

Jeanette Winterson,
Oranges Are Not the Only Fruit

But how to refer to an irreversible past, that is, a past
which this very reference would not bring back, like memory which retrieves the past, like signs which recapture the
signified? What would be needed would be an indication
that would reveal the withdrawal of the indicated, instead
of a reference that rejoins it. Such is a trace, in its empti-
ness and desolation. Its desolation is not made of evoca-
tions but of forgettings, forgettings in process, putting
aside the past.

Emmanuel Levinas,
"Enigma and Phenomenon"

Posing at work for the ethnographer

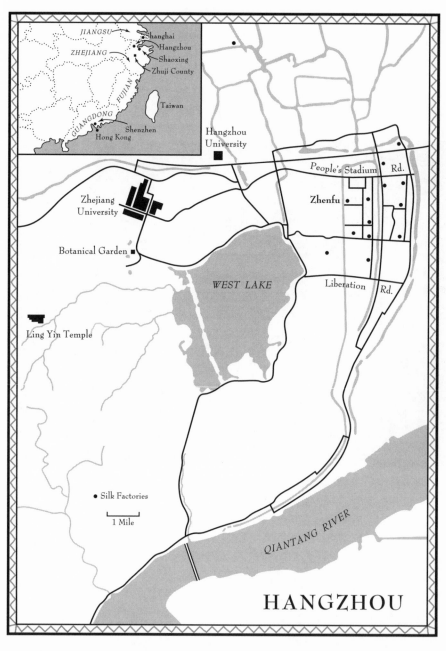

Hangzhou. Source: *Hangzhou Travel Maps,* compiled by Jin Qinyu and Lu Xianjian; text by Chen Qiaoyi (Hangzhou: Hangzhou People's Press).

1 Liberation Stories

We were enjoying the midday break for cadres. Yu Shifu, Tang Shan, and I had gathered in our customary spot, Zhenfu's cramped reception office. Though I spent the bulk of my days in the workshops with women workers, the cadres responsible for me at Zhenfu urged me to lunch with them during their hour in the dining hall rather than in the earlier rushed and noisy half hour when workers hurriedly gulped down their food. My lunches were, relative to workers', luxurious stretches of quiet time.

With economic reform in full swing, Zhenfu's reception office had the air of a train station, what with factory staff running in to use one of the few available phones, or with visiting engineers and cadres, at Zhenfu for collaborative meetings, coming in to grab teacups and thermoses of boiled water. But at this moment, when most cadres were resting after lunch, the office was unusually still.

Tang Shan was then an earnest twenty-seven-year-old who had been a former worker and had the unusual fortune to be promoted to cadre. She had been assigned to take care of my needs. Yu Shifu, then in her late forties, was also a former prep worker as well as weaver. She had been in the factory much longer, indeed since before the socialist revolution, for she had entered Zhenfu as a child laborer. Some ten years earlier she had managed to secure the much less onerous position of factory receptionist. Yu Shifu averred that the factory leadership had "looked after" her because she had become tired and weak. Others confided that Yu Shifu had previously had a position in the weaving shop

41

next to the woman who was the current party secretary. During the Cultural Revolution, Yu Shifu had sided with her when the radical faction had attacked; the receptionist's job was her reward.

Many at Zhenfu gave Yu Shifu the unofficial title of "backbone cadre" in recognition of her long years of devotion to the party. Some said it with admiration and others with a barely perceptible sardonic tone. Yu Shifu, like Tang Shan, was one of the few who stood by the party. In the mid-1980s, Yu Shifu persisted in invoking the socialist guiding phrase "Serve the people," and she dressed in the simple, unadorned blue jacket and pants that signified an earlier era of class politics. No one could have leveled against her the increasingly common accusation about party cadres: corruption of politics for personal gain. On her own initiative, Yu Shifu had assumed toward me the position of surrogate mother and ideological guide. When I arrived at the factory in the morning, she offered me tea to ward off the winter chill; during the day she kept a check on my movements and contacts within Zhenfu; and, occasionally, she sang the praises of the party to me.

Over the weeks, I realized that Yu Shifu was exerting great effort to do "thought work" (*sixiang gongzuo*) with me, to educate and convince me, the outsider, about all the positive transformations in China since Liberation. One point on which she held especially strong views was the liberation of women in China. "Women and men are equal now in China," she would insist to me over lunch, during walks, while we sipped our tea. "Women can go out and work, just like men." "Women have been liberated," she would continue in a slightly anxious and overly eager tone.

I silently disagreed with Yu Shifu, but I always politely nodded my head. I took her comments with an equal measure of respectful interest and political frustration. Anthropologists have laid to rest the myth of the classic participant-observer who merely listens and records. Through numerous self-reflexive descriptions, we have acknowledged that the anthropologist's presence is inevitably a complicated matter of involvement.[1] Yet much experimental ethnography portrays the anthropological encounter as a dialogue that ultimately culminates in a relation of equitable and harmonious exchange. Challenging Yu Shifu, I knew, could be a much more acrimonious affair. I was well aware of how closely the question of women's liberation in China was tied to a defense of the nation. Any challenge to her would operate through a long history of asymmetrical engagements between China and the West.

But that day in the office the strain of anthropological and political disinterest had become too great. I decided to engage her. I was moved to do so, in part, because of the pervasive controversies I was hearing in the silk factories about the effects of the new modernization policies—debates in which women's voices were vociferous. In addition, just the previous day I had been a bemused bystander to a playful argument between Yu Shifu and one of the inspection shop's rakish young men over whether women or men had a more burdensome life. Yu Shifu claimed that women were more burdened, what with shopping at the crack of dawn, cooking time-consuming meals, washing everyone's clothes by hand, and then having to go to work besides. Her interlocutor, in the midst of languidly cleaning his bicycle, pointed at his vehicle, arguing that men had to shoulder all the dirty work women couldn't handle. (Cleaning bicycles, not unlike waxing cars in the United States, is considered "men's work.")

Yu Shifu's convictions about women seemed to me starkly contradictory. I decided to be direct. "If women and men are equal," I challenged, "how is it that there are so many competent women in this factory who don't get promoted to be managers?" My question took her by surprise, less because of its content than its tone. We had negotiated a careful but nonetheless warm relationship over the weeks. My directness suddenly intruded, threatening to break the tentative threads of cautious friendship. The atmosphere in the office changed from one of placid sociability to tense wariness. "Men and women are equal," Yu Shifu replied. "But they are different. Men are more suited to managerial work." I pressed the point, asking bluntly what those different qualities were. My bluntness, I could see, further chilled the air. "Men are stronger than women," Yu Shifu slowly answered, obviously trying to weigh where I was taking the conversation. Assuming she referred to biological traits, I countered that "strength does not lead to intelligence." Shifting the framework of discussion, I pointed out that "since the Cultural Revolution, everyone has gone to great pains to emphasize the difference between physical and intellectual talents." (This was part of a wider repudiation of class labels and class struggle, together with support for the ascension of intellectuals.) Yu Shifu appeared to be without a response. Or perhaps she thought the situation had skidded dangerously close to a breach of the relatively unconstrained relationship we had built. Whatever the reason, she broke off the discussion. Tang Shan, who had stood watching silently from the sidelines, looked both amused at my comments and slightly appalled at my brazen challenge, which might easily have caused Yu Shifu to lose face.

The issue of women's liberation provided one of the most critical terrains on which China endeavored to construct its modernity. At a certain moment, Chinese women's liberation also figured centrally within western feminism as a means for structuring its own forms of knowledge and politics. This chapter explores the multiple deployments of meaning and power constituting "women's liberation" as it reconsiders the heterogeneous processes through which a small group of women felt galvanized to adopt the kinds of revolutionary subject-positions that the socialist regime provided for them. I focus on the oldest cohort of women workers, who came of age with the 1950s nationalization of urban industries, for they were the ones who experienced this radical transition. In Hangzhou's silk factories, a particular fraction of this oldest cohort repeated to me, with much insistence, that the revolution had liberated them. Their commentary is situated within the intersections of a number of discourses: changing cultural logics of gender and work, official socialist narratives, local cultural politics of the silk industry in Hangzhou, nationalism, and, finally, a cross-cultural dialogue with western feminists. In light of the latter, my consideration of the various contestations and investments in the meaning of women's liberation entails simultaneous attention to the politics of feminist ethnography.

For the Chinese state, especially during the Maoist era (that is, from the 1949 revolution to the end of the Cultural Revolution in 1976), woman was a sign of the nation and its possibilities for reaching modernity. By officially interpreting women's liberation as an already-achieved stage in China's history, the state in effect provides a story about the success of the socialist regime in casting off semicolonialism as well as the "feudalism" of Confucian culture that—from their different positions—western colonizers and orientalist scholars, Chinese intellectuals and activists alike invented and debated as they tried to define the essential cause of China's subordination to the West. Projects of modernity during the Maoist era thus revolved centrally around instituting women's liberation.

As the new socialist regime rearranged local economies and social relations in its search for modernity, it crafted the means for sedimenting powerful representations that nonetheless periodically unleashed a vociferous politics about how to interpret and represent the "socialist real." Hangzhou, far from serving as a center of revolutionary fervor, had a reputation, as residents still told me, of harboring the Guomindang opposition. Chiang Kai-shek's native place, people whispered, was not far from Hangzhou.[2] Like most other coastal cities, Hangzhou witnessed the arrival of the revolution after the fact—that is, after the Chinese Communist Party had won the war in the countryside and taken formal hold of the central place of government in Beijing. Cadres representing the new government quickly descended on Hangzhou from Shanghai, a center of revolutionary activity. Older workers remembered a few "underground revolutionaries" in Hangzhou coming forth to lead the new regime, but most learned about the revolution from their Shanghainese visitors and from the northern cadres of peasant background who formed the backbone of the revolution.

The process of learning how to reconceptualize and therefore rework the meaning of experience in every aspect of their lives remains vivid in the memories of older residents. The new regime effectively saturated social life with overlapping political networks. Cadres quickly assembled branches of the Women's Federation, the party, and the youth league within the municipal government, the few factories in existence, and every neighborhood. These committees taught the populace how to conceive of their new lives, emphasizing in particular the joining together of two aspects of socialist modernity as interpreted by the new regime: first, that people now had a future, and that future would become infinitely better; second, that this progress into the future depended on instituting social equality. Cadres thus initiated a rearrangement of social relations that would have unexpected and explosive consequences in the future, as they assigned a class label to every single person. For the urban areas, these included the labels of worker, petty bourgeoisie, national bourgeoisie, and bureaucratic bourgeoisie. Once differentiated, those with the same label were placed together in political meetings, discussion groups, literacy classes, and entertainment activities to learn how to speak and think as socialist subjects. No one remained unaffected. Over the decades, citizens became political adepts at reading the ciphers of socialist power.

The all-too-real fantasies of modernity combined the production of these new identities with economic production. Rapid industrial expansion took center stage in projects of socialist modernity. Having just thrown out the western imperialist powers, China turned to its socialist neighbor, the Soviet Union, for aid and guidance. Massive factories, mighty housing projects, and monumental state-run markets mimicked Soviet development. They transfigured urban landscapes, as at the same time revolutionary operas and heroic films of the peasant and working classes filled the space of public representation. The Hangzhou municipal government followed central government directives in nationalizing all economic activity by the mid-1950s. Tiny "factories," like Zhenfu, of no more than twenty people, were pushed together with the other few silk "factories" to replicate the Soviet larger-than-life socialist realist vision. Owners of silk shops became employees of state-run distribution centers, while capitalist managers became socialist managers. Appearances as much as supposed economies of scale were crucial to the dream of reaching modernity. But Hangzhou retained its reputation as a center of handicraft production, remaining a place where the beauty of its classical landscape lured new political elites rather than tourists, even as a belching steel mill grew on its outskirts. The silk industry, dependent on exports, had a steady if uncertain existence in the ensuing years as it fed mainly Russian tastes before China and the Soviet Union broke off relations in 1962; it also surreptitiously—with a wink and nod of the

Central Textile Bureau—funneled products through Hong Kong (and thus ultimately to the western imperialists).

"Women's liberation" fed on these socialist projects of modernity. In the first years after the socialist revolution, few women thought of their lives in terms of the socialist discourse of women's liberation. Yet there existed a small group of women workers who immediately embraced the new revolutionary categories and became representatives of the party in speaking for women. They joined the party and also took up the political work of the Women's Federation. They made the links, when necessary, with the neighborhood committees that organized women to "labor" for the new state. But their situated interpretations of women's liberation diverged in unanticipated ways from those of both the state and western feminism. The heroism still reflected in their tales was not exactly on the state's terms. The specific gender divisions within Hangzhou's local silk industry also lent an unexpected twist to the way these women became heroic socialist subjects.

At various moments, Chinese women have had as central a place within western feminism as within China. Representations of Chinese women by U.S. feminists have served to counter imperialism, hegemonic notions about socialism's possibilities among the Left, right-wing politics about abortion and reproduction, and the western solipsism of feminist theory, even as they did not operate wholly outside of these frameworks. Yet Chinese women have also served as our radical third world others. At times they appeared in typical, abstract terms. Eventually, western feminists critical of the Chinese party-state definitively concluded that Chinese women were not liberated by socialism. My long engagement with this activist scholarship, with its formative knowledge about Chinese women and its power to authorize feminism, informed my explosive dispute with Yu Shifu and was partially responsible for my strong retorts. After the argument, however, I continued to be troubled by our encounter. I had to confront its ethnographic challenge: how was I to take seriously the words of Yu Shifu?

I could not dismiss her convictions. But what was I to make of our differences? Dominant representations by both the Chinese state and western feminists, despite their radically opposed perspectives, share the tendency to overlook the heterogeneity among Chinese women produced by the revolution. Both sets of interpretations tend to confer on the matter of women's liberation an ontological status; it implicitly depends on a modernist story of linear progress that paradoxically creates a singular, ahistorical theory of both gender identities and feminism. But the troubling nature of my ethnographic encounter, taken together with postcolonial critiques in anthropology and feminism, eventually led me to a different appreciation of Yu Shifu's position and, by extension, to a new set of questions about cross-cultural gender differentiation and feminism.

Understanding why these women enthusiastically took up the language of liberation to organize their lives requires a genealogy of the meanings through which "women's liberation" gained its representational force. Crucially, the party imposed a modern functional discourse of gender subordination, one that revolved around a dichotomy of family and work, on an already existing cultural system of gender that depended on an entirely different cultural dichotomy, a sociospatial logic of inside/outside. The women like Yu Shifu who appropriated the socialist discourse of liberation did so as a way to challenge this gendered culture of space that had earlier constituted appropriate and inappropriate femininity.

To explore the cultural practices that imaginatively constituted women's liberation in China is to address the question of agency and its relationship to the discursive production of social identities. The manner in which these women workers came to conceive of themselves as revolutionary women speaks to the heart of concerns that have preoccupied both recent cultural theory and new social movements. What are the relations among knowledge, power, and action? How do people come to speak as subjects with radical political convictions? What manner of subjectivity supports political change? What is the relationship between theories about subalterns and the practice of subaltern politics?

In theorizing about these multiple concerns, I write fragmented stories in this chapter to highlight the contingency of ethnographic truths and the importance nonetheless of constructing them. Stories of modernity are consequential: not merely transparent windows on otherwise "objective," "material" reality, they—together with other practices—form that which people come to comprehend at a given historical moment as their reality. But the closure imposed on narratives in the name of modernity must be challenged. The fragmentation of the stories reflects one way in which people in China expressed their own shifting locations within postsocialist contentions about modernity. These women confounded, even as they also upheld, the hegemony of the desire for modernity in China. They made room for subtle ruptures in the state's official allegory of liberation. Their stories—and mine—simultaneously decenter ethnographic authority and deconstruct powerful narratives about socialist state power, modernity, and the figure of "woman" who represents them. If, as feminists have recently theorized, gender identity is never fixed but is rather contingent on practice, performance, and context, then the stories that follow mimic in their form how women in China enacted their radically transformed identities. In presenting fragments, I draw out what is implicit in women workers' descriptions of work. Their commentary was at times indirect; the meaning came through in the way they approached their daily engagement with work. My analysis of the meanings of liberation emerges in the juxtaposition of commentary and practice.

DECENTERING THE INTERLOCUTOR

My encounter with Yu Shifu disturbed me on several levels. I thought at the time that an anthropologist was not supposed to argue with her informants and that therefore I had blundered. With few exceptions (Briggs 1970; Visweswaran 1994), anthropologists have rarely portrayed interactions that end in acrimony. Romantic allegories of affinity and acceptance are more often deployed. Culturally, I had stepped beyond the bounds of caring about another person's "face," which I should have placed above the desire to win an argument no matter the social relation. Moreover, I knew that in speaking out about the issue of feminism in China I was treading on nationalist sentiments born out of a colonial history. I felt caught and found myself stumbling into representing a West critical of China.

My heated engagement with Yu Shifu was far from being an act by a neutral observer with a disinterested curiosity about women workers in post-Mao China. The subject of women's liberation in China has perhaps been one of the most vexed questions for Euro-American feminists such as myself who write about the lives of women in third world countries. When the discussions about this particular question were most intense, I had not yet begun to write about Chinese women. Nonetheless, I was actively involved in public feminist debates about socialism and feminism that used Chinese women as our "case." I thus share the history I trace below.

It has become a commonplace that third world women have served as the site of colonial knowledge about the inexorability of "tradition" that marks the third world difference from the West. This insight lies at the heart of critiques of orientalism. Chinese women, however, played an indispensable role in debates among western socialists about the progress of revolutionary world history: U.S. feminists wrote about Chinese women as part of a counterdiscourse to the masculinist heroics of socialism. In fighting against a total erasure of women's subjectivities, they recognized a form of agency in Chinese women that inspired white, Asian American, and other feminists of color. Perhaps justly, some people have criticized these interventions into socialist politics for sharing its colonizing gestures, but feminists did not reproduce the same universalizing rhetorical strategies or homogenizing effects of a uniform world history as did socialist critiques that ignored gender.[3]

Representations of Chinese women divide into two periods. From the late 1960s to the mid-1970s, the Chinese woman held a special place in anglophone feminist writings. Western feminists, like male socialists, looked to China as the utopian answer to our political dilemmas. Chinese women became our heroes. Within a broader feminist framework that shifted theories of modernization to discussions of women's oppression, European and American feminists argued that Chinese women had battled the oppression of traditional Chinese patriarchy; in the vanguard of the revolution, they had fought to abolish footbinding, insisted on "free" marriages and "free" divorces, and claimed the right to something called "work."[4]

This earlier romantic period gave way, under the weight of western feminists' disillusionment with the Left, to an increasing critique of women as caught in the structures of a patriarchal socialist state. Gone were the larger-than-life portraits of iron women who held up half the sky. Chastened by stories that filtered out about the chaos of the Cultural Revolution, feminists situated in the West began another revision of Chinese women's story: women continued to be subordinated by a communist state that had used ideological rhetoric to mislead them. In this version, Chinese women were still oppressed, though now by a new form of socialistic patriarchal family; socialist working conditions, far from having liberated women, doubly burdened them.[5] Those women who proclaimed themselves liberated by the Chinese Communist Party were perhaps the unfortunate objects of the power of ideology. The idea that women in China had been liberated was treated not merely as the socialist state's instrumental use of women but as the state's ideological investment in woman as sign of socialist modernity. Given that the role and position of women had been of central concern to the architects of the Maoist polity, Euro-American feminists felt cruelly betrayed.

These feminist recuperations of Chinese women were essential in breaking new political ground in an international discourse on national liberation movements that had either ignored questions of gender or had implicitly addressed the colonial gaze by invigorating a masculine politics of nationalism.[6] But in the latter accounts of objectification, Chinese women never rose above the generalizations about them to become subjects of a counterhistory. The problem here was not orientalist portrayals of people living in a timeless culture. To the contrary, we were concerned with the progressive movement of Chinese women in history. Rather, the problem with these representations lay in the binary divisions we utilized to forge a singular feminism: socialism versus capitalism, Chinese traditions versus Chinese socialism, and Chinese feminism versus western feminism. We made "socialism" operate as an overarching category of oppression in the same way that religion, family, or the veil have been invoked by those speaking of women in the Middle East (Mohanty 1991).

This long history of representations informed my edgy encounter with Yu Shifu that day in Zhenfu's office. Her insistence in her analysis—shared by many other women of her cohort—that Chinese women had experienced liberation and my initial refusal of her judgment forced open a gap in these cross-cultural feminist dialogues. To disentangle the possibilities in that gap it is necessary to replace liberation's ontology with its historicity. Yu Shifu had, inadvertently, started the process of my own "liberation" from a field of Eurocentric hegemonies.[7]

To move in a different direction requires pulling apart the singularity of the Chinese woman and then holding that multiplicity in tension with a refusal to establish a unitary referent for what constitutes feminism. I thus turn to the cohort of older women workers as feminist analysts of the initial socialist imaginary of modernity in China. I begin with a description of the gender relations and cultural geography of silk production to establish the local meanings of femininity and labor that these women would be moved to contest.

HOUSEHOLD WORKSHOPS

A genealogy of the multiple meanings of "women's liberation" for silk workers must begin with women's relationship to the local silk industry at the time of the revolution. Hangzhou has long been one of China's centers for producing silk. When I first arrived, I assumed that the silk industry there would resemble what I had read about Shanghai—it would be an old industry that experienced early industrialization, since the 1930s it would have been thoroughly imbricated in a global political economy, and women would have filled the factories. I believed that the gendered divisions of labor in the silk industry would be obvious. The university scholars in China who had kindly agreed to supervise my research did nothing to contradict my initial assumptions. When I expressed interest in gender and the cultural divisions of labor, they repeated a popular aphorism: "Men plow, women weave." They presented it as a natural fact of life and as a long feudal tradition. This assumption has also found its way into feminist writings in China. Unlike my university mentors, however, scholars such as Meng Yue and Dai Jinhua analyze the division as the social basis of women's subordination:

> Throughout its long history, China has been an autarkic agricultural society. This form of agricultural life, with food as its basis, meant that the sexual difference in the social division of labor—that men plow and women weave—carried a certain significance of dominance and subordination. It suggested the dominant position men occupied in social production and the dependent or supplementary role of women. . . . It became one of the most basic elements of patriarchal rule. (1990:5)

The stories told me by older workers still working in Hangzhou's silk factories, both men and women, were therefore quite unexpected. They spoke of a world before the revolution and until the mid-1950s nationalization of industries in which silk weaving was the most highly coveted skill in Hangzhou and was entirely dominated by men. Indeed, silk weaving was considered exclusively "men's work" until well after the Great Leap Forward (1958–60), when women in Hangzhou were first encouraged to enter the industry in large numbers. Men dominated silk weaving, moreover, in the context of household workshops that produced the vast majority of the silk in Hangzhou. As everyone readily told me, there were only five "large" factories in existence in 1949, each with a mere thirty to one hundred workers. The elaborate Suzhou brocades, crepes de chine, and Paris brocades for which Hangzhou had gained such renown depended on the painstaking, highly skilled craft of families who generally owned one, hand-operated loom—at most, two. They organized their laboring through their family relations. These household workshops—over several thousand, some estimated—were densely clustered in the working-class districts on the east side and what is now the downtown area. Many of the older workers, both men and women, whom I met in the 1980s traced their genealogies to these family workshops. Their parents, the workshops' last owners before nationalization, had almost all passed away, but these older workers had vivid memories of learning the skills of silk production as children within their households.

Ding Zhuren, for example, the head of the Number 3 weaving shop at Zhenfu, recalls a long lineage in silk weaving from grandfather to father to son: "My father learned from his father. I am the third generation. My grandfather had the hand-operated loom. It didn't use electricity. My father's had electricity. My father was an only son. He didn't even graduate from elementary school. I have six brothers and sisters. I was the oldest. We had only one loom, but we had ten people in the family, so it was hard. My father didn't have any education. You needed that to be a real boss."

His is a tale of patriarchal descent and inheritance, and Ding Zhuren does not wonder about or reflect on this arrangement. To him, even reminiscing from the vantage point of the 1980s, patriarchal power appears natural. What strikes him now, after the repudiation of Maoism, as most unnatural is the loss of that petty capital to the state—that is, his loss, as the oldest son. Ding Zhuren was sixteen when he entered Zhenfu in 1956. Had it not been for nationalization before he had the chance to take over the family loom, he would undoubtedly have become what was later given the class label of *xiao yezhu*, or petty bourgeoisie.

Though only a few years from retirement when I met him, Ding Zhuren was restless. He was known throughout the factory as someone who was quick to exploit the new reforms and who chafed under continued restraints. Once, when Ding Zhuren spoke with me of his disquiet and discontent, he mentioned wistfully that had things been different, he could have been a capitalist by now. In the context of economic reform, positive talk about past bourgeois genealogies is part of the repudiation of Maoism, as the desire to be a capitalist has become a sign of daring, the site of risk, glory, individual achievement, and masculine strength. Ding Zhuren implied that Maoism had forsaken his—and by extension the nation's—latent potentialities, which one inherits through the male line.

There were others scattered throughout the silk industry who traced silk lineages similar to that of Ding Zhuren. Tao Changzhang, director of Chunguang Silk Weaving Factory, attributes his successful rise to his silk heritage passed down from his father. Chen Shifu, whose story I tell at length below, grew up a daughter in a silk-producing household. These personal histories cast a distinctive light on the party's interpretation of gender and liberation. The cultural imbrication of family relations and work relations in a male-dominated craft—virtually the only major craft in Hangzhou—provides one of the meaningful contexts for understanding how certain women in the oldest cohort became inspired to take up a socialist discourse that provided women with a quite different gender identity.

For these household workshops produced not only silk but unequal gender relations within the family. Gender conceptions framed the contours of the household economy even as the workshop relations of production in turn gendered family members and generated positioned interests. Although men and women worked together as family, they were differentially positioned by cultural conceptions embedded in a labor process that doubled as family life.

It was the custom in Hangzhou, I was often told, to think that only men were capable of doing the weaving. The word "custom" carried shades of a normalizing practice through which specific and arbitrary arrangements of gender and labor were made to appear natural. As men's work, silk weaving was a highly sought after skill. Men who migrated from the countryside felt fortunate if they could learn the craft, for male weavers cautiously guarded their knowledge. They generally passed it on only to close relatives or those who hailed from the same native place. Jin Zhuren, head of Zhenfu's inspection shop, arrived in Hangzhou from the rural surrounds of Shaoxing (just south of Hangzhou) on the eve of the revolution, when he was fourteen. He was intent on learning a "skill," for the countryside was poor. Jin Zhuren had a connection through a neighbor in his village who, in turn, had a connection with a weaver in Hangzhou who was from the same village. Only in this way could Jin Zhuren enter the world of silk.

The "mastery" of silk weaving, according to older workers, involved not only skill but "autonomy" for men who could establish family workshops. They were simultaneously skilled artisans, petty proprietors, and heads of households. Each role reinforced the other. The possibility of autonomy rested on the ability of the male head of household to oversee the "outside" realm of the family business; that is, to interact with non-kin in the various realms of commerce in silk. These workshops commonly worked on consignment for silk stores, which provided them with the raw materials and sold the finished silk cloth to colonial importers. Given the uncertainty of the economic situation in China during the wars of the 1940s and the vagaries of the world market in silk, the male head of a silk household needed to be agile in negotiating relations of commerce. If he failed, he might be forced to enter one of the factories, bringing his loom with him. He thus represented the labor of "his" household to those in the outside world as if it were coextensive with his own person. Men in this way not only achieved a skill and a business but, through that business, they also achieved the project of manhood.

The Communist Party would develop an official discourse on women's liberation that interpreted women's lives in functional terms of subordination in a "domestic" sphere of nonlabor. This discourse would radically recast the meanings of women's place in silk-producing households. It would erase any recognition that women in these households had engaged in "laboring" activities. Older workers readily acknowledge, however, that their mothers worked in their family workshops. They did the "women's work" of preparing the silk yarn for their husbands to weave, and occasionally they even did the weaving. Ding Zhuren recalled that "my mother learned before 1956 [when families moved into the factories with nationalization]. Because she was at home. Father had to go out to sell goods. So she would turn on and operate the loom. A lot of women knew how to do this. They didn't know how to repair them."

For Ding Zhuren, as for others, the laboring activity of their mothers was not a cause for shame or awkwardness. It did not lower the social standing of their families, for their mothers engaged in silk production inside the home. Women's subordination in this cultural system was not due, as the party would later reinterpret it, to "material" divisions of labor between the "private" sphere of family and the "public" sphere of work. Instead, women's subordination on the eve of the socialist revolution was organized through a cultural topography that shaped spatial relations in terms of sexual difference. Divisions of labor were not the causal foundations so much as exemplifications of a larger cultural construction of gender.

Before turning to a discussion of that spatial topography, however, I offer Chen Shifu's story of growing up in a silk-producing household. Chen Shifu, a much admired senior silk weaver at Zhenfu, was one of the first women to enter the male domain of silk weaving in the 1950s. Her narrative highlights the different gender positionings within the cultural economy of silk production. The women and men in these household workshops did not always share a unified cultural perspective. Nor did the cultural logics of this economy always go unchallenged. Though often taken for granted, they could also be the site of conflict and gendered insubordination. Household workshops, as a node of social life and a field of power, reproduced sociospatial representations of femininity and masculinity characteristic of urban Chinese culture in the first half of the twentieth century. This specificity produced its own set of critical gendered commentary. Chen Shifu's story provides one such commentary.

A DAUGHTER, NOT A SON

Chen Shifu's is a tale about the downfall of a household workshop, and it is not in any sense typical. The tenuous circumstances of her early life thwarted the hegemony of gender differentiation in silk households. It is through just such gaps that alternative visions can slip, as other discursive practices lodge there. In Chen Shifu's story, then, we begin to discern the way in which the socialist state's production of knowledge about women's liberation was able to take such powerful hold in the imaginations of particular women.

I first met Chen Shifu on a late autumn day at Zhenfu when a rare moment of respite had quieted the looms. The lack of sufficient electrical power in the city meant that each district was required to follow a rotating schedule of halting electrical use for several hours every week.

The city government tried to spare industrial work units, but it was Zhenfu's turn, and so the usual hum and racket of the looms and spindles briefly died away. Several workers, especially the older ones, discreetly tried to appear busy, as not being occupied could be interpreted as a political stance, echoing Cultural Revolution work morality. Others were less concerned; young men dragged on their cigarettes while young women chatted among themselves. Workshop cadres tried to prove their "efficiency" by calling production meetings. I took advantage of the calm to tell Tang Shan that I wished to speak with an older weaver, as most of my more intimate contacts had been with young women in the prep shop. She promptly brought Chen Shifu over from one of the weaving shops to meet with me in the small, spare office off the elaborately stuffed reception room in what workers colloquially called the "higher ups' " building: that is, where the administration lodged itself. Workers rarely entered it; they would tell me they didn't have the qualifications to do so. When one or the other of the women from the prep shop would, on occasion, wander over to look for me, they peered awkwardly into the entrance, unsure how to conduct themselves in this unknown place. They knew no one there; to them, the higher ups, the cadres in charge of the factory, were strangers.

But Chen Shifu had none of these qualities. She entered the room with a firm gait, as if the trappings of power in the place where cadres resided contained little that could shake her. Unlike some others, she was not shy or hesitant with the foreigner. In her mid-forties, Chen Shifu was, as the phrase went, "willing to talk." Since the Cultural Revolution was still fresh in people's minds, a "willingness to talk" indicated a lack of fear of political retribution. When used to refer to women, such ability to speak up also meant resemblance to a man, for women were supposed to be inarticulate and timid with strangers. Yang Zhuren proudly introduced Chen Shifu as one of the factory's two "model workers" chosen by the city's silk bureau for the last several years because of her high productivity.[8] Her "modelness" may have designated her as a person who could speak and whose speech had value, but it did not entirely determine the content of her speech. Her critique of economic reform was sharp and pointed, as was her dismissal of the qualities of cadres. They all got there through connections, she once said.

Chen Shifu and I had several lengthy conversations, as well as more informal contact thereafter. Our interactions were made possible in a multilayered network of geopolitics. Yet our conversations did not simply reflect this geopolitical territory, for we both maneuvered at unpredictable counterangles to the forces that had brought us together.

Chen Shifu identified herself strongly as a skilled master of her trade, in part because she could call upon a long history with silk. Chen Shifu, like Ding Zhuren, grew up surrounded by silk production in a household workshop and from there entered Zhenfu in 1956, at the age of fourteen. But unlike Ding Zhuren, as a young girl Chen Shifu could never expect to inherit and run the family loom. Her position as a girl but also the oldest child in the family workshop, coupled with the unexpected trajectory of her household fortunes, made it possible for Chen Shifu to rebel against the cultural economy of gendered silk work.

I asked Chen Shifu to tell me the history of her involvement in the silk industry. We sat one across from the other, at one of the cadres' desks. Her story emerged gradually. "My circumstances were rather special. I was a 'family laborer' (*jiating gong*). But my pa died when I was seven. My ma was not very capable. My pa was a weaver; my ma did all the yarn preparation (*fansi*) and everything. I had a younger brother; it was just the two of us. He later became a carpenter." Chen Shifu's initial comments were cursory and to the point. Containing none of the embellishments and indirection of educated elite speech, they placed people and their activities. Yet I was struck by the brief moment in which she figured her mother with ambiguous hints of criticism, for it was rare to hear someone criticize her or his parents. Our conversation meandered to the increased work pressures these days and to the unfairness of her situation: "My wages have always been a little strange. I was so young as an apprentice. I didn't even get the usual 'clothing expense.' So there's always been a big difference between my wages and others. I was an apprentice for three years. They didn't really have apprentices. I was in the household. My mother and I entered the factory. I was a household laborer, but because I was so young they treated me like an apprentice even though they didn't have any. So every time they raised wages I went up with the young workers because my wages were always lower. We didn't know before about the government documents that talked about raising wages, about who should get raises. So I really lost out. But I don't want to haggle over it. It's more important to do good work."

But stronger emotions emerged inadvertently, when I asked about her education. Chen Shifu self-consciously explained, "I didn't have a chance to study. In 1956, when I entered the factory, I was a little illiterate person. I went to night school then. I studied for a couple of years and can recognize a few characters. But we didn't have as good conditions then. And women were not as important then." That "women were not as important then" was said casually; the socialist historiography embedded in the comment is noticeable only in its taken-for-granted quality.

Chen Shifu's tone grew harder, though, in what she told me next. The visceral emotion in her voice as she related the losses she experienced marks the substantive weight she continues to place on these events in explaining her sense of what it means to be a woman weaver. There were undoubtedly complex reasons for the demise of her family's silk workshop. It is therefore important to listen closely to the manner in which Chen Shifu's unequivocal memories of her experience tell a story that highlights the ability of men to betray women who are ill-equipped to confront the world of outside social relations.

She continued, "My father definitely would have let me study. 'My money is enough for her to study at the university.' Those were his words when he was dying; he said it to my ma. But my ma couldn't even write her own name. She didn't know how to do things. So she was cheated out of the money by others, because she couldn't read." Chen Shifu paused, and I hesitantly pushed her to tell me the story. "Friends, who were like brothers," she said with strong feeling, but also as if the events stood on a distant horizon. "They were not my own family. They said they would take the silk cloth and sell it and give her the money. But they didn't give her the money." "Did you ever see them again?" I asked. "We still had contact with them after that. But when I was thirteen and could understand things, then we didn't have any dealings with them anymore."

Chen Shifu herself, she implied, took control at a young age and began to order the household economy. What might have otherwise been a seamless cultural economy of gender operating through her family's workshop fissured as a result of her father's death. In the gap that opened, Chen Shifu began to glimpse the arbitrariness of gender relations that left women at such a critical disadvantage.

In her narrative, Chen Shifu casts herself as the wise and tough daughter who could have saved the household workshop had she been raised as a son or had she not been constricted by conventional femininity. Chen Shifu's tale creates a young girl with implicit desires—and the ability—to transgress gender boundaries. This young girl strains against the conventions of femininity and masculinity that keep her on the "inside" of the business and arbitrarily place men in a position of dominance. That Chen Shifu attributes these insights to herself as a young girl reveals as much about the possibilities she later found in the socialist state's discourse on women to cast off "traditional" femininity as about the circumstances that produced her desire to embrace it.

But the story of her troubles did not end here. One afternoon I asked if we could speak more about the 1950s. Chen Shifu said she was hoping to hang out her laundry to dry, since the weather was clear and she was on the evening shift. Perhaps out of politeness to the foreigner, though, she acceded to my request. Before I could ask any questions, she launched in: "It was a set rule [when they nationalized the industry] that for each loom you brought in, you could bring in two and a half people. One person who did the light, cleanup work, sweeping, pouring water, that person counted as half a person. Ma came in and did the *fansi*. We didn't have a main worker in our family. Ma and I were not. I counted as a child laborer. There wasn't any eldest brother and my younger brother was too young. Ma counted as a regular worker, so we made up one and a half people." The last time we talked, Chen Shifu had mentioned the presence of an older cousin in her family's workshop. Confused, I asked what happened to him. "Yeah, my older cousin counted as a worker. He was the main labor power." An older cousin working in the household workshop would, under most circumstances, have been considered a member of the family. I was struck by Chen Shifu's initial deliberate exclusion of her cousin from counting toward the two and a half people who could be nationalized. Why had he not been part of the family history? I delicately wondered aloud if her cousin knew how to weave when he came to work in her family. Chen Shifu's story about her cousin poured out:

"My cousin couldn't do anything when he first came. He was from the countryside. Pa had called him in. He was pa's older brother's son. We were too young to help. My cousin was fourteen. It was after pa had returned from Shanghai, then he taught him. Pa was a worker in a factory in Shanghai. A big factory there. We weren't born yet. It was around Liberation. They closed the factory and gave him money. Pa rented a house in Hangzhou and bought a loom.

"He and ma married late. After he returned from Shanghai. Ma was from the countryside. They married just at Liberation. I didn't grow up in Hangzhou. Pa worked in Hangzhou by himself. After a couple of years, he brought in my cousin and ma to live there. We two kids stayed in the countryside. We lived in a small temple that we fixed up. We built three rooms and lived there.

"But after I was six, I came to Hangzhou. Labor power was tense. Pa was sick, but he was still working. I was small, but I still had to do the work. I cooked and I studied *fansi, juansi* (reeling and twisting the yarn). Ma had no time to do this work. Ma's mind wasn't quick. So by the time I was seven, I learned these skills. Things were tense and I was the biggest child. There was no time to study. If I had an older brother or an older sister, I coulda gone to study. Then after three years, we formed the cooperative. That was 1956.

"We weren't doing good business. It shoulda been good. We coulda done well. My cousin, we were like brother and sister. He shoulda helped us. But his conscience (*liangxin*) was no good. There was planned production by then. Each month we got fifteen bolts of silk yarn. We were supposed to weave them. But you got fined if you didn't finish the work you got from them. My cousin, he wasn't willing to do the work. His skill wasn't any good besides. So we had defective cloth. If you made defective cloth, then you lost even your money to cover the costs. And the next time they gave you less to work on. So our family, slowly we had less wages. He didn't have his heart in succeeding. So cousin felt like, let's just go into the cooperative and be done with it. Ma, she didn't have any learning to run a business. We shoulda done well. Some families did well."

As an afterthought, she added, "My cousin had a bad temper. So they sent him to another factory back in 1959. A cotton textile factory [where labor was much less highly skilled]. Now he just sweeps the floor. We don't have much contact with him."

In this narrative about her family's silk workshop, Chen Shifu crafts a story of her past in which an older male cousin, who should have acted like the oldest son, allows the family workshop instead to sink into ruin. She casts her mother as a symbol of the incompetencies of traditional womanhood. She plays the part of the wise daughter who, if she had been the oldest son, could have saved her family. In the background lie larger socioeconomic forces—in particular, the new regime's gradual centralization of production, which meant both economic stability and increasing constraints on the petty entrepreneurs who led silk households. While Chen Shifu recognizes their structural importance, socioeconomic forces are not deterministic; indeed, within their frame, the cultural politics of gender loom much larger. Chen Shifu's narrative challenges essentialist notions of homogeneous gender identities, portraying instead telling moments when desires contrary to dominant, seemingly taken-for-granted practices might arise. That the language of gender politics captures such moments has everything to do with the party's representations of women, which began to reach Chen Shifu just at the time of her story, in the mid-1950s. That discourse sparked her imagination to envision a different female subjectivity, one that came to view the gender differentiation in her household as a contingent cultural form rather than a natural artifact of fate. The socialist state's representations of women enabled, even as it obscured, what might otherwise have been a more muted and inchoate contestation to the cultural hegemony of her early life.

We might further note that male weavers–cum–household heads in the Hangzhou silk industry did not find much liberation in Liberation. For them, it was a process of proletarianization of skilled artisans. One former manager who was around at that time spoke of these men as "unruly and undisciplined." With nationalization, the state deliberately redistributed their looms for others to use, trying to break their identification with private property. The older male weavers insisted on constantly checking their own looms, refusing to accept the state's erasure of the link between loom, property, and manhood. Most retired early; a few stayed; a few became managers, as the relational boundary between "women's work" and "men's work" shifted; and a few of the younger ones joined the radical faction in the Cultural Revolution, still protesting their lost manhood.

INSIDE/OUTSIDE

Chen Shifu contested the boundaries of female respectability that constrained her "inside" her family's workshop.[9] Yu Shifu, in contrast, never found herself presented with the chance to achieve respectable femininity. Yu Shifu and other poverty-stricken women were forced to work "outside" in Hangzhou's few factories. On the outside, they found themselves on the other side of the border of respectability. The shame of their activity lay not in the labor itself but in its location. Only gradually did I come to realize how a cultural topography based on a dichotomy of inside and outside critically informed the meaning of liberation for women already located in factories. Their shame, or lack of social virtue, served as another central site for inducing ardent political convictions about socialist liberation, though not entirely in the state's terms.[10] Shame is not easy to recall or embellish on. It surfaced only indirectly and in brief moments in women's narratives about life prior to the revolution. To grasp the import of what are necessarily fragments of stories that evoke shame, it is necessary to consider the cultural meanings of inside/outside that produced a loss of social virtue.

Inside/outside is a pervasive cultural construction of space embedded in implicit social knowledge. It is a doxa, or cultural schema (Bourdieu 1977), whose simplicity lends itself to multiple renderings. This cultural binary is not unique to silk-producing households or to Hangzhou. It

applies more generally to relations between those within and those outside of kinship networks, as well as to relations between villages, na-
tionalities, people of different native places, and even, since 1949, between work units. I came across this doxa in almost every aspect of life.
People would say of those not from Hangzhou that they were "outsiders." Government organs, such as the police, refer to their organization
as "inside," in relation to the public outside. The "foreign affairs office"
of the local university—most work units also had one—is literally the
"outside affairs office." It deals not only with foreigners from abroad
but with anyone who is outside of, or does not belong to, the university.
Internal or "inside" documents (*neibu*) are documents that anyone not
of the government organ that issued them or at a certain level of party
hierarchy is forbidden to read. Those who are skilled in a particular craft
or excel at a certain type of commerce or are up on the latest fashions
are known as "insiders" (*neihang*), while those who don't have the same
knowledge are "outsiders" (*waihang*). And, of course, when cadres
would not allow me to do something or go somewhere, they would say,
"You know, there's always a line between insiders and outsiders."

Strikingly, by the 1980s this cultural dichotomy of inside/outside did
not map onto gender. Only once did I hear a very senior professor introduce his wife as "my inside person" (*neiren*). Yet, prior to 1949, this
spatial distinction was gendered in its conception and application.[11] Conversely, gender categories were spatialized. Such gendering of space
was, in turn, given cultural weighting through class hierarchies. These
mutual imbrications suggest the cultural force of inside/outside distinctions prior to the revolution in differentiating the boundaries of social
respectability.[12] "Respectable" women of the gentry and urban upper
classes had the means to remain inside the bounds of kinship relations.
Working-class women and poor peasant women were more vulnerable.
Yet they too struggled to remain inside, for such a location defined female subjectivity. Transgressing the historically variable border of in-
side/outside, then, meant the loss of full female personhood within one's
kinship world, which is to say within one's social world. As Margery
Wolf aptly puts it: "Only women who had gone out of the family and
were therefore outside the rules of respectability appeared openly in the

streets. These were the beggar women, the slave girls, the prostitutes, the vendors, the servants. Few women, no matter how close to starvation, made the decision to go out easily, for there was no going back" (1985:12). In turning to the fragmentary stories that follow, we need only add to Wolf's list women factory workers before the revolution.

Yu Shifu would, on occasion, walk me back to my place in the weft preparation shop after lunch, with a combination of care and gentle surveillance. Ten years had passed since Yu Shifu had left this space of production activity that is gendered female. In a gesture half playful, half serious, Yu Shifu once took up a place on the line, her old place. This is how we used to do it, she instructed. Then she deftly bit off the ends of a broken silk yarn and retied it all in one motion, working so quickly I barely caught the act with my eye. She became absorbed in her task, demonstrating how it was done all by hand and teeth in those days, not with the pair of wide scissors that young men nowadays hang from their ear and women more discreetly place in their work bibs. One of the young women standing alongside of me murmured, "That's why they say we silk workers 'eat' silk food." Yu Shifu's performance, her show for us, evoked a sense of the long distance from the recent past, of memories at once nostalgic and alive, of the inseparability of the heroics of labor and its bitterness in the early 1950s, when the meaning of one's position as a woman worker underwent a revolution—a liberation for some, like Yu Shifu. Her actions hinted that the signification of her labor power lay not just in the task but in its creation of her as a particular gendered subject.

We are strolling in the Hangzhou Botanical Gardens, Yu Shifu and I. The end of winter is near, but the air is still brisk and the famed flowers and blossoming trees that once drew Song dynasty painters to this spot and currently draw hordes of tourists have yet to appear. That morning, Yu Shifu had invited me to her home for lunch. As Yu Shifu's husband is an army X-ray technician, they had recently gained the privilege of living in the army compound, in the wooded hills on the west side of West Lake, not far from the famous Buddhist temple, Linyin. Yu Shifu was proud of how far she had risen; she wanted to show off her new home to me. She had not realized that foreigners were forbidden from entering army areas.

When I arrive, she hurriedly meets me at the gate to explain, with much embarrassment. We eat at the temple and then spend a desultory afternoon in the gardens, located just beyond the army compound on the other side from the temple. Yu Shifu is chatting volubly about her daughter's recent wedding. Her daughter is one of the assistant accountants at Zhenfu. Yu Shifu is especially pleased with the enormous amount she has been able to give her daughter as wedding money to buy furniture for their new home and to go on a honeymoon. She then waxes eloquent about her comfortable home, with its trees all around and the nearly free hot water; the high wages that she and her husband together bring home; and the latest soap opera she and I are in the midst of following. Her relative rise in status and success still strike her with wonder, and she draws me in to share her pleasure.

I press her to go back and remember for me the beginnings of her life in the silk factory. Yu Shifu's tone and mood change perceptibly. She becomes more reticent. There is nothing to be proud of here, at least not in the early years. Later, I will take her reticence itself to be significant, because I will have seen it in others who spoke to me about pre-Liberation times. It reveals how the party's official stories of liberation effaced particular kinds of shame attached to women, but in such a way that the memory of that shame could never turn into the heroic tales of class suffering that workers would learn to tell. Yu Shifu passes on a quick sketch, lacking the embellishment she has just given to her family's current glories.

"I began [working in a silk factory] when I was ten years old. Before that, I had grown up in the countryside. Then, because Japan had invaded China, everybody was fleeing from them. We fled to the city. To Hangzhou. But it was hard to find work, so we fled again to the countryside. My father died when I was only six. My mother had to go out to work then; she became a maidservant and took care of someone else's children. Then she met my stepfather and married him. Then we moved to Hangzhou. Of course, a stepfather is never the same as a father. So I decided it was best to go out and find work.

"I found a job through friends. In those days, it was like that. A friend of yours worked in a factory—they were all small factories in those days, with only a few people. We had to light candles and bow to our boss. That's all.

"We were all silk reelers. It was all by hand then. We put the silk thread on the wide frame and turned it and then the silk thread turned onto the shuttle. It was very bitter, then. You couldn't produce much, in one day, maybe only a few ounces. Now you can produce several hundred. Then they began, after Liberation, they began to have the machines and the work was partly by hand, partly by machine. You pull the thread out of the cocoon, that's by hand, but then you connect it to the machine.

"My mother didn't work in the silk industry; she stayed at home, looking after my younger brother—the child she had with my stepfather."

Yu Shifu was forced, by the winds of history blowing her family back and forth, to go out to work as a child. She must go out, even as her mother has found the means to come back in. Though she quickly turns the conversation to the challenges of the technology, one can discern in her narrative the tacit allusions to the enormity of her movement to the outside and of her mother's movement first outside and then back inside. Only severe disasters—a large-scale war over empire, the death of a father—could have compelled her to take this step. Such a journey marks not merely functional movement through space but an enormous cultural transgression that brings dishonor and devaluation. The degradation of having done so exists at several registers in the narrative—as implicit social knowledge so obvious it needs no further elaboration, as submerged fragments in her party-inspired political convictions that offered a divergent interpretation of the originary causes of women's oppression, and as a still dynamic sentiment of discomfort with the implications of the shame.

We are walking down the alleyway leading off from the front gate of Zhenfu. Yu Shifu, Tang Shan, and the young assistant to the factory's party secretary are accompanying me in search of new shoes. We are laughing about the large size of my feet compared to those of Chinese people; they warn that I might not find anything that fits. They are right.

This begins a discussion of Chinese women's feet. "In the past," Yu Shifu intones, "women bound their feet because it was thought to be beautiful." "Was it really thought to be beautiful?" I inquire. The young man avows that it was. Yu Shifu turns the conversation into another lesson about liberation. "Also, they did it to keep women in place so they couldn't run away." The others erupt into laughter at her exegesis, but Yu Shifu becomes earnest. "It's true. Women weren't supposed to go out; this way they couldn't rebel. Now women are liberated, they can do what they want. Women go out to work."[13]

Here, in a more humorous mood, she was willing to talk about the issue of women going out of the appropriate social sphere.

I am conducting a formal interview with two older women workers at Zhenfu: Yang Wanfen, head of the trade union, and Si Zhaoding, head of security. Si Zhaoding's name means "beckoning certainty," an optimistic name for someone born amid the chaos of the Anti-Japanese War. Si Zhaoding is a short, tough, wiry woman with a smoker's cough and black shadow under one eye that made her look like a boxer who didn't shy away from a fight. It was unusual for a woman to be head of security. Si Zhaoding had a local reputation. Just the year before, a young man from Zhenfu threatened to kill his girlfriend for having rejected him. He wrapped a bomb around his body and planned to throw himself on her. Si Zhaoding went to his home and talked to him through the entire night until she had talked him out of it. This event became a story of heroism in the local news. Si Zhaoding traces the "bravery" and "frankness" that she says make her suitable for security work back to the 1950s. Yang Wanfen is taller, rounder, and softer than Si. They both appear more versed and less hesitant in telling their stories of suffering before Liberation than Yu Shifu. Both had come from Zhuji county to work as child laborers at Zhenfu before Liberation. They entered the factory together in 1947, at the age of thirteen: "That was old for child labor." Most of the workers were child laborers then, they explain, "because capitalists wanted to make more money." They came from the countryside: "Country people know how to 'eat bitterness' and work hard; that work was a real hardship." Most of the work was reeling, and so almost all the workers were women. Yang Wanfen did reeling, but Si Zhaoding, because she was so short, was assigned straightening-up work. Each had family already working at Zhenfu, who served as their guarantors—Yang's mother and Si's father's sister.

They stress the exploitation: the virtual lack of wages for children, who received only small material goods; the unconscionably long work hours—"The roosters called us out of the house and the ghosts sent us back in"; the literal pain of the work—"The water was so hot in the reeling that the skin on your hands softened and then fell off in pieces"; and the constant surveillance of their activities—"We couldn't go out of the factory. If a relative came to visit, we talked to each other through the window."

Yet they also emphasize the specific hierarchies by gender. Everything, it seemed, was distinguished by male and female. Wages were set by gender, no matter which tasks women and men performed. The four-level scale of wages established the relevant categories: skilled, male, female, child. "Even men who swept the floor received higher wages than women reelers." The food at the factory also distinguished among levels. "The women's rice and vegetables were the most inferior." They recalled that the male workers had four dishes and a soup; the women only a few dishes of old vegetables. The skilled personnel ate from ten dishes while the high-level management had dishes they could order prepared especially for them. For year-end bonuses, male workers received two month's wages while women workers received objects, such as rings.

Only at the very end did they touch on the shame of women going out to work, and only in answer to my direct question. Here, I found the same reticence as Yu Shifu had shown: a brief answer, no elaboration. "If the family had means, of course they didn't let women go out to work. Only if they were very poor." The emphasis was on the word "out" rather than "work."

Men with authoritative voices are more willing to elucidate the source of this shame. A retired teacher from the Zhejiang Silk Institute has kindly agreed to speak with me. Zhao Junshan, a rotund, ebullient man

in his late seventies, speaks without fear of castigation for giving information to the foreigner, though he was formerly labeled a small capitalist. But his experiential knowledge of silk from before the socialist
revolution has become a desired object in the post-Mao state. He has
been resurrected to save the industry from its Maoist excesses. Zhao's
class label has been transformed into new symbolic capital.

He enjoys reminiscing, and I warm to him. His life is filled with the
adventures of the silk business both before and after the revolution. In
his narrative each of his experiences is iconographic, as he sweeps their
import into historical forces larger than himself. His early beginnings in
the business were in a silk store in 1925 at the age of thirteen, in his
hometown of Shaoxing.[14] Silk handicrafts formed the backbone of the
local economy of this area from Shanghai south of the Yangze River
along the coast. Except for Shanghai, the rest of the area depended on
small workshops and stores and peasant families that grew silkworms
in the surrounding lush countryside rather than on any large-scale industrialization.

These beginnings become lessons in the class innocence of youth, before the revolution. "I was young. But I had an idea. When I first entered
the store, I bowed to the god of wealth and then to the boss, saying
'Master' (*Xiansheng*). I then had an idea. Even though I didn't know how
I was to make money, I thought the master was extraordinary. I wanted
to be a great master. A manager. I envied them. I wanted to be well
disciplined, honest, have means and a skill. I didn't know at that time
that if you open a store you exploit people, I didn't know about this
Marxism."

Zhao eventually opened his own silk store, in Hangzhou, after the
Anti-Japanese War (1937–45). It was a risky time to open a store, as
Hangzhou was in the midst of recovering from wartime chaos. Inflation
and instability threatened the silk industry, which was highly dependent
on exports. Attached to Zhao's store was a small factory, with twenty
workers. I ask if there were any women workers in the factory. "No, no
women workers. Preparation work was done at home. No women came
out to go to work. If a woman went out to work, nobody wanted her."
When I press for an explanation, he offers an aphorism: "Women fall

into the factory like a horse falls on the battlefield." I press for more, getting closer to the source of the shame. "If a woman fell into the factory, it was the same as an injured horse. Nobody wanted her."

What Zhao means is that nobody wanted these women as a respectable marriage partner. They were damaged goods, no longer sexually virtuous, because they had transgressed the appropriate sexual boundaries for where women should work. Again, it was not the fact of their labor but its location. These women were vulnerable to the gaze of male strangers, which was enough to sully any claims to being virtuous women. Women who worked outside in factories were placed in the same category as other "fallen" women. They were, as one person said, just like "broken shoes," a slang term for prostitutes. Their shame was sexual. After all, Zhao said, this was not the "sin city" of Shanghai, where anything went, where women could work in factories because all manner of "sin" was going on anyway.

Another authoritative man confirms this view. Professor Wu of the history department at the local university reels off a brief history of Hangzhou's silk industry for me. Then he comments about conditions before the revolution: "Workers' lives were very bitter, especially women workers. They did reeling in a big factory, where it was extremely hot from the water they soaked the cocoons in. They did everything by hand; there was no machinery. Their work was arduous. They wore undershirts and shorts. When I went to look inside the factories in the early 1950s, we didn't dare enter because we were too embarrassed to see these women."

It was that male gaze that shamed these women.

Inside/outside as implicit social knowledge of space is not homologous with dichotomies that oppose "family" or "domestic life" to "work" or "public" life. Women's inside activities were not construed primarily in relation to motherhood or to "housework." In contrast to an American middle-class cultural dichotomy of domestic versus public, inside/outside was not based on a misrecognition of activities within the household as nonlabor, or as arising from women's psychological propensities to nurture. None of those involved in either household workshops or in the factories spoke of their relationships with their mothers in terms of the quality of emotional caretaking or the amount of attention they received. Some of the women who had been child laborers freely admitted being sent to the countryside to live with other relatives without portraying it as a time of lost mothering, or alternatively as a lost childhood.

While women's activities inside family workshops were not construed in terms of American white, middle-class notions of domesticity, neither were they cast in opposition to a category labeled "work." Ding Zhuren and others readily acknowledged that their mothers labored in preparing the silk yarn or operating the loom; the femininity and honor of these women and their families were not challenged by such activity.

Lou Shengzhi confirms this interpretation. Lou Shengzhi is known locally as "the woman capitalist," for she is the only woman to have owned and managed one of Hangzhou's silk factories prior to the revolution. She is a slight woman in her sixties, with vital, expressive eyes. The first time I speak with Lou Shengzhi, I express my curiosity about how a woman in the 1940s came to run a silk factory. Lou Shengzhi responds that her "old man" (i.e., her husband), then a wealthy silk entrepreneur, gave her the means to do so. But what, I want to know, did people think of her as a woman running a factory. There was no problem, she quickly asserted, because in managing the factory she was inside her home. Lou Shengzhi and her family lived inside the factory, in rooms located above the shop floor.

Unlike the gender segregation described for women elsewhere (Abu-Lughod 1993; Boddy 1989), the inside space of the family, at least for urban entrepreneurial families, was not demarcated into separate sexual spaces. It was a hetero-gendered space where women interacted with men connected to them through familial ties, thus making such social interactions appropriate. It was heterosexual rather than feminine. Social space outside of the family, by contrast, was marked masculine. The resulting opposition was one of heterosexual versus masculine rather than feminine versus masculine.[15]

The cultural construction of appropriate femininity and masculinity thus framed activities of labor, but not in the manner that the state's discourse on women's liberation would later pose. Work outside in the few factories that existed in Hangzhou before the revolution was fraught with shame and dishonor for the women forced to engage in it. These women workers' continuing need to cast narratives of their past in terms of force—that only historical, familial, economic, or other powers beyond a self-respecting woman's control would induce her to enter a factory—underscores the extent of the shame. The source of that disrepute, however, lay not in the work itself, either the general activity of labor or the particular tasks—in this case reeling and preparation of the thread—to which women were assigned. That is, it was not the idea that they were women who *worked* that marked them as "fallen horses" or "broken shoes." Rather the disgrace lay in its social location; the factories pulled women outside the social spheres where proper women maintained their femininity. The social location of work shifted the terms of their femininity. Being outside, in factories, turned them into women whose sex was a matter of humiliation. This shame, as evidenced in the men's comments as well as in the women's continued reticence, operated through the way that men such as these, who had no familial connection to the factory women, could nonetheless gaze upon them.[16]

Even as gender became normalized through this configuration of space, space was naturalized in terms of gender. This cultural schema of inside/outside did not merely describe social space but made it meaningful. Gendered subjects were constituted as they moved through spaces marked as appropriate or inappropriate. Inside/outside was not a template imposed on already sexed bodies but created the sexual markings of those bodies. Women and men achieved their gender identities as they moved in this cultural schema. But once women lost their virtue by stepping into a factory, there was, as Wolf remarked, no turning back.

FROM "BROKEN SHOE"
TO LIBERATED REVOLUTIONARY

1948: The Anti-Japanese War has drawn to a close and the People's Liberation Army is fighting the Guomindang regime, backed by the United

States. Liberation, it will turn out, is only a year away. The Chinese Communist Party is preparing for its entrance into the cities from its bases in the countryside as a prelude to establishing a new state. Central to this preparation is the creation of a socialist imaginary that would legitimate this new state. Crafting such a visionary politics depends on an interpretation of women as active subjects freeing themselves from history:

> Women, who form half the population, have played a big role and have become an indispensable force for defeating the enemy and building a new China. . . . The central task in woman-work is to organize women to take an active part in production. . . . [I]n some districts conscientious care has not been given to eliminating the survivals of feudalism which hold women back. . . . The attitude of valuing men and despising women handed down from the old society, all kinds of constraining feudal customs, especially the economic dependence of women on men and the handicaps of not excelling at all sorts of labour and even despising it, have obstructed the rapid realization by women of the rights already granted to them in law. . . . *[A]bove all they must be made to understand fully the importance of labour and must look on it as glorious* [emphasis added].[17]

Labor. Production. The new China. The old feudal customs. These elements coalesce in the document quoted, one among many on this topic, all designed to bring into existence the new revolutionary woman. The concrete, pragmatic tone of these powerful pronouncements evokes an epistemology of scientific realism that almost allows us to forget that this was a specific—and revolutionary—mode of representation, one that made socialist sense out of the oppression in women's lives. The revolution was made out of the barrel of a gun, but it was also made through socialist realist metaphor: a functional metaphor that made "productive labor" the definitive mark of a fully social being and the standard for measuring human worth. This socialist production of subjectivity only partially replaced the previous system's evaluation of humanness according to kinship relations. If, until recently, this logic of a political economy of labor has appeared translucent and rather acultural, it is only because we have forgotten the sense in which Marx's critique was also testimonial to a revolution and therefore was a form of cultural praxis.

In Chinese Marxist discourse, "work" (*laodong*) was constructed as a new cultural category: it became equated with "productive" activity, which in turn was defined as activity that produced surplus value for the state, acknowledged with a wage. Certain activities and not others became valued as work. Activities confined inside the family became either signs of the feudal constraints that held women back from liberation or petty-bourgeois (i.e., nonproductive) labor, privatized and therefore opposed to the interests of the state. This functional metaphor of production versus home created a radically different cultural framework for evaluating Chinese womanhood. It led to a certain interested "forgetting" of the sociospatial metaphor of inside/outside that had so recently produced appropriate and inappropriate femininity.

In this revolutionary discourse, the new Chinese woman, along with the new China, was constituted as a subject who, through production, freed herself from the "tradition" of feudalism and stood against imperialism. The party thus told a new story of women's lives, one that made some truths transparent and erased others. It did not speak of the shame of sex in laboring inappropriately. It invented a tradition of feudalism that was ahistorical and erased women's agency in the past, as well as any sense that they had labored previously. Yet it also enabled Yu Shifu and many other women already laboring in factories to speak what had previously been unspeakable, in the sense that they had had no words to speak it: the bitterness of being female in a world where the spatial location of their labor led to shame. The socialist realist version of women's lives enabled a pervasive critique of what had so recently appeared an inevitable aspect of social life, an analytical skill that the oldest cohort of women workers would never lose. The promise of the revolutionary dream that would free women from the oppressiveness of gender itself—this promise is what Yu Shifu's and other older women's memories of their liberation captured for me.

The socialist discourse on women's liberation would soon become the official and dominant one, institutionalized through numerous active methods. Ongoing cultural work to make this discourse appear to be a transparent description of gender rather than a normative representation included "thought work" (*sixiang gongzuo*) to encourage women to speak this narrative themselves. Older women workers recall that shortly after the new state was established, activist party members came to their factories to explain what "women's liberation" was all about. They learned to speak it in their literacy classes and in the political study sessions that were frequently held in the evenings after work. They saw it in popular theater productions and movies and heard it on the radio. They heard it, too, from the neighborhood committees formed to establish socialist order in the cities. The state Women's Federation also organized numerous activities that addressed women and told them how their liberation was a formative aspect of the new nation. Women were not merely the grounds of this project, the means through which a new China was to be born: they may have been the objects of this discourse on liberation, but women needed to become active subjects speaking this discourse for it to constitute a new social reality. Through narrative performances of women's liberation, a small group of women workers first came to participate in this particular mode of knowing reality. In narrating their newly acquired political convictions, they reshaped the meaning of their past as part of a collective reordering of memories.

The fundamental irony lies in the way that this new political construction—and regulation—of appropriate and inappropriate female agency in terms of "freedom to labor" felt most liberating to those already laboring in factories. Yu Shifu and the other women shamed in the factories were the most enthusiastic "voices" of this new discourse. Yu Shifu was liberated not to labor but to reposition herself as a woman worker. These new social categories of class provided a small group of women workers with the agency to shift the terms of pride and shame, to invert the social bottom and top, and to transform the foundational assumptions of gender that had established the meaning of their positioning "outside" in a silk factory. Their gender identities transfigured from "broken shoes" who had transgressed the appropriate cultural borders of gender to revolutionary, liberated women—indeed, they could become political models. They were no longer fallen women unfit for respectable marriage but working-class exemplars, heroic in their labor.

Their very gender transgressions marked them as courageous women. They were an active sign of the utopian socialist imaginary. Yu Shifu, Si Zhaoding, Yang Wanfen, and other women workers quickly joined the party. They became ardent participants in producing a discourse of women's liberation through labor that, in turn, produced them as new kinds of women. Within this metaphysics of labor, they could nearly forget their shame.

The party's cultural and political reconstitution of femaleness was also liberating to a few young women, like Chen Shifu, who chafed under the hegemony of gender differentiation within household workshops. It allowed her as well to take up a subject-position that could challenge the male domination of silk production. Chen Shifu and all those who labored in household workshops were eventually organized by the Central Silk Bureau, first into cooperatives and then into the factories. By 1956, she found herself laboring alongside Yu Shifu and the other women already in the factories, though a different class trajectory had brought her there. These women not only embraced official state feminism but were galvanized by it to exceed the initial terms of its discourse even as they spoke and acted through its categories. They began to challenge the gender differentiations of labor in which men had claimed weaving as their domain. Women like Chen Shifu crossed this border to become weavers, but not at the behest of party cadres. She described this process as a battle, a struggle involving great determination on her part. The battle was not against state power, which was on her side in this one. The fight, Chen Shifu said, was against the "conservative consciousness" of the male weavers, who refused to pass on the secrets of their knowledge and skill to women. To describe the male weavers as having "conservative consciousness" was, of course, to use the new language of liberation. She remembered, "Even my cousin was not willing to teach me. I had to study myself, and to 'beg' the men, but I had to show that I had some ability."

Chen Shifu's story traces the contours of a heroism in which she and the other women who joined her, including Yu Shifu, went to great lengths to engage in the most strenuous, most exhausting, yet most "skilled" work in the factory. Recall that silk weaving was thought to be highly skilled, and not simply in relation to the other tasks of silk production. In Hangzhou in the early 1950s, silk was the only industry around—and thus virtually by definition it was the most "advanced." Their entry was a conscious transgression of gender boundaries, a heady moment of challenge to a male dominance that they now had a language not only to describe but to expose as contingent and crafted rather than transcendent and immutable. The customs of silk weaving that had so pervasively fashioned Hangzhou's social world and had made the replication of past gender relations seem natural and seamless were suddenly placed in a novel temporal framework. The new language of liberation led these women to interrogate the hegemony of customary ways of living and to "sentence" those customs to a temporality in which the past would now be superseded by a teleology of the future.

The transgressions that enabled them to inhabit liberated identities taught them, moreover, that becoming one of the new revolutionary women was a matter of activity, not of social location. Judith Butler (1993) has argued that the materialization of sex emerges in a matrix of differentiating relations in which gendered subjects are produced by way of performative reiterations of powerful norms. The group of women who shed their shame in the creation of new political convictions about gender materialized their sex in the discursive practices of state-defined labor. They performed new gender identities in the transformed meanings of that labor.

Through disjunctions, refusals, bitterness, pride, laughter, reflexive commentary, contradictions, and a heroic display of hard work, Yu Shifu and Chen Shifu marked their gendered, generational histories of class. Their stories show us that "Chinese woman" is not a fixed identity but is shifting, multiple, and subject to change. Attempts to create a dialogue along only one axis—for example, class, family, or sex—obscure this multiplicity, which exists not just as differences between Chinese and western women but as differences among Chinese women.

In this liberation, there was a simultaneous marking and erasing of sexual difference. Official discourse did not simply address these women workers; it led them to set in motion the performance and narration of an altogether different gender identity. Chen Shifu and Yu Shifu were women doing the weaving, and in the fact of their gender lay their liberation. But they were not doing the weaving *as* women. Their transgression was part of a larger process that would later redraw the boundaries of what counted as "women's work" and "men's work." But for this generation, the embrace of a class position appeared to make femaleness irrelevant to the one marker that counted—"work" itself. In negotiating the gendered terrain of liberation, the oldest cohort's stories speak to but also go beyond recent feminist theoretical assertions that "woman" is not an essentialized locus of experience but a shifting subject-position not reducible to any essence (Butler and Scott 1992). The transformative dislocations in their lives reveal multiple meanings of liberation and thus of woman. But they also lead us to entertain the possibility that at certain historical moments and in distinct places, "being" a woman is not relevant.[18] Real liberation could be found in that irrelevance, for a time.

A WOMAN CAPITALIST

Yet not all women were liberated by Liberation. Official feminism and the heroics of labor transgressions may distinguish the gender identities of this oldest cohort of women workers from those of the two younger cohorts, but cohorts are not uniform. Members neither have a unified agenda nor think of the challenges of femininity in exactly the same way. There are other stories about the changing cultural meanings of gender at the time of the revolution that do not fit neatly within the dominant discourse that authorized what counted as liberation for women. Put another way, the novel foundational discourses of women's liberation operated through differential and exclusionary means, disqualifying some women—and certain activities—from becoming the subjects of a liberated womanhood.

Perhaps the person I gained the most insight from in this regard was Lou Shengzhi, the former owner of one of the major silk factories in Hangzhou. I had heard of her by chance one day when I went to interview the party secretary of the Fudan Silk Weaving Factory she used to own. In offering me the official history of the factory in its transition from capitalism to socialism, he mentioned the "woman capitalist" who had run the factory and still lived around the corner. There were only a few capitalists in Hangzhou's barely industrialized silk industry before the revolution. They were all locally famous, the "woman capitalist" among them. I eagerly requested a meeting with her and he reluctantly agreed. Over the next year, I often visited with Lou Shengzhi and enjoyed long, leisurely conversations with her in her home.

I had initially assumed—given the official histories I heard in all the silk factories, as well as what I already knew about socialist state politics—that she would tell me a story about her struggles with having been labeled a woman *capitalist*. As you will see, Lou Shengzhi did sometimes talk about her bitterness at having to take up that identity under socialism. But she also led me to recognize the ways in which I had been stereotyping her as a capitalist. Hearing her stories about the gender challenges she faced, I began to think about her as a *woman* capitalist. She opened up for me an appreciation of the gender politics that had led to her capitalist activity. I came to ask a new question: What kind of gender constitutes a capitalist?

Lou Shengzhi told a story specifically highlighting a gender politics of marriage that disrupts and challenges the homogenizing discourse of socialist state feminism. The heroism she portrays in her gender transgressions does not fit the parable of capitalism and socialist modernity that others try to tell about her. Her story is positioned eccentrically in relation to the dominant discourse, which brushes past and partially occludes its powerful import. She nonetheless disrupts the official norms of gendered knowledge, offering possibilities for conceiving of other heroisms in reconfiguring gender identity. I hope, in the way I tell her story below, that I honor how Lou Shengzhi led me to join her in going against the grain of the stories told about her.

The first time I spoke with Lou Shengzhi, two cadres from Fudan's party committee insisted on accompanying me to her home. Lou Shengzhi would confide, much later, that because Fudan's party representatives had never formally apologized to her for their treatment of her during the Cultural Revolution, they were particularly concerned about what she would say to a foreigner. She remarked, with satisfaction, that my visit prompted them to say at last, "We wronged you."

Fudan's cadres, Lou Shengzhi, and I sat in her two-room courtyard home crammed with layers of objects that silently spoke about the various periods of her life: prerevolution bed and armoire of dark red wood, Singer sewing machine, bright new refrigerator, and various knick-knacks. Then in her mid-sixties, Lou Shengzhi was a slight woman with vital, sparkling eyes and a severely hunched back. She told a fairly conventional story that day, with much officious interruption by cadres she had barely spoken with in the fifteen years since she had left the factory.

In 1949, just before the Communist Party came to state power, her husband, who already owned and managed a silk store, bought Fudan from the man who ran the Bank of China; the seller wanted to get rid of some of his holdings and sold it cheaply. It was one of only five existing silk factories in Hangzhou. Her husband knew very little about the production aspects of silk and a previous factory he owned had gone bankrupt. He wanted to buy a luxury home by West Lake, but she insisted he buy a factory. She ran the factory while her husband ran the store. Her determination turned the factory from a losing venture into a success. After the revolution, the state reorganized the factory. Her husband was appointed the manager, she the assistant manager, and her husband's cousin, who was a silk "insider," became the factory director. At first, they still owned the factory, working the raw material that the newly established state-run silk bureau distributed to them. But times were so hard that they cut their own salaries in half, also making a gesture to show workers they had the right attitude. The silk bureau, impressed by her skill and attitude, appointed her to be the accountant after the factory was nationalized. Though workers complained, she instituted a successful system to keep a close accounting of the production process. In 1965—she had no need to clarify, especially in the presence of these cadres, that this year was the prelude to the Cultural Revolution—she was sent down to work in the weft preparation shop. Former capitalists—actually she used the term *sifang*, or "private persons," as a euphemism for her class label—were no longer allowed to work in the administration. She learned prep work quickly and after only a short period was able to do all the different kinds of spinning in the shop. Originally she was afraid of how difficult the work would be, but after she went to work there, she saw that it was fine. She also learned a great deal about how workers' lives were different from her own. In 1971, at the age of fifty-one, she retired (early and in anger, she would later tell me, before the Cultural Revolution had ended). Currently, she was helping one of her sons manage a dry goods store that he opened in Hangzhou.

That was the story she told that day. As I sat there, I felt like I was only a marginal participant in the conversation, listening while the important and indirect communication was taking place between Lou Shengzhi and the party. She was telling the party committee that she only ever did what was needed, that she respected workers, that she was willing to do whatever was demanded of her, even spinning thread on the shop floor, and, by the deadpan tone in which she recited the story, that she had no feelings about the past. I was, frankly, disappointed and bored. Like the workers, Lou Shengzhi had been brought to speak a class-inflected narrative about her life. She had been taught to express public humility about her class background and to demonstrate that she had undergone a change of "consciousness" about class. I was certain (but felt it inopportune to ask) that she had been "struggled against" during various political campaigns aimed at individuals with bad class labels. Of course. That was why the party cadres were there, to make sure I avoided those questions.

Over the weeks and months that followed, however, as Lou Shengzhi told me a story about her life that had a quite different gender inflection, I came to realize the importance of having first heard this more-or-less official story. It was not grumbling about mistreatment that made the contrast between the two kinds of storytelling so vivid. Rather, her subsequent narrative amplifies how her first story normalizes her identity by excluding and foreclosing the gender challenges whose transgressions, from her perspective, propelled her to become a capitalist. Lou Shengzhi pulled her resources from several overlapping cultural frameworks—namely, a system of filial piety, polygamous marriage, and capitalism—to formulate oppositional commentary, barely audible from the edges, about sexuality, gender, and the construction of political knowledge.

Filiality

Filiality in China is often described as the domain of men. It is the reason men live with or near their parents, and the reason it is so important for men to have sons. Sons carry the family line in this patrilineal kinship system and thus fulfill their filial obligation to parents and ancestors. They must also support their elderly parents. Women marry out; they must help their husbands carry on their husband's family line by giving birth to sons. Families that give birth only to girls are said to have experienced tragedy. But Lou Shengzhi inverted the gendering of this cultural logic.

My mother and father had only one child. Mother couldn't have any more. Father had a wife before, but she died. He was already forty-five when he married my mother. He regretted that he had no son. But then he decided that daughters and sons were the same.

As Lou Shengzhi spoke of her family background, I was struck by how she placed a tale of her very unusual life trajectory in a conventional cultural form of respect toward her parents. Her story could have been a parable about gender paradoxes, about how she flouted the proprieties of the period. Instead, she utilizes the conventions of filial piety and places herself in an obeisant position within them. She respectfully attributes her ability to blur gender identities to her father. Hers is a tale not of rebelling against customary parental strictures but rather of fulfilling them. Thus her father supported her later studies at the university, when such education was unusual for women.

I studied music at Nanjing University. There were only two or three women students in each school. My father had progressive thinking. He said that women must have ability (benshi). Otherwise, if their husband turns out not to be good, there's nothing they can do about it. I also wanted to study. But after my marriage, I had to throw out my music.

I thought, as Lou Shengzhi continued her story, that she was describing in effect how she became a surrogate son for her father. Her father wanted to ensure that his only child, his "son," was properly educated and trained. Since this son would need to marry a husband, it was all the more imperative to provide her with the means for becoming self-reliant. Lou Shengzhi attributes much prescience to her father in his thinking about husbands. In effect, she makes him the wise and learned father who foresaw her life. It seemed to me that Lou Shengzhi, in turn, assumed the responsibilities of a filial son.

Father worked in the Salt Administration. First he was a teacher in a family; the head of the family was in the Salt Administration. He saw that my father had ability, especially with foreign languages, so he asked him to come work in the Salt Administration.

The Salt Administration, which oversaw the collection of taxes on salt, was one of the key ministries of the Republican government.

Father had money in the bank, ¥20,000 GMD [Guomindang] money [one yuan equaled approximately thirty-five cents before the war]. Then with the Anti-Japanese War, there was chaos. My father's money was worthless. You could only buy a few socks with it.

In telling a story of the dramatic misfortunes of her parents, Lou Sheng-zhi presents herself as "naturally" pulled by filial desires to follow the course she pursued within the constraints of gender.

I married because I needed to care for my parents. Originally, we could live well off the interest from his [her father's] money. But suddenly, there was no money. So I had to go out to work. But there was a problem with going to work. Women were like flower vases, you had to be like that with the boss. But I wasn't willing. The best work was to teach, but that was not enough to support my parents.

Listening to Lou Shengzhi slowly unfold the story of her marriage, I realized that it was largely about reluctance. Only because disaster faced her parents did she consider this step. Sexual harassment—the require-ment to "be like that" with the boss—and the lack of remunerative work for women also forced her down what she implies is a road she wished she never had to take.

Lou Shengzhi told me these details about her life not long after our first meeting. I had pressed for further explanation about how a woman in the 1940s had managed the unusual feat of owning and running a factory. For some time after that, I took Lou Shengzhi's story about her reluctance to marry as indicative of a culturally appropriate response of many women of her time, though not all, toward marriage (Silber 1994). There were some who told me otherwise. The elder Lius, for example, loved to regale me with memories of their passionate attraction for one another. They pulled out photos to show me what a beauty Liu Bomu had been as a young woman, as if to explain why Liu Lao couldn't help his sexual desire for her. But they also told their story to me in a tone that delighted in the brazenness of their open acknowledgment. For many young women at that time, too forthright a display of interest in men and marriage was considered socially unacceptable. Thus, I did not think Lou Shengzhi's story particularly remarkable.

A Tale of Polygamy

But I was curious as to the whereabouts of her husband. Occasionally, she would mention that her "old man" had been by, and that she had told him about our friendship. That surprised me, because she seemed to be living just with one of her sons and at first I had assumed her husband had died. It was only after we had known one another nearly a year that she unexpectedly offered me the rest of her story. One day, she said she was ready to tell me.

He already had an old lady. His mother made him marry her. He didn't want to. She agreed to let him marry again if he married her. He pursued me; he went up to my college for me. I had one condition. I love my parents. I said he must live with my parents. I was the only child and wanted to look after my parents. At that time, they didn't used to have this, a daughter having her parents live with her. He agreed.

This is a story of love: her husband's love for her and her love for her parents. In Lou Shengzhi's telling, her husband's relationship with his first wife was one of obligation; with her, of romance. She hardly resembles the conventional image of the second wife, or concubine, as a beautiful plaything acquired to enhance the status of the man. She demands proof of her husband's love and threatens his status by insisting on a form of marriage that only poor men usually agreed to, a uxorilocal marriage whereby the husband moves in with the wife's family (Wolf and Huang 1980). Of course, to this day her husband goes back and forth between the two households of his two wives. Still, Lou Shengzhi reverses the established conventions of polygamy. Her marriage would usually have been a matter of shame for women of her class, signifying a loss of status for her family. Instead, Lou Shengzhi transforms it into a narrative of her unusual bravery. She uses the accepted prescriptions of filial piety as the source of her strength to challenge the strictures of polygamy.

Shortly after the revolution, her husband wanted her to flee to Hong Kong with him.

He said he wanted to go to Hong Kong. He wanted me to go with him. I had four children. He wanted only me to go, also his mother and the other one [i.e., his first wife]. He only wanted me to go because I was able to help him with the business. I wanted to take all of my children and my parents. He wouldn't go if I didn't go. So we stayed.

Lou Shengzhi resignifies her experience of the socialist revolution, stressing not its meaning for her as a capitalist but its role in revealing her husband's devotion to her, his second wife.

Lou Shengzhi had four children in rapid succession. Then she insisted that she and her husband buy a factory for her to run, so that she could continue to care for her parents and raise her children.

My husband owned two silk stores, one in Hangzhou and one in Shanghai. He wanted to buy a house next to West Lake, but I told him we should buy a factory. I told him that the factory he had before went bankrupt because he didn't get involved closely in the production. My husband didn't want me to go out to work. He said I would only be a flower vase, a showpiece to attract business. My father got angry. He thought all my studying should not go to waste.

In the version of her story encouraged and managed by Fudan's party committee, Lou Shengzhi had emphasized her husband's importance in buying the factory. Here, she changes the description not so much of herself as a capitalist but of the politics of marriage that led to her becoming a capitalist. And the details of capitalist investment that she now offers emphasize her independence from her husband.

Some of it was my husband's money, but I had money. I sold all of my dowry. Jewelry, real pearls, gold. Some women like to save their money, to satisfy their small pleasures, but I don't care for that. I thought I should make a living. What are small pleasures? I thought I needed to study a skill. My husband's part came from Li Daoshi, a wealthy Buddhist monk who had money given to him by people who wanted him to pray for them or build statues of gods for them. He was a good friend of my husband.

Her husband should not even have been given credit for his portion of the investment.

I only wanted to be together with my parents. I never had anything to do with them [i.e., her husband's family with his other wife]. If I had money from this factory, I could raise my family. Zili gengsheng. Popo [mother-in-law] thought I was capable. She said, "Her parents don't eat up our food for nothing." None of her other daughters-in-law lived with their mothers. Only me. I gave her money. She said, "No one else does this. Even my sons don't give money to me." She told her children I gave her money.

Lou Shengzhi mixes in contemporary official language—*zili gengsheng,* or "self-reliance"—to describe herself. Yet from the official story of her life she wrests and disposes of the idea that her husband was a key figure in the factory, either in its purchase or its management. Running the factory herself is critical to her inversion of conventional stories about second wives. Buying the factory, for Lou Shengzhi, was both a continuation of filial piety and a way to distance herself from the potentially demeaning status of second wife.

And she was no plaything:

I was never like the other wives with their cards, poker, and dancing. I wasn't willing to learn. If you learn to dance, then after marriage, your husband "eats vinegar" [i.e., gets jealous or gets cuckolded].

She reiterated this point in another conversation:

Women like to chat, gossip, play cards, eat at each other's homes. They spend their money on little things. Like in Dream of the Red Chamber *[a famous eighteenth-century novel of a wealthy gentry family]. I don't like that. They said I was aloof, that I thought I was too good.*

Engendering Capitalism

Many times, Lou Shengzhi spoke to me about her anger with the socialist state and with Fudan's party members for their treatment of her and her children. Her list of grievances was long. Speaking of problems with her health, she once said, "My trachea tore open during the Cultural Revolution. It tore open out of anger." She also attributed her hunched back to working so hard in the prep shop during that time. Her children never had opportunities for education because of her class status; they had to scatter to various "remote" areas. The government never fully reimbursed her for her capital investment in the factory; the factory's party cadres never admitted any wrongdoing until they had to speak to her about my visit.

Since the state began to introduce capitalist means of acquiring wealth, the party committee has sought out her knowledge. "They asked me to write down my methods. I said they are too old. They asked me to write down my experiences. I said I forgot." A few years before we met, Lou Shengzhi had become a Christian, and perhaps that gave her a way to grapple with the pain of her past. Sometimes, she said, she used her Christian forgiveness to overcome her animosity. But her Christian desire to forgive continued to war with her anger.

Yet alongside this bitterness, Lou Shengzhi offered a different commentary that implicitly challenged the gender politics of the party's inscription of her into their critique of capitalism. After my first visit, Lou Shengzhi took great pains to correct the party's placement of her as subordinate to her husband. Eventually, as the story I have already told makes clear, she also challenged the socialist pretense that her class status as a capitalist grew out of a monogamous marriage. The party had long championed monogamy as one means to liberate women from "feudal" marriage arrangements and after the revolution prescribed it in the socialist constitution.[19] Party members had embraced and fostered monogamous marriages as part of an Enlightenment project begun in the May Fourth Movement of 1919. Socialists and nonsocialists alike advocated a thorough cultural revolution to strengthen China in the face of imperialism. They had viewed radical transformations of the Chinese family as critical to modernizing Chinese culture. The end of polygamy would free women, they believed, but it also would help poor peasant men acquire a wife. In the countryside, the party explicitly ended polygamy as part of a larger campaign to challenge wealthy elites. Party cadres in the cities, for reasons unclear to me, merely insisted on the appearance of monogamy when men had more than one wife.

Recall that shortly after the revolution, before the nationalization of industries, the Central Silk Bureau had appointed Lou Shengzhi's husband to be the manager. They did so because the ownership of the factory was technically in his name. She became the assistant manager; their valuation of her in relation to her husband was marked by the lower salary she received. This ironically reinscribed the kind of subordinate relationship through marriage that Lou Shengzhi had taken such pains to subvert.

My husband didn't pay attention to the factory at all. I took care of everything. He had two stores. He took care of selling the goods once they were produced. He didn't understand the factory business. He depended on me for everything.

As she explained during another conversation, "The concrete work, he didn't do any of that." The success of the factory, both before and after the revolution, was due to her initiative.

I didn't know anything, but I was determined. I did it "with one heart and one mind." When the weavers talked, I listened carefully. I often went to the workshop and listened to their analysis. Then I finally understood "the talk of the profession."

Lou Shengzhi changed her name when she acquired the factory, to get rid of the flowery and feminine connotations of the characters in her name. She chose a masculine-sounding name.

Originally, my name was Shengzhu. I changed it to "zhi" because "Shengzhu" didn't sound good for going out and doing business, it didn't have boldness. "Shengzhi" means to succeed at things, to conquer all.

Eventually, even the party had to recognize who was really in charge.

In 1956, of all the capitalists, I was the only one whose wages they increased. The others had their wages cut. They made me the accountant and they sent my old man to another industry.

The party's portrayal of the "woman capitalist" obscured Lou Shengzhi's narrative of herself as someone who set into motion particular transgressions of gender that led her to capitalism. Everyone involved at Fudan in the early years surely knew of her marital circumstances, which could hardly have been a secret. I can only guess that in the aftermath of the revolution the party decided, discreetly, to ignore her situation and act as if she were monogamous. In so doing, the party glossed over the importance of her imagination and initiative in addressing a politics of gender they suppressed. But they, too, showed a certain degree of imagination in deciding to treat Lou Shengzhi as if she had a modern socialist marriage and family. In 1986 the neighborhood committee awarded Lou Shengzhi with the title of "the five goods household" in recognition of her sterling family life.

By gendering capitalism, Lou Shengzhi led me to appreciate the kinds of struggles that are barely discernible in any of the multiple meanings of women's liberation in China. She does not simply fail to conform to a unified project of liberation for women of her cohort. Her tactics for maneuvering the gendered obstacles she faced are the fugitive methods of someone whose project never opened into a larger agenda for women. Her own story has no public life, despite her reputation as the "woman capitalist." By offering her story to me, however, she refused to fully accede to the official stories about her. Her critical perspective helped me to think through the unexpected connections one should always seek among gender, class, and political convictions that challenge hegemonies of power and knowledge.

Stories of freeing oneself from the confines of patriarchal households, inverting sociospatial cultural logics that defined female virtue, challenging the male dominance of silk weaving, and surmounting a polygamous marriage by way of capitalism, as well as my own story of repositioning my previous political convictions—these liberation narratives could not have been told without a modern socialist revolution or international feminism. A small group of women from the oldest cohort felt "hailed," to borrow a term from Althusser (1971), by the discursive power of the socialist state because of the unprecedented possibilities it extended to them. They spoke enthusiastically as subjects of the new state, even as—or perhaps precisely because—its version of women's liberation effaced the alternate meanings liberation had for them as women already working in silk households and factories. Others, like Lou Shengzhi, nearly lost the capability of narrating her version of liberation, caught in the storm of class struggle. And as for myself, I learned to topple the figure of the Chinese woman as she had been conceived by U.S. feminists, with our modernist aspirations, in dialogue with a Chinese state reaching for a postcolonial modernity.

Together, these liberation stories reveal the specificity of cultural imaginations that shape the longing for modernity. They indicate precisely how these cultural imaginations are forged within global networks of unequal power and how they are also located in time and space, in culture and history. Then, too, they rupture the referential solidity of modern imaginaries, which rest on allegories of gender. For the multiple meanings of liberation cannot be contained in a singular, homogeneous master narrative of modernity. We find instead the articulations of particular histories formed in the phenomenal existence of desires for modernity—desires that motivate western feminism no less than the Chinese state. The long legacy of colonial dynamics has reached down into these transnational investments in modernity, as a socialist state speaks back to the West and western and Chinese feminists speak back to Chinese state power. But these women's stories reframe that dialogue. They reveal the ongoing but shifting process of pursuing agendas of modernity in the conjoined histories of "East" and "West." And the gaps that they disclose show the historicity of transcendental claims for modernity and feminist theory, as well as of the changing gender meanings that have accompanied those claims.

Yu Shifu's analysis, along with the others', makes possible an engagement while simultaneously breaking down the dichotomy of western self/non-western other. This dichotomy continues to inform certain "dialogical" versions of experimental ethnography. A somewhat cartoonish description of that dialogue posits a unified and coherent self, usually male, meeting a unified and coherent other, usually male, and the two, as representatives of their respective cultures, finding a common ground. It might have been possible for me to construct such a narrative. In the factories, at least, male managers encouraged me to take up a position as honored western expert and talk with them, one "man" to another, about how "we" in the West think about efficiency and productivity. They were alternately perplexed and worried that I wanted to spend so much time with the women. "They have nothing to say," they would invariably insist. "They don't understand very much." As Trinh T. Minh-ha has noted, "Difference is not difference to some ears, but awkwardness or incompleteness" (1989:80). Yet these "inarticulate" women taught me how to reconceive the meaning of liberation. In so doing, they ultimately led me to see the imaginary quality in modernity, which rests so intimately on categories and meanings of gender. Yu Shifu and others were not "informants" but analysts and producers of feminist discourse in their own right. They were interlocutors with whom I might, in fact, disagree.

My deconstruction of liberation feminism in light of their stories has made it more difficult, I hope, to approach Yu Shifu, Chen Shifu, Lou

Shengzhi, and other women of the oldest cohort as unreflexive recipients of state ideology with a "contradictory consciousness" (Gramsci 1971) apparent to the western observer. They are not, in fact, in that sense ideologically constructed at all. Their interpretation of liberation leads us to the insight that "women's liberation" is not a state of being that, once achieved, exists suspended outside of time and space. It cannot claim an ontological status as such, or a "metaphysics of presence" (Butler 1989; Derrida 1974; Kondo 1990); nor can the modernity that rests on such contentions.

The manner in which women workers of the senior cohort came to conceive of themselves as revolutionary women reveals the power of political narratives to produce activist subjectivities. By enabling women to render as arbitrary the gendered meanings of inside/outside, the functional discourse of liberation generated political convictions—not for all women, but for those women who could then leave behind in the hazy shadows of "feudal custom" their inarticulate shame and frustration as women. Their liberation from that shame—their ability to conceive of themselves as unmarked by their gender—led this small group of women to become staunch proponents of the new regime's ultimately exclusive power to construct gender difference. It led them, as well, to embrace a broader teleology of modernity that shaped their experience as one of linear "progress" toward a coherent future.

To younger generations of women, this oldest group came to represent the hegemony of official feminism. Feminists in post-Mao China have argued that the dominance of this liberation discourse excluded and foreclosed a gender consciousness for women (see Barlow 1994, 1997; X. Li 1990; Meng and Dai 1990). Certainly Lou Shengzhi's story bears them out. The most important political challenge, in their view, is to reconceptualize themselves as women. Their argument is analogous to feminist critiques in the United States that have pointed out how the domination of the women's movement by white, middle-class women continues to exclude other gender projects. As we will see in considering the younger cohorts in China, the dominance of this liberation discourse is precisely what they will perceive as in need of challenge in order to rediscover how their gender should be marked. Their rebellions consist, however, not in rejecting modernity as their goal but in recasting its deferred enchantments.

The oldest cohort, too, has lived through the rejection of Maoism in the post-Mao reforms. As these women became marginalized by new imaginaries of modernity, their stories of liberation held but a faint echo of their former power to inspire. These tales exist instead as nostalgic traces in the clamorous insistence on a market economy that will finally, many hope, bring China to the threshold of a modernity globally recognized as such.

2 The Poetics of Productivity

Workers in post-Mao China live as what one might call an "absent presence." This is surprising, perhaps, since Maoist socialism rhetorically cast workers, along with peasants, as the central heroes of the nation. Maoism established their revolutionary consciousness as that which would bring China to a socialist modernity beyond western capitalism, and the current regime, though it has thoroughly repudiated the Maoist period, continues to identify itself as socialist. Yet in the discussions of how China can reach modernity encouraged by national political culture in the 1980s and 1990s, the most striking feature is how rarely workers figure at all. They are never portrayed as the kind of people deemed to be the appropriate subjects of a post-Mao—and for many, a postsocialist—modernity, who instead are those who know how to invigorate the economy and social life without the support of the state.

On the contrary, workers appear in official and elite commentary on the obstacles that might hinder China from ever reaching modernity. Those desiring broad social transformations represent workers as the quintessential embodiment of a Maoist past, marking a "historical lack" that China must overcome. They are depicted as both cause and consequence of the ills said to have befallen China as a result of the Cultural Revolution. Workers thus appear both outside of and as a hindrance to a reconstituted imaginary of modernity. Consequently, the state has subjected them to a novel disciplinary regime, whose epistemic violence is wedded to the coercions of rational initiatives for development. This postsocialist decentering of workers turns on China's own decentered relationship to those countries, especially the United States and Japan, that continue to produce modernity as a realm of unequal power. At the local level, these complex dynamics play themselves out in reconfiguring Hangzhou's world of silk production.

How have women workers negotiated this process of marginalization? How have they endured such a profound transformation in public representations of their place in a story of national progress? On the whole, it seems fair to say that workers reject the image of themselves as a "dilemma," accompanied as it is by negative valuations of their moral being and essential predilections. Yet the emergence of new gender meanings and relations have further complicated workers' engagement with this pervasive devaluation of themselves. The Maoist woman who heroically overcame her gender quickly became a parodic figure. She was roundly derided in comedy routines, soap operas, newspaper editorials, and even in some post-Mao feminist writings. It became nearly impossible to believe that anyone had ever taken her seriously. How could a modern nation support such nonsense, the jokes implied.

The ground of masculinity has also shifted. Official and popular discourses alike represent the gendered activity that will bring modernity not, as with Maoism, as a transgression of feminine identity in the state sector via labor, but rather as an assertion of a natural masculinity in the market via risk-taking exploits. As Lyn Jeffery (1995) has argued, the post-Mao imaginary of modernity feminizes the state sector as the realm of passive inactivity and loss, while the market economy signifies masculine prowess. Feminized subalterns—men and women who continue to work in the state sector—are marginalized as those who are dragging into the present the "socialist tradition" that hinders modernity.

This chapter traces how the post-Mao pursuit of modernity, known as "economic reform," constructs mobile discourses of dominance in which national priorities for development normalize workers even as they cast workers to the side of history. My descriptions rest on the assumption that the identity of subaltern selves is not intrinsic in the relations of production. Rather than accepting as transparent the identities of workers, one must ask how they are culturally produced, embraced, performed, challenged, and denied. As I argue throughout the book, changing parameters of meaning and power, in which gender, class, and the state intersect, produce a historically variable range of subaltern and other identities.

The first section of this chapter examines discourse on the recent socialist past and how it represents workers as embodying that past. The second section addresses new regimes of productivity that operate through the cool violence of statistics, turning on doubled practices of individuation and differentiation. The third section tells a story about an incident between a silk inspection worker and her supervisor at Zhenfu in which I played the catalyst. The story illuminates the cultural peripheries of history where workers negotiate the disjunctures in projects of modernity in the post-Mao era.

''EATING OUT OF ONE BIG POT''

When I arrived in China at the end of 1984, "economic reform" had just begun to seep cautiously and deliberately into the cities.[1] One can easily describe the prosaic aims of this policy: to thoroughly readjust the role of the state in economic development. Reform has led to the introduction of a market economy, the appearance of privately owned companies, a reduction in the scope of mandatory state planning, the devolution of centralized planning to the local levels, the restriction of party cadres' interventions in the economic plans of their local work units, increased autonomy for technical managers of state-run enterprises, the establishment of "special economic zones" to attract foreign investment, and the introduction of new wage systems to increase productivity. Such radical change has brought China fully onto the playing field of transnational capitalism. It also has reinvigorated the deferred desires for modernity.

Yet economic reform is not a simple matter of economic policy. Nor does a view of political economy in which "materiality" and "culture" are structurally separable though linked sufficiently capture the process. As a means of radical disengagement from Maoist socialism, economic reform is also and most significantly a space of imagination. Dreams pile up, one upon another, in this space. The state and its hierarchically positioned citizens conjure up a future that can rid China of the haunting excesses of Maoism. Visions thrive of a wealthy and powerful nation that will finally disprove the predictions of colonial history. The party-state fantasizes about how it can re-create its moral authority. Factory managers creatively maneuver in the newly opened gaps of state power, finding ways to bring their factories to life and make profits that are not exactly against state policies and not exactly within state policies, because their methods are dreamed up in the process of trying them out. At any moment, these activities are equally likely to land them in jail or make them new model citizens. And finally, the populace dreams of a life beyond any political culture—a fantasy, one might add, often nourished by the state. These imaginings reside in edicts from the state; projects of local bureaus of labor, textile, and foreign trade; meetings between party cadres and factory managers; new factory rules and regulations concerning worker discipline; television soap operas, erudite novels, and karaoke bars; endless newscasts of production statistics; social science surveys of "public opinion"; frenzied consumption; and quiet conversations between friends.

But these imaginings are not unified. For economic reform has given rein to the kinds of economic inequities and class stratification whose eradication once formed the basis of the moral authority of the Chinese Communist Party (CCP). At the same time, the post-Mao regime has officially abolished the class-status system under which party cadres, in dialogue with local communities, assigned each person a class label based on a combination of individual or family level of economic exploitation, status, and potential for revolutionary consciousness (Chan, Madsen, and Unger 1992; Hinton 1966). Good class labels included poor and middle peasant, proletariat, cadre, revolutionary martyr, and revolutionary intellectual (assigned to those who had joined Mao before the revolution). Bad class labels included landlord, rich peasant, bureaucratic capitalist, counterrevolutionary, rightist, and bad element. Class labels that wavered between good and bad included petty bourgeoisie and national capitalist (who were considered patriotic because they did not flee after the revolution). The purpose of the labels was manifold: to

indicate how to redistribute wealth, to divide those who had revolutionary virtue from those who did not, to clarify the lines of class struggle,
and to instill a "consciousness of class" so that individuals would re-
orient their social identities and make revolution against those with
whom they had formerly sought identification. The party cadres who
instituted this system believed in language's creative role. To classify
meant to create possibilities for action. Both those in the party and those
nearby used class labels as an index of each person's moral worth. Abstract classifications became lived representations as each person's entire
social reality was defined in terms of her or his class label. Access to
material wealth and power were inextricable from adjudications of socialist morality (Billeter 1985; Kraus 1981; J. Watson 1984).

Thought to be temporary when they were first assigned just after the
socialist revolution, class labels became hereditary statuses through the
paternal line. The creative moments of classification and its possibilities
to incite transformations here gave place to naturalizing reification.
Women and children were assigned the class label of their husband's
family. As a result, marriage practices came to involve matching one's
children with a partner who had a good class label. New forms of hierarchy arose, as those with "good" class labels became the arbiters of
state power and cadres became a class status unto themselves (Billeter
1985; G. White 1976).

This classificatory system was always a process in which people interpreted "class" in specific local circumstances. Individuals' "material
conditions" did not always fit objective measurement; other circumstances of local importance came into play, and the "subjective" matter
of "revolutionary consciousness" created instabilities in indexing political virtue (Chan, Madsen, and Unger 1992; J. Watson 1984). In these
respects, it might be more useful to think of class in China as analogous
to race in the United States, overwhelmingly defining a person's social
value and wavering, in politically explosive ways, between being understood as a social construction and being treated "commonsensically"
as a natural inheritance. Taken together, the hereditary nature of the
system, the unresolved tension between material conditions and consciousness, and the new forms of hierarchy that evolved out of the sys-

tem eventually exploded into the Cultural Revolution (Billeter 1985; Kraus 1981; G. White 1976). Moreover, global cold war politics also contributed to the way these class identities continued to resonate in a national imaginary. With both the United States and, after 1960, the Soviet Union its superpower global enemies, the Chinese state was ever alert for enemies within and without. Cadres measured citizens' loyalties to the new regime by how closely they approximated "good" class consciousness.

With the repudiation of this class-status system, new roads to wealth and power through the accumulation of capital emerged to replace the accumulation of socialist moral wealth. New forms of knowledge also arose to explain social inequality and difference. One fundamental change was in the language of class. Most people I knew, including party cadres, studiously avoided the class labels of the previous era. They referred to someone's "social identity" (*shenfen*) rather than "class background" (*jieji chengfen*). They spoke of "workers" (*gongren*), but not the "proletariat" (*wuchan jieji*). They were likely to say "employee" (*gongzuo renyuan*) to refer not only to a vast array of people who worked in offices, department stores, or factories but also to engineers or designers. The term "city residents" (*shimin*) had replaced "the working class" (*gongren jieji*), and "the populace" or "the public" (*minzhong* or *dazhong*) was invoked rather than "the masses" (*laobaixing*). This shift in everyday terms of address displaces the figure of the subaltern as the subject of China's advance toward modernity.

Official language also made an ambiguous transition in the moral discourse on wealth (Anagnost 1997). Party pronouncements renounced the egalitarianism and collectivization of the Maoist era as decided hindrances to modernity. Many instead underscored the need to allow individuals to express their inherent talents in order to reinvigorate China's possibility of emerging into modernity. The idea of the pure individual mingled, however, with the sense that those social classes which had been the objects of attack under Maoism deserved recognition from the state.

Intellectuals, one of the major categories under attack during the Maoist period, especially emphasized their need to be recompensed. The

Deng regime regarded intellectuals as essential to China's development. Official discourse both praised intellectuals and warned them about their proper place. Intellectuals I knew from the local university felt strongly that they were the ones with the talents most important to further China's pursuit of modernity. Many hailed China's long imperial history of rule by the gentry-literati to remonstrate with the Deng regime, arguing that they still lacked their deserved social position and their rightful access to political and moral leadership. Not a few sported lapel stickers with Confucian aphorisms, as if to conjure up those lost glorious days.

As intellectuals negotiated the shifting meanings of their status within a system in which the state is still the main arbiter, market activity led to new forms of wealth and an incipient bourgeoisie emerged with the potential to usurp what many intellectuals viewed as their natural place as elites.[2] The markets that flourished on the streets of Hangzhou were filled with peasants from the surrounding countryside and mainly young, unmarried men of working-class backgrounds. Less visible markets "behind" the street scenes—markets in foreign currency, illegally imported goods, and weapons—were run by high-level cadres and their children. Peasants sold produce directly from their household plots, while young men set up stands to sell the latest fashions from Hong Kong and America. Many of the latter were unemployed youth or those who had returned to Hangzhou after having been sent to the countryside during the Cultural Revolution and held no permanent position. There were also young male workers from the factories who refused to continue in their state-appointed jobs, preferring instead the lure of the market. Although markets appeared all over the country, the south of China—further away from the center of power—moved more quickly to experiment with them. People in Hangzhou prided themselves on being, as they put it, "quicker" than Chinese people to the north. The local government and party worked to stimulate rather than hinder this activity, sometimes sheltering the full knowledge of it from the central government.

A dangerous and exciting masculinity thrived in this arena. Popular discourse focused on the ability to take "risks" as necessary for success in market endeavors. Those who were most capable of taking risks were said to be young, unmarried men who could prove their worth as men in such exploits, showing their daring, savvy, strength, and ability to entice. They had to travel long distances to obtain goods from Canton, near Hong Kong, and avoid being taken advantage of along the way. They had to have an ever-widening network of social connections to lay their hands on these golden goods—the latest fashions. They had to appear publicly in the market, hawking their wares brazenly, though at any moment "the state" might shut them down in a campaign against spiritual pollution. Women who appeared as sellers in the market were, by contrast, viewed as too brazen, as bad women. They had, people hinted, an air of prostitution about them. How could women, especially unmarried women, do that kind of traveling and haggling with men, that kind of networking, without there being something unsavory about it? "Getting taken advantage of" had a wholly different meaning for them.

"I don't have the courage to do that," Xiao Bao, a young woman silk worker once commented to me. "Men can do that." The risk involved not merely the potential loss of money but engaging in moneymaking activities in the midst of a political culture in which the moral discourse on commercial wealth was ambivalent. Another risk was of abandoning the security of the state's social welfare system of lifetime job guarantees and benefits. Popular wisdom had it that these young men were hooligans or that they used unsavory means to gain wealth. Others remarked on the less visible markets in highly valued imports, nodding knowingly about the sons and daughters of high-level cadres who could take advantage of their family's power to conduct scams. Official discourse took pains to distinguish "selfish" means of garnering wealth from legitimate activity that contributed to the nation, but the line was difficult to draw with any certainty. Most people I knew, including workers, rejected the "radical egalitarianism" of the Maoist period, when wealth was supposed to be shared and only small differences in income were visible. Yet traces of the previous morality remained. In this turbulent moment, it wasn't clear which type of person should represent the nation, which group of people the state should favor in its post-Mao vision of modernity.

The Maoist past haunts these new regimes of truth, for post-Mao social differentiations are caught within the very social forms they are meant to overcome. Economic reform is meant to signal an abrupt break, an entirely new road to modernity that leaves the past far behind. But history paradoxically provides the very grounds on which people negotiate this new road. Invoking Walter Benjamin's image of the angel of history (Benjamin 1968:257–58), one can imagine Maoism as that pile of debris whose wreckage continues to grow as the storm of progress blows China forward. One cannot understand the post-Mao moment's relationship to the Maoist past unless one pursues Benjamin's task of dispelling the myth of a single, unfolding history.

We must begin with Benedict Anderson's insight (1991) that national histories are often a matter of forgetting, or rather of remembering to forget.[3] Even as official discourse in China exhorts people to forget what is often called "the ten years of chaos," it continuously revives the specter of Maoism and the need to overcome it in order to provide a source of moral authority for the post-Mao state.[4] The differences that are so necessary to claims of modernity, differences often created between unequal nations to enable the colonizing of noncitizen others, can be reproduced equally within the nation to enable the disciplining of citizenselves. The state needs to prove over and over again how it can vanquish Maoism. It would be easy enough, otherwise, to let the Cultural Revolution fade into the deep shadows of forgotten history. Instead, we find the Cultural Revolution is continually marked, remarked on, and used as a base point for all discussion of modernity, and tales of its meaninglessness and horrors are repeated and repeated. So long as the post-Mao regime is in power, the Cultural Revolution does not stand in danger of oblivion. History here offers a road to modernity strewn with national degradation and becomes, pace Nicholas Dirks (1990), not so much a sign of the modern as the uncertain site where the possibilities for modernity are construed.

The cultural reinscription of workers is intimately connected to this uneven and highly contested understanding of China's socialist history. More than any other group, workers became the most salient illustration of the socialist history that virtually everyone wished to overcome. Official and popular discourse represented them as literally embodying the past. This characterization was initially brought home to me, most startlingly, at a banquet my mentor instructed me to host not long after my arrival in China. I scarcely understood the import of the event at first. Under the aegis of Chen Li, president emeritus of the university, I invited the president of the provincial silk college, the chief engineer of the Hangzhou silk bureau, and a senior technical adviser to the provincial silk bureau. In addition, Chen Li and several professors from the university attended. Only gradually did I grasp that this banquet was not simply an occasion for a formal interview with my distinguished guests but a gesture critical to building a network of connections, or *guanxi*, that would smooth my way into the silk factories to speak with workers.

Chen Li advised me to submit written questions about the silk industry. Each of my illustrious guests—who, in turn, as a result of this banquet would become hosts of my research—had prepared formal written responses. They all had long years of experience in the silk industry, stretching back to the decade prior to the socialist revolution. That history had made them first targets of attack for engaging in capitalist exploitation and now objects of emulation for that same capitalist knowledge. Their comments were a mixture of facts, figures, and personal reminiscences. Having gone through the formalities, we launched into our meal. In the midst of awkward pleasantries, I asked a question about the problems workers now faced. Suddenly, everyone laughingly chimed in with an obviously clichéd and popular rhyme: "You work well, you work poorly, it's all the same; you work a lot, you work a little, it's all the same; you work or you don't work, it's all the same." They explained its meaning with much good humor: workers lacked the proper discipline for work. They had learned during the Cultural Revolution that they would be rewarded in the same way no matter what kind of effort they put into their work. They had learned laziness as a work ethic, my guests argued.

Workers had certainly challenged the discipline of the workplace during the Cultural Revolution. They had actively assaulted managerial authority, sometimes beating their managers as well. But the moral of that evening's verses, as I took it, was that workers had become flawed because of the failed promises of Maoism. Moreover, this flaw had settled into their natural disposition.

Thus we find the inscription of a new mythopoesis onto workers. No longer treating the subaltern as the hero of socialist progress, the state and nonparty elites have decentered and reconstituted her as one of the central obstacles that needs to be addressed if China is to move forward into modernity. Many, including some workers themselves, compel workers to signify internal lack, potentially hindering China from reaching modernity because they bring the past into the present in their very existence. In a conflicted process, the postsocialist construction of otherness fixes the subaltern worker in the position of historical otherness. The state tries to naturalize the historical difference that it has made workers represent. But as in relations between the colonizer and the colonized, there exists both a tacit acknowledgment and a disavowal of the relations of power that have made workers represent historical difference. On the one hand, it is recognized that Maoism produced a certain consciousness in workers; on the other hand, this historical variability is adamantly denied. The production of new forms of class and gender inequalities are at once tacitly admitted and vigorously disclaimed.

There thus exists a paradox, the simultaneous acknowledgment and disavowal of the conditions that are expressed in the stereotyping of workers. Desires, anxieties, and affirmations of China's postsocialist quest for modernity figure in the body of the worker. The official and popular representations of workers acknowledge the global conditions that force China to create new relations of exploitation but disavow that exploitation—and the dependency of China's modernity on workers— by displacing it onto the workers themselves. Attempts proliferate to fix and normalize workers so that their activity will support capitalist development. But these new forms of disciplining workers are displaced onto the history of socialism in China. And as with colonial discourses of difference, one detects a certain anxiety about the need to make a pure and clean historical break and perhaps the impossibility of doing so, as history bleeds into the present in the figure of the worker.

Workers embody history. They are said to live in what we might call, following Anne McClintock (1995), anachronistic space. According to this trope, workers do not inhabit history proper but exist in a permanently anterior time as anachronistic people. But in official representations, history is an ingestible substance that has been transformed into part of the essential nature of subalterns, replacing their mutable consciousness. Moreover, this process has led to a certain degeneracy. Newspaper editorials and casual comments alike implied that history had created an abnormality among workers, causing harm within the body politic and possibly inheritable tendencies that threatened the "quality" (suzhi) of the Chinese populace. This ambivalence about workers—viewing their behavior as the fallout of history yet naturalizing their collective character—pervaded the everyday commentary on them by others. My intellectual friends at the university took pains to explain that workers lacked a "high consciousness," that they were incapable of dreaming about the future, that they only cared about material goods and wages—as if workers' arguments about wages and material comfort were distinct in kind from those I heard from intellectuals rather than being very similar, that is, a richly symbolic dialogue about social worth and status.

One young professor, Wang Hangsheng, sympathetic to workers and from a worker background himself, invoked Confucius: "We have a saying from Confucius, 'Canglin shi er zhi lijie' [when the granary is full, then one can know the proper manners; i.e., only the wealthy can have the leisure to learn proper etiquette]. Common workers, very few are motivated to have a high consciousness. How can they? They have to worry about just getting food to eat." Yet workers in state-run factories have a guaranteed lifetime income. Indeed, for all intents and purposes their granaries are full, if not exactly overflowing. Professor Wang's interpretation of the Confucian aphorism inverts their reality. He casts workers as those for whom "consciousness" of the future is the opposite of the materiality of the present, where they are thought to be rooted. One finds workers so treated in western scholarship as well, where measurement of workers' wages and productivity are assumed to offer a transparent means to perceive their behavior (see Walder 1987, 1991). Such use of quantitative measures contributes to the reification of workers, treating them as a commodity-form befitting capitalist relations of production and lending justification to the new disciplinary regime.

The essentialization of a disposition in workers toward laziness, disorderliness, and transient material desires—characteristics that establish them as hindering China's efforts to realize modernity—perhaps nowhere made itself more evident than in the accusation that the Cultural Revolution had taught workers to "eat out of one big pot" (*chi daguo fan*). Over the ensuing months I heard this cliché often enough; it had quickly turned into another hackneyed political phrase in the newspapers as well as a form of jesting—for example, mothers used it in teasing their children about their reluctance to do household chores. The expression refers to an extended family that shares both its food and living quarters.[5] "Eating out of one big pot" happens—literally—only within the family. However, within the family it serves as a metaphor for the sharing of the family food and money "pot" without keeping close track of how much each individual has contributed. When I asked silk factory workers, both parents and children, about family finances, for example, they would insist no precise calculations existed among family members, even as they could easily tell me how much money children in their family handed over to their parents every month.

The linking of finances to food within the family makes this phrase a powerful representation of work relations in China. When used to refer to factory workers, "eating out of one big pot" means that no matter how much or how little workers produced, they all ate the same "food," that is, received the same wages.[6] Those who continued to work hard, so I was told, were not given their just "desserts." The metaphor has still deeper resonance for factories. The work unit in China, until recently, operated in a manner analogous to a family, with large work units, like Zhenfu, taking care of all its workers' needs. They had everything from a hair salon to a medical clinic within the factory grounds. The work unit dispensed all social benefits, from ration tickets to medical care to retirement pensions; it continues to give permission to marry and to help resolve a variety of personal conflicts, such as spousal conflict. In this manner, the state provided socialist support and also sought to pull citizens into an overarching loyalty to itself rather than to their familial relations. In the name of modernity, the post-Mao state castigates workers for having accustomed themselves to living as socialists in this way. Such criticism at once breaks with previous forms of knowledge about socialism and institutes new modes of discipline.

To cast workers as having fallen into an antimodern work ethic inverts and obscures the political history of workers' activities during the Cultural Revolution. That political history continues to be a highly emotional matter, for its evaluation necessarily reaches to the very foundations of socialism. Historical judgments of the causes and aftermath of the Cultural Revolution assign guilt and innocence from the highest levels of the state to the local struggles between people whose bonds had been thought to be inalienable—students and teachers, workers and managers, children and parents—as well as among peers, friends, and co-workers. An ambivalence thus pervades the new truth regime about workers, reflecting a larger paradox about how to unravel the past and thus how to morally evaluate the present. History provides the allegory of workers' fallen condition but it simultaneously is erased as their habits and competencies are naturalized. In this post-Mao story about workers, the socialist past becomes reified as a substantive force that appears to exist apart from human relations. It can do things to people and make people become what they originally were not. It resides in people as if it were a removable substance. One might call this reification a form of historical fetishism (see Taussig 1992). Like commodity fetishism, historical fetishism turns the Maoist past into an object whose effectiveness in the world appears to stand apart from specific social relations. The "Cultural Revolution," people now say, kept China from reaching modernity. This emotionally wrought ambivalence about Maoism underlies the equivocal acknowledgment and disavowal of workers' consciousness as agents in history.

This historical fetishism recalls Lukács's discussion of reification (1971). Lukács argued that with commodity fetishism, the human qualities of workers appear increasingly as "mere sources of error" (p. 89) when contrasted with the rationalization of abstract laws governing modern production. For Lukács, the structure of reification occurs not merely within the labor process; it becomes the dominant characteristic of modern society, sinking deeply into human consciousness and all modes of rational knowledge production. Thus every manifestation of life is treated as if it exhibited a necessity subject to strict, abstract laws and a totality ruled entirely by chance.

Although History decentered workers, they in turn decentered

History by telling local stories of their specific pasts. None of the workers I knew ever characterized her- or himself as "eating out of one big pot." They all spoke instead of heroic exertions, volatile political struggles, and radically different forms of discipline than those of economic reform. While they sometimes spoke of the Maoist past as if it were a disembodied substance, they also destabilized this dominant discourse by recalling what it meant to be a worker during that time. Nor did they think of themselves as a natural collectivity. They distinguished themselves from one another in manifold ways, including by the different political campaigns that they felt had established their life trajectories, by specific experiences of the Cultural Revolution, by gender, by family history with silk production, and by class background prior to entering the factory. These diverse histories also led many workers to deny their difference from the rest of society, which has marginalized them and placed them on the other side of a vast gulf. For many, "worker," at least as it was re-created in an abject form, was not an obvious identification. Their challenges to the dominant meaning of their work identities were effected by the telling of different kinds of histories. This was one place where the radical transformations of the post-Mao period were exposed, where the very meanings, images, and subject positioning of workers were renegotiated. Official, elite, and popular commentary all rewrite Chinese history through the vision of a post-Mao modernity and, in so doing, bring that vision into existence and give it a universalizing force. Workers' local stories, however, cast doubt on the universal as they trace subtle differences in the phantasm of a singular modernity.

PRODUCING CULTURE

In the winter of 1985, still close to the beginnings of my fieldwork, the Central Textile Bureau instituted a new wage and bonus system, along with new disciplinary measures, for all textile-related industries. They called it, in a kind of fantasy of stationary permanence, the "position-wage system" (*gangwei gongzi zhi*). State cadres hoped these measures would be the heart of China's modernization program in state-run industries. They designed them to raise workers' productivity by joining punitive regulations to precise statistical measurements. The position-wage system, which applies to workers but not to cadres, replaces the old system based on seniority with one based entirely on the job position, or category. Jobs are divided into five main categories, in descending hierarchical order: (1) weaving, (2) warp preparation, (3) weft preparation and inspection, (4) transport, and (5) miscellaneous work—sweeping, machine cleaning, dining hall work. Weavers occupy the top category and receive the highest wages, with the other categories following in increments of five to ten yuan less at each step.[7] Workers just entering the factory for the first time are placed on this new wage scale, although they do not receive the official wages set for each category until they work for six and a half years. As for workers already at the factory, older workers whose seniority in the old system put their pay above the scale retain their original wages until retirement; those not yet receiving top wages are gradually given raises.

Bonuses for workers in this new system are based on individual piece-work. After workers fulfill a predetermined quota, which represents their basic wage as set by job category, they earn the rest of their income through individual bonuses (though the range of the bonus is also differentiated by job category). The quotas are set such that workers must exceed them to make a living wage—in effect, the wages for each category include the bonus. The problematic nature of the bonus portion of the wage is reflected in the way that workers in the silk factory talk about it: most speak of their bonus being deducted if they fail to reach the maximum amount rather than of earning an extra amount. The wage thus actually has two components: one fixed and one variable.

Party cadres and technical managers in the silk industry explained to me that the position-wage system would rid workers of their tendency to "eat out of one big pot." They cast it as a way to liberate work relations from the constraining political categories of the Cultural Revolution and, indeed, of the entire Maoist era. In this way, the state displaces the issue of exploitation onto workers themselves. Party cadres and nonparty managers in the silk factories were unified on this matter, although much confusion and uncertainty remained: How was power to be divided

between them? How autonomous would they be? How would they rec-
oncile the factory's role in a centrally planned socialist economy, based
on handing over their finished product to the state, with the novel demand—paradoxically by the state—that the factory begin to make a
profit? Party cadres inside the factories seemed at once superfluous and
still powerful in their ability to gain various advantages by invoking the
name of the state.

Theoretically, a smooth, vertical chain of command exists from the
central government's Textile Bureau to the Zhejiang provincial silk bureau to the Hangzhou municipal silk bureau to each of the thirty or so
of Hangzhou's silk factories under its aegis. A parallel line exists from
the Central Party Committee down to the branch party secretaries and
party committees in each factory and in each workshop of each factory.
Yet, while cleaving to this form of power, those at its center also wished
to shake off its unwieldiness and thereby invigorate "the economy."
They hoped that managers of state-run factories would turn a profit but
not stray too far from the strictures of socialist control. The moral discourse on wealth reflected these dizzying extremes of anticipation and
anxiety. All along the "descent lines" of socialist power, innovators developed active, creative means to maneuver in the postsocialist breaches
that had opened. At any moment, they could be shut down and declared
exemplars of spiritual pollution—or they could be declared models of
the road to modernity. By whom? By any level of the government, anyone speaking in the name of the state.

The central government devolved much of the responsibility for economic planning to the provincial and municipal levels. The Zhejiang
provincial silk bureau now set production demands, ultimately answer-
ing to a higher level but with increasing independence, particularly in
managing the lucrative export market. China's silk found eager buyers
all over the world, but especially in Hong Kong, Taiwan (indirectly),
Europe, and the United States. Hangzhou was one of the two or three
major centers for this treasured trade. The windfall from silk exports
gave rise to much dispute, as everyone, including the central government, desired a piece of it for their own ends. Factories had a certain
amount of autonomy in expanding production, but they were not supposed to control directly any aspect of foreign trade. Still, factory man-

agers quickly found ways to increase exports, even as their innovations could be declared dangerous or corrupt at any moment. These contentious, hope-filled maneuverings took on added urgency as everyone feared that the appropriate moment to seize the opportunity for wealth had just passed them by.

Thus newly created desires provided the impetus for the novel regime of truth and discipline embedded in the position-wage system. The state had never before permitted but also had never conceived of such closely refined statistical measurements. Managers viewed these statistics as a neutral and fair means to assess rewards for those who worked hard and punishments for those who did not, and they assumed that I would support their efforts and join in a discussion about the best ways to implement these modern forms of scientific management. After all, I was from the belly of the capitalist beast; I should know best. Their presumptions led me to realize that workers' interpretations of management's interpretations of "productivity" was one site where local histories were expressed.

Commentary on the new position-wage system among workers was open and heated. It eventually led to a tense confrontation with the top directors by one group of workers. Their range of engaged responses makes it impossible for me to treat the new system as an objective method of gathering statistical facts about a transparent reality. Rather, I understand statistical measures to be a means of establishing the authority of a certain vision of social order (Hacking 1991; Porter 1986; Joan Scott 1988b). In the case of China, that vision rests foremost with the state. At the same time, the statistical measures of third world workers like those in Hangzhou's silk factories are taken up and made into productive knowledge by the World Bank, western scholars, and transnational capitalist investors.

Individuation

The position-wage system pressures workers to labor more intensely by transforming the "collectivity" of Maoist production into individuated measurement. In the previous era, workers shared the responsibilities of production as well as its rewards in the form of small bonuses. They were collectively bound to one another in two ways: within each shift, small groups of workers, divided by job task, shared the burden of production; and within the shift rotation system, all workers who had operated the same machine shared the responsibility for production problems. Under the position-wage system, each worker is held responsible for her or his own position within the shift. At Zhenfu, each bolt of woven cloth, for example, carries the name of the worker who produced it. In the shops where the yarn is spun, matters are not as simple. In Zhenfu's weft preparation shop, the shop supervisor pulled one worker off the line and assigned her the task of counting how many broken threads each position had; each worker was docked accordingly.

This individuation of workers resonates with a broader national discourse on the need for individuals to distinguish themselves. The cultural production of individualism speaks at once across time and space: to the Maoist era of collective identification, now said to have hindered China from reaching modernity, and to western orientalism, which describes Asian cultures as lacking a modern concept of individual freedom. Thus a news article on the youth of Shenzhen, the export-oriented special economic zone (SEZ) created near Hong Kong, exemplifies official praise of the need for individual distinction. By lauding the Shenzhen youth, the statement instructs all Chinese citizens on the eight methods for individuating themselves:

> 1) [they have] the courage to assert themselves, to volunteer their services to become factory director; 2) they regard standing on their own feet, earning their own living, and striving to improve themselves as glorious; 3) [they realize that] time is money, time is efficiency; 4) they are particular about bearing and appearance, hoping to draw people's attention; 5) they strive to be a "bird whose head sticks out," to be in the limelight. They dare to compete to be first in their field. They dare to be first to wear a new style of clothing. Very few now believe that one should "know one's place" or that one should not seek to forge ahead. This is a quality youth should have. Jealousy now breeds not a feeling that the crowd should beat down him who "sticks out his head" but a competitive spirit to be better. 6) [They have] the daring to plan for themselves, be able to think it is always the other mountain that

looks higher; 7) [they know that] social contact is for gaining information . . . ; 8) [they have] a feeling of responsibility that unites individual
pursuits with the country's welfare. They have changed the view of the
1950s and 1960s that the pursuit of wealth is only for society's welfare.
(*News Digest*, 13 September 1985, p. 3)

These new individuals need to be freed not simply from socialist moor-
ings but from the stifling force of the crowd, from cultural strictures that
hold them back. But since people do not live simply in "crowds," the
article implicitly refers also to the particular social worlds in which people are enmeshed—families, networks of peers, and the hierarchical
world of work. Modern subjects are those who have the strength to deny
the power of the group. They place modern desires onto their very bodies—in the way their heads "stick out," in the clothes they wear, and in
their display of emotions. As the final method discloses, this discursive
production of individualism is part of the process of imagining a postsocialist modernity for China. It does not seek to liberate individuals so
much as to constitute them as citizens of a post-Mao nation-state (L. Liu
1995).[8]

Age

The individuation of workers leads to rewarding those who are most
"productive." Yet this individuation operates through changing notions
of cultural differentiation embedded in the very concept of productivity.
These notions include "youthful energies," the "bitterness" of weaving,
and gender difference. I first learned about the importance of youth from
Yang Zhuren. Yang Zhuren, who held the modest post of secretary to
the party office, had come forward to speak with me on my initial visits
to Zhenfu. I had naively assumed at first that he must be a relatively
unimportant figure with much time on his hands, the kind of time usefully spent receiving a relatively unimportant foreigner. Yang Zhuren
himself downplayed his position to me. But as I later learned from
others, Yang Zhuren's background in the army, his assignment to
Zhenfu in 1970 to quell the Cultural Revolution, and his subsequent
talent for amassing connections had enabled his gradual rise to become

Zhenfu's most powerful party cadre. Yang Zhuren liked to regale me with stories about his simple peasant background and could enumerate with nostalgic pleasure the elaborate customs of his home village not far from Hangzhou. But he also was keenly aware of everything going on in the factory.

We spent long days discussing and disputing economic reform. As Yang Zhuren explained it,

> The previous system wasn't appropriate. With textile workers, when they are old, the quality of their work is not good. They say of textile workers, "They mature early, they contribute early, they deteriorate early." When someone has just entered the factory, after a few years, around twenty years old is when they produce the highest quality. But they were getting the lowest wages. It wasn't fair.

This representation of youths as the most productive workers stands in radical opposition to the former notion that older workers, as *shifu*, or masters in their trade, should be rewarded for their knowledge and experience. Such reverence for youth accords with the view, vigorously propagated in the 1990s, that people are their most creative and contribute most effectively to the advancement of society in the early years of their career.[9] Indeed, this is a pervasive trope in many nations' discourses of modernity: the child or youth carries the promise of a new beginning in transcending a decayed and corrupted cultural tradition. It has certainly been thematized in China before but perhaps never with such concerted attention to the discipline of the laboring body.[10]

Much talk in China circulates about the need to "juvenize" (*qingnian-hua*), to encourage older people to step aside for the more capable youths now stuck in junior positions. This discursive elaboration of the positive qualities of youth represents a fundamental challenge to the kind of seniority still prevalent in the party, many workplaces, and the family. The assumption that the young have greater capacity also implies a direct relationship between biology and productivity. This notion owes much of its credibility to a milieu in which science has replaced Marxism as the ultimate arbiter of reality.

The new position-wage system privileges youths in that young people who enter the factory will, after only a few years, receive the same wages as those who have worked there for twenty or thirty years. Moreover, older workers who have reached the top of the scale will receive no further wage increases. Thus the wages at the senior end of the scale are effectively lowered. The system, based on changing interpretations of productivity, rewards a category of workers—youths—based on the hegemonic representation of their possessing greater potential capacity to produce. That youths do not always produce more is clear. They are often, as one assistant director of a collective silk-weaving factory put it, "the 'naughty' boys. After work they go out and play. They play late, so they have no energy to work the next day." These are the workers who have their pay docked most frequently. But the gap between youths' variable work performance and the current belief in their capacity has in no way diminished that belief or lessened its role in forming the position-wage system.

The disciplinary regime of post-Mao modernity thus depends on a fundamental transformation in notions of "productivity," a far from transparent process. Workers, as well as certain managers, provided outspoken commentary. Older workers offered me their perspective on the new system. Chen Shifu, only three years from retirement, was direct: she had begun silk work as a young child, had fought hard to become a weaver, and had worked diligently for thirty years. In the past, older workers could transfer to less strenuous jobs without losing any wages in their last few years before retiring, and Chen Shifu had looked forward to becoming a security gatekeeper. She felt she was entitled; she thought the "higher ups"—a common term for politically powerful superiors—should "look after" (zhaogu) her. But with the new position-wage system, transfer to another job category would mean a reduction in pay. Chen Shifu was angry. "These new changes," she said, "xin bu-tong" (won't go through my heart; i.e., my heart won't accept them).

Bitterness

Not only the cultural category of age but also various job categories were given new meaning by the position-wage system. Managers explained that weaving takes greater skill and labor intensity than the other tasks. Indeed, historically silk weaving was the most highly skilled craft in Hangzhou. But in the mid-1980s people in Hangzhou began to consider work in the silk industry to require virtually no skill relative to other, flashier industries like electronics or foreign tourism, then newly introduced into China. No young urban person wished to go into the silk industry. Hangzhou is now a center of light industry and tourism. Young people envied service employees in foreign hotels or tour guides; they fancied work in banks or computer chip factories. And, of course, young men who dared to do so worked in the emerging markets. Since 1982, when everyone but university students could "choose" to seek out their own job instead of receiving a mandatory job assignment from the state Labor Bureau, silk factories have desperately searched for labor, semi-illegally relying on migrant women from the countryside.

While all silk work is virtually indistinguishable in this wider perspective, within the silk industry weaving is recognized as taking more time to learn than prep work; more discrete tasks are involved. But as I quickly learned at Zhenfu, the "productivity" and skill of weaving are most closely tied to interpreting the job as "bitter" work. To "eat bitterness"—that is, to suffer hardship—was once the stuff of socialist pride. In the post-Mao period, however, the heroic glory of eating bitterness had faded. Postsocialist modernity requires not tales of loss but tales of gain.

The bitterness of weaving, as I learned during the time I spent at Zhenfu, comes from the fact that almost all the defects found in the finished cloth are blamed on the weaver. Everyone readily admits that such automatic condemnation is unjust—the fault is not always the weaver's. But the silk process makes it difficult to trace mistakes to any other source. I was in the weaving shop one day when an argument ensued between a weaver and several people representing other shops; the participants included Dai Hongyun, the prep shop's union leader and master worker. The vociferous dispute centered on a problem in the cloth still sitting in the weaver's loom. Yelling over the deafening noise of hundreds of looms, the weaver insisted that poor thread preparation in the prep shop led to the snag in the cloth. Dai Hongyun yelled back that the weaver's inattention when the thread got caught in his loom caused the problem. Qiu Shifu, the assistant shift supervisor, suspected the transport workers, who perhaps were too careless in carrying the bulky but delicate roll of warp over from the steam shop. The argument had to be settled before the weaver continued and the evidence disappeared, and its resolution rested in who could tell a more convincing story, who could talk the other person into giving way. They went back and forth for a long time; ultimately, the weaver yielded, but only because he could talk no one else into taking responsibility. The objective measures of productivity thus rest on local interpretations of work "experience." More than any other silk workers, weavers regularly have their pay docked for falling short of the new, more stringent quality standards. In this sense, their work is more bitter.

Gender

These cultural interpretations of status and skill that inform statistical measures of productivity are in turn shaped by changing conceptions of how gender relates to silk work. The understanding of productivity itself is clearly gendered, for the position-wage system applies only to what is increasingly considered women's work—weaving, prep, and inspection. Tasks such as machine repair and transport (including truck driving) are categorized as skilled technical labor and defined as men's work. The division between management and workers in the silk industry is also increasingly made along gender lines. Those who do the women's tasks (including those men who do so) are thereby produced as feminine subjects. Conversely, women and men who engaged in tasks designated as appropriate for men were seen as masculine. Many comments flowed freely among women workers, for example, about the masculinity of those women who prepared the warp or were shop supervisors.

As the previous chapter demonstrated, silk work in Hangzhou was not always women's work. Until well into the 1960s, local culture reserved silk weaving, as well as warp preparation, for men and for women who could demonstrate masculinity. Women prepared the weft thread and spun the thread out of the cocoons. With the 1958 Great Leap

Forward campaigns to bring more women into the workforce, women in Hangzhou began to take on more of the weaving. By the mid-1960s, Hangzhou's silk industry was witnessing a decided feminization of its workforce. But this trend was halted during and just after the Cultural Revolution, when urban youth sent down to the countryside who wished to return were allowed to inherit their parents' factory jobs if their parents retired early. Young men entered the silk factories and took up jobs as weavers, machine repairmen, and transport workers. Even in the 1980s, nearly half of the silk weavers in Hangzhou were men. This gendered division of labor exists as a matter of historical contingency, dependent not on an inner structural logic or an inherent teleology in the relations of production but on political campaigns that construct specific meanings of gender.

With economic reform, an increasingly rigid distinction emerged between the production line jobs of weaving, prep, and inspection work, construed as manual labor, and those jobs more highly valued as skilled technical and mental labor—machine repair, transport, and managerial work. As part of this process, the manual labor tasks became women's work, while the technical and mental tasks were assigned to men and women thought to be masculine enough to handle them. This gendered division of labor has taken shape through gendered interpretations of work capabilities; women and men were and are said to have different capacities uniquely suited to these divergent tasks. Yang Zhuren, in a casual aside, once told me that the new system was created to categorize tasks considered boring, tasks requiring energy but little skill. Realizing the import of his remarks, he then quickly moved on to speak of other problems. Managers repeatedly told me that women are most suited to such tasks—they have the requisite patience, complain less about boring work, and have nimble fingers. Because gender capabilities are defined in opposition to one another, men are thought to be innately more capable of technical tasks. To the extent that particular women in the silk factories are viewed as able to do men's work, they are said to resemble men.

Representations of the appropriate managerial qualifications also operate through gender. Most important, people would comment that women lacked the necessary leadership qualities to be managers. In particular, women don't know how to talk people into doing things; they thus lack the skill needed to resolve disputes and make the social connections so necessary for getting anything done. Talking, or verbal persuasion, is at once a political, cultural, and social skill. The party operates most effectively and most powerfully when a party cadre can persuade someone verbally to do as the party wishes. To excel in this art means to lead the person who is the object of persuasion into embracing the party's wishes as her or his own; that is, to become the subject of these desires. Zhenfu was filled with such artful verbal maneuvers: supervisors talking workers into staying on the job rather than taking sick leave for the day; the youth league secretary attempting to talk young men back into the factory rather than skipping work to make money in the market. In honing this skill, leaders had to be authoritative but not authoritarian; compelling in their combination of moral, social, and emotional reasoning rather than blunt. Those who were most artful would remind a worker of her or his obligations to other workers—how much other workers would be unduly burdened if she or he refused to work. A worker might also be reminded of the importance of her contributions to the welfare of her factory, her family, and her country. Those few women acknowledged to have mastered the art of verbal persuasion were said to be just like men in their ability to talk.

The state certainly took the initiative in gendering work but, as in earlier eras, these differentiations took their power from diverse sources. That is, state cadres did not stand outside of culture, manipulating it from above. They and others naturalized and in the process materialized these gender relations. Educated women, for example, also insisted to me that women talked of petty things, that "they" lacked the ability to settle human affairs. It is possible, too, that the global conditions of textile labor, in which women predominate, have helped shape local changes in Hangzhou. Women workers themselves both accepted and recast these gendered work relations. While they never overtly challenged this mapping of gender onto work, neither were they patient, silent, or meek. Indeed, the major challenge that supervisors faced was keeping these women in their place—a subtle, never-ending contest that supervisors lost as often as they won. The more experienced *shifu* also had to teach new workers how to have "nimble fingers." Sometimes they complained of the migrant women from the countryside that their hands were too "stupid," that they weren't "quick" like city women. As the combination of global markets and diverse competing party and managerial interests within China continued to devalue the women's work of silk production, women workers in Hangzhou's silk factories tried desperately, and sometimes successfully, to leave their place in silk work altogether.[11] They fled to new work that was no less gendered. In Hangzhou, the most alluring was the world of foreign tourism, where young women could serve as the "Asian beauties" that foreign businessmen sought.

Cultural notions of gender thus construct work relations. Work relations, in turn, instill gender identities. Women and men participating in the dailiness of work activities come to embody gender distinctions as they imperceptibly take upon themselves the discursive regime of labor. In China, "labor"—rather than, say, family, sexual desire, the psyche, consumption, religion, or any number of other realms of human activity—under socialism served as the principal cultural site for the production of identities. The processes and practices associated with labor became infused with gender ideologies that, in turn, structured possibilities for women and men. Labor played such a critical role not because of its supposed objective materiality—after all, we are talking about a rather short period of history—but because of the party-state's success in discursively producing it as the critical site. That is, the state made labor the cultural arena in which women and men crafted the meaning of "liberation," proved their socialist moral worth, expressed their nationalist sentiments, and received their rewards—or punishments—from the state. Labor furnished the means by which the state measured its own modernity.

Political economy here becomes not the material ground of women's experiences, nor the objective framework for them; rather, it is a discourse like any other. It creates its object of knowledge and its construction of reality.[12] That people labor and are exploited in the process is clear. But the meaning of labor is always contingent. Political economy, then, is a Marxist discourse that produces the meaning of labor and was, in socialist China, the primary means of producing modern identities.[13]

Because labor has provided such a vexed cultural site, in the post-socialist era it continues to be the focus of a number of cultural struggles—over "productivity," to be sure, but also over the meaning of socialism and capitalism, one's relationship to the state, one's identity as a woman or man, and one's future as a modern subject. Yet it now competes with other cultural realms. The state has enabled the "market" to become one such field for the intertwining of modernity and masculinity. The market—not construed as labor—is a new site for the cultural production of "liberated" modern subjects. Here, masculine men, not liberated women, transgress what people now call "traditional socialist" values. The invention of the psyche and of sexuality cultivate still other forms of modern identities. In the process, women workers became the feminized subjects of a reconceived state-run arena that, everyone complains, holds China back from reaching modernity.

A MOMENT OF INSPECTION

Contestations over gender and work identities sometimes came in explosive outbursts or grumbling back talk. At other times, they were enacted in the subtle dailiness of work. My presence at Zhenfu more than once gave rise to such performances, as the following story attests.

It was a cold, wintry morning in early December of 1985, about two weeks after I had begun my daily visits to Zhenfu. I had decided to wander over to the inspection shop to learn more about the work that went on there, for inspection of the silk cloth prior to export increasingly served as the nodal point where the local political economy of the silk industry met globally inflected desires for consumption—and thus where the fetishism of commodities intersected with the fetishism of Chinese workers' labor.

The inspection shop felt quiet and peaceful, a refreshing contrast to the frenetic noise of the weaving and prep shops, where speaking to anyone meant yelling with one's lips close to her or his ear or leaving the shop floor altogether. In the inspection shop, men calmly bolted the cloth for transport after women and men methodically inspected meter after meter of cloth for "defects." A small group of women sat in front of sewing machines, embroidering numbers into the cloth to identify which workers had worked on each bolt of cloth. Another group of women arrayed down the length of a wooden table restitched the "defects" by hand.

The calm of the shop belied its central importance. The assessment performed in the inspection shop seemed to me a late-twentieth-century analog of the imperial examinations (see Miyazaki 1976). Instead of deciding who would be rewarded or denied the honor of serving the imperium as literati-bureaucrats, this version castigated with lower pay those who had produced "defective" silk cloth or honored with a bonus those who succeeded in making the nearly flawless cloth western consumers demanded. Indeed, the question of "quality," as I gradually learned, was the crux of the discourse on "productivity" in this export-oriented industry. The new, more intense pressures for higher quality, as most workers were well aware, resulted directly from western expectations. "You foreigners have such picky taste," I was told over and over again as Hangzhou's silk factories scrambled to make their cloth into the "first-grade" type the Foreign Export Bureau insisted upon for shipment to Hong Kong, the United States, and Europe. "The Russians," someone once explained, "are not nearly as demanding."

I sat that morning, bundled in my down jacket and hugging a hot water bottle in my hands, on a stool in front of Du Shifu's inspection table. (The inspection shop had no heat, unlike the other shops, which were kept warmer to protect the tensile quality of the thread.) Du Shifu, a woman in her late forties, had worked at Zhenfu for twenty-seven years. As one of the senior inspection workers, she led the group who inspected the cloth. Du Shifu—wearing only a thinly padded jacket and no gloves—energetically gave me a lecture on her work and, via her work, on the entire technology of silk production. I tried, occasionally, to chat about other, more personal things, but Du Shifu stayed intent on her lecture.

We began with silk lining (*dianlifang*). Du Shifu laid out the first meter of the pure white cloth over her table. The black curtain separating her table from the rest of the room blocked the glare of the sun so that the "defects" would stand out. "This cloth uses a double-threaded yarn in the warp," she lectured, illuminating the silk weave under her small, handheld magnifying glass. "It should have a twenty-two over twenty density, with thirty-two threads per centimeter and two folds of width." She briskly moved her magnifying glass with its centimeter gauge over different portions of the cloth and measured. I was bewildered by the amount and detail of information she threw out at me so quickly. Du Shifu promptly took the pen out of my hand and began to write down the main points of her lesson for me in my notebook. She continued: "The weft is triple-threaded yarn, with a twenty over eighteen density."

"How did you learn all of this?" I asked, unsure of what else to venture about so much technical information and hoping once again to turn the conversation to her own life. While she was a weaver for thirteen years, she stated without wasting any words, she studied in the factory-run school. She had been an inspection worker for the past fourteen years. Then my apprenticing lesson continued: "The two most common defects are 'broken silkworm gut' (*canjiao po*) and 'single end' (*dantou*). Broken silkworm gut occurs when the weaver tries to fix a problem by pulling out several weft threads. Then you can see two different colors in the cloth. The bottom warp shows through the top weave; the 'gut' of the silk cloth is broken. *Dantou* is when there is one less weft thread than the cloth should have. With each broken silkworm gut, we dock [the weaver] two points. With each *dantou*, two points for every fifteen millimeters. Twelve and a half points equals a defective cloth." Defective cloth was, by definition, silk that could not be exported to the West and thus could only be sold for domestic consumption, lowering its profitability.

Du Shifu then laid out a magnificent brocade quilt cover, a product for which Zhenfu was famous. Five large white phoenixes, one in each corner and one in the middle, luxuriantly displayed their golden plumes. Surrounded by bright blue and green flowers, they stood against a brilliant red background. This silk cloth was one of the popular marriage quilts women brought as part of their dowry. Du Shifu continued the lesson. She explained that it was easier to inspect this kind of patterned brocade, partially woven with "man-made" silk, or rayon, than plain natural silk. The "defects" stand out more clearly.

Just at this point, the assistant supervisor of the inspection shop approached. He was a young man in his early thirties who had recently been "plucked up," as they colloquially said, out of Zhenfu's workforce to be groomed for modern management. That grooming, it seemed from his self-presentation, consisted of learning a bit of English and reading management journals. One of the few people at Zhenfu who dressed in a western-style suit, this young supervisor strained to perform his intended role of modern manager. He approached me to impress us with his western knowledge, hoping that a performance acknowledged by the foreigner would then garner more accolades from others. With hesitancy and bravado, he stood just behind us. Du Shifu ignored him.

Du Shifu: "The two most common defects in this quilt cover are 'too much rising' [*duoqi*] and 'too little rising' [*xiaoqi*]."

The assistant supervisor, lobbing the word over my right shoulder, said in English: "Dyeing."

I turned around to find him grinning with his sense of accomplishment. Du Shifu glared at him over her shoulder. She continued, as if a pesky fly had been buzzing in our ear: "With 'too much rising,' the weft thread comes up one too many times when it shouldn't have, so it doesn't get woven in. For each mistake, we dock two points."

The assistant supervisor again lobbed the word over our shoulders: "Machine," he said in English.

Du Shifu spoke forcefully, leaving her back turned to him: "Sometimes the problem is in the loom. But we dock the weaver anyway because she should catch it and pull out the thread."

The assistant supervisor then shoved a fistful of management journals in my face. Du Shifu threw him a withering look. I realized that my giving face to one of them meant taking face away from the other. Defeated in his efforts to capture the foreigner's attention with his version of silk production knowledge, the assistant supervisor finally slunk away.

The tensions over knowledge and worthiness in this performance, for which I was supposed to play both audience and arbiter, reflect the hopes, dreams, and frustrations circulating in the post-Mao imaginary of modernity. The troubled negotiations in this brief encounter spoke tersely, with no need for further elaboration, about the cleavages in China's deferred desires for modernity. They raise questions that I pursue in the remaining chapters: How do women workers negotiate their "double consciousness" of being in but not of a post-Mao allegory of modernity? How is this imaginary shaped within uneven global relations of power, in which, for China, the United States is such a central figure? How do women assert, perform, and remember their identities as women workers in the midst of such marked splits? What of the heterogeneity among women who, through different political campaigns, came to desire distinctive gender identities? While the upheavals of post-Mao narratives of modernity explicitly decentered workers, the cultural struggles of diverse cohorts revealed modernity to be a mutable project developed in unequal cross-cultural dialogues and contentions. How do women workers inhabit the uninhabitable edges of modernity?

3 Socialist Nostalgia

History is not kind to us
we restitch it with living
past memory   forward
into desire

Audre Lorde,
"On My Way Out
I Passed Over You and
the Verrazano Bridge"

Stories of liberation, as I situated them previously, speak about a seemingly distant past. As a history of the 1950s, they trace the specificities of cultural challenges that made transgressions of sexual difference a central practice of imagining a socialist modernity. They illuminate how and why a small group of women became such enthusiastic subjects of a Maoist discourse on liberation. Yet we cannot forget that these women shared their stories with me in the contemporary moment of post-Mao reform. In this context, their tales of gender transgressions appear to be anachronistic, incongruous in today's very different regime of modernity. I heard their commentary, then, as an arc of interpretation that swept from the 1950s to the 1990s and back again. Older women workers proffered these stories to me as if they were reminiscing over photographs from an old national family album. But these were not sepia-hued snapshots of moments frozen in time. Though steeped in nostalgia, they were instead selective genealogies of socialist subjectivity, insistently fashioned against a current of marginalization in the post-Mao era. They were, to quote Audre Lorde, "past memory forward / into desire" (1986:57).

In this chapter, I bring us back to these liberation stories to reflect on them from another angle, considering them as memory, or what I prefer to call "memory-practice." As nostalgic memory, they raise questions about how people come to reinterpret their history. They lead us to consider how representations of the past are discursively produced and deployed. I draw attention to their nostalgic quality in order to discern how that nostalgia is produced out of and positions women of the oldest cohort in relation to post-Mao visions of modernity. The post-Mao imaginary of modernity, as I argued in the previous chapter, decenters workers and makes them the embodiment of a troubled history. As managers and party cadres sought to reinvigorate the silk industry in order to produce exports profitable for the state, they invoked a dominant form of nostalgia that imagined how workers in the period before the Cultural Revolution used to be more obedient, more dedicated, and too naive or too afraid to speak out.

Older women workers implicitly complicate that construction of the past by remembering themselves instead as socialist heroes. Their nostalgia resides not only in the content but in the form of their stories, which is known as "speaking bitterness." By speaking bitterness in the post-Mao era, women workers in their turn unsettle the most recent universalizing vision of modernity that has displaced them. Analysis of this interplay will require a more nuanced interpretation of nostalgia than its usual and somewhat dismissive portrayal as an "always already" insidious structure of sentiment. We must pay attention as well to the dynamic and contested nature of historical identities.

By turning a doubled angle of vision on these stories—seeing how they speak not just to the past out of the present but also to the present out of the past—I necessarily explore the writing of history in anthropology. History provides a critical ground from which scholars challenge the allochronism of culture as that approach was developed in colonial anthropology. By "allochronism" I mean, following Fabian (1983:32), the use of "naturalized-spatialized Time" as a distancing device that supported a systematic tendency to deny the coevalness in time between the subjects of anthropological writings and the anthropologist. Anthropologists have, for some time, contended that non-European peoples "have" not only history (E. Wolf 1982) but the art of historical inquiry (Faubion 1993; Price 1983; Rosaldo 1980). They have explored how history both disrupts and reinforces culture, as well as how culture is an effect of history (Rosaldo 1980; Yanagisako 1985). While certain anthropologists have, in a problematic vein, discerned a "cultural logic" that reproduces itself through historical events, thus purportedly demonstrating cultural autonomy (Sahlins 1985), others have demonstrated how history can be used to tell a story of forced cultural syncretism in colonial worlds of unequal power (Comaroff and Comaroff 1991). Though many of these critical approaches have unraveled the colonial conception of culture as timeless tradition, they have failed to explore the politics of knowledge in constructing narratives that count as history.

Recent anthropological work along these lines has developed from critiques of Hegelian historiography (Chakrabarty 1992; Duara 1995; Prakash 1990; H. White 1987; Young 1990). These critiques have unveiled how Enlightenment assumptions of linear progress relegated contemporary histories of struggles over power and meaning to the shadowy background of ahistorical cultural difference. Classical Marxist versions of such linear tales were similarly flawed, reducing all forms of subalternity to a story of class oppression. Such Enlightenment histories narratively incorporated colonized peoples by forcing on them the kinds of progressive histories that kept Europe and the United States at the center of modernity. Indeed, the very concept of modernity derives from hypostatizing History as a story of progress. For this reason Foucault, though he ignored colonialism, intentionally disrupted linear narratives of progress with genealogies that traced the recent invention of concepts and practices that lie at the heart of modernity.

Simply proving that non-western others also have History thus does not undo the link between structures of historical knowledge and forms of domination. Such uncoupling requires open-minded scrutiny of the relations of power in the creation of historical narratives—relations of power that reside, for example, in narrative genres. As Hayden White

(1987) has argued, the content of history is found in the form. These genres include biography and autobiography (Gagnier 1991; Steedman 1986), statistical studies (Joan Scott 1988b), and tales of the rise of class subjectivity (Thompson 1963). Such relations of power also inhabit the politics of history as discourse (Chakrabarty 1992; Spivak 1991), whereby historians construct the very terms of a past they believe they merely describe. And finally, power dwells in the heterogeneous sites where these narratives have a contested existence—in struggles, for example, over cultural citizenship that challenge linear tales of the nation or, in this case, over the politics of gender that challenge progressive stories of modernity.[1]

This chapter, then, draws attention to the discursive production of history. I by no means intend its argument to supplant that of chapter 1 for the continued need to understand the historical production of discourse (in this case, discourses of women's liberation). Rather, in juxtaposing the two chapters I explore the creative tension between them— between the way discourses of women's liberation were historically generated and the way history is discursively deployed.

If nations, states, and peoples deploy history as a sign of the modern, then the past becomes a site through which multiple voices can contest specific projects of modernity. The oldest cohort's stories of liberation, when revisited with an ear to their nostalgia, open up a space for women of this cohort to remember themselves as creative political actors in a world that now denies them this ability. To be sure, the nostalgia was not theirs alone. A nostalgia for the utopian dream of socialism, and for the first years after the revolution when people believed in that dream, pervaded national political culture. Older women workers drew on this dominant form of socialist nostalgia, which portrays an innocent state at one with its citizens. They, too, remembered a time when they sacrificed on behalf of the new state. But their memories diverged from the history created by the state. For in remembering that during that time they were heroes in the eyes of the state, they provided an implicit social commentary on the post-Mao regime's current vision of modernity. They unsettled the naturalization of that vision and the effort to rewrite history that such naturalization requires.

THE GOLDEN ERA

A recurrent nostalgia for the initial years of socialism underlies official and popular rejection of Maoism. Indeed, many people told me that "Maoism" began only after the halcyon early years of the 1950s. National political culture, including both official and unofficial revisionist histories, novels, television programs, and informal commentary, encourages a nostalgic view of those years as utopian perfection, utter social harmony, and the innocent belief in the unity of Chinese citizens and their new socialist state. Many—not only older workers but also a significant number of intellectuals—share in this nostalgia. Their sense of loss is tinged with a nationalist longing for a future of rapid and infinite progress. The longing speaks of a desire to have China regain a dignified and powerful position in relation to the West; lost is the hope that China would lead the way out of the social degradations generated in the history of western capitalism. Michael Dutton (1995), borrowing from Walter Benjamin, has called this period China's "dream time."[2]

Incorruptibility

The reminiscences of Yang Zhuren brought out one prevalent nostalgic image of the 1950s—that of a society that was incorruptible. Yang Zhuren held the modest title of secretary to Zhenfu's party office but was perhaps the most powerful man in the factory. Like others who expressed nostalgia for that time, Yang Zhuren allowed his ruminations to emerge in momentary and unexpected snatches. At times, people reminisced in response to my direct questions about their lives right after the revolution, but just as often, their nostalgia punctuated commentary on other topics.

Yang Zhuren was a consummate storyteller. He had a firm grasp of the politics of speech, a skill that was essential to his political power. He was also a virtuoso at discretion, sometimes turning stories into oblique illuminations of contemporary political dilemmas and at other times just using them to distract my attention. I had gone to Zhenfu numerous times to interview Yang Zhuren and others before I received permission to visit on a daily basis. When the latter project began, I spent the first full day with Yang Zhuren again. This time I tried to be more assertive in pressing him on the deep problems Zhenfu faced because of economic reform. Echoing popular explanations, Yang Zhuren blamed their problems on the Cultural Revolution. When I asked which specific practices still lingered from that period, Yang Zhuren deftly skirted my question.

"Before the Cultural Revolution," he began, "people helped one another. It was not an economic relationship. We did not have 'going through the back door,' 'the winds of corruption,' 'opportunism and profiteering.' " Yang Zhuren invoked phrases familiar from official denunciations and ordinary conversation alike. The post-Mao government had disengaged the act of accumulating wealth from questions about the mode of its acquisition or the relations of inequality structured by it. Yet a lively and heated moral discourse on wealth nonetheless continued, raising questions about who should be allowed to make money and in which ways. As he and I both knew, the most pointed critiques of corruption were directed toward party cadres and their families for using their political power to gain unfair advantage. Even the central party-state leaders felt compelled to announce periodically, with much rhetorical fanfare, the latest campaign to sweep out corruption in the party. Local citizens merely shook their heads cynically.

He continued, "Before the Cultural Revolution, there existed 'honesty in the performance of official duties.' Government officials did not seek personal [i.e., selfish] gain." Yang Zhuren had tellingly switched his mode of political discourse. His language here reflects a presocialist language of governance, replete with a four-character phrase from classical Confucian prescriptions and a term for "government officials," *guan*, that harks back to the imperium. Then he grabbed a piece of the factory's stationery and held it up to me: "For example, you wouldn't even use this paper to write your own letter. You would buy your own paper. Then it was glorious not to use what belonged to the public."

No Thieves

The public sphere then was built on mutual trust—or so people remembered. One day after her retirement, Yu Shifu and I met for a long walk. I had just returned to China after a four-year hiatus. We caught up on past news. Had I finished my dissertation, she wanted to know? And did I have a job? Reassured on that account, Yu Shifu waxed eloquent about her newfound leisure time. We lingered over unraveling episodes of the soap opera *Yearnings* that she and many others were devoted to watching. Then I turned the conversation to her past. There were details I wanted to fill in. I began by asking her what her first impressions were of "this liberation stuff."

"Good, very good," she answered. "Because then we had wages. It wasn't like now, with people so particular about nice clothes and good things to eat. Then we just cared about getting enough wages to eat at all. And that was when I finally learned how to read. I was thirteen years old. I hadn't gone to any schooling before that; we were too poor and things were too chaotic.

"And it was so much more calm and stable then. Oh, it was really good. No one dared steal anything, it was very stable. People's relationships with one another were really good."

"How did people get rid of the thieves?" I asked.

"Whenever someone took anything," she replied, "for example, if someone took something on the bus, then they would post his picture and say he had stolen on this bus. Then he wouldn't dare do it again. Or if someone beat someone, then they would post his picture where it happened and say that this person had beaten someone in this spot. So people didn't dare do it anymore. So the 1950s were good. Very safe. And people were very trusting. Friends had a sense of loyalty."

Sacrifice

Citizens willingly made sacrifices for their new state—or such was the sense conveyed to me by various people's nostalgic memories. Yang Wanfen and Si Zhaoding, Zhenfu's trade union leader and head of security, respectively, fondly remembered their self-denial. "Just after Liberation," Si Zhaoding recalled, "workers' zeal was so high. We thought, after Liberation, life couldn't be better. Then, workers were obedient. Now, people just want money. We had a few bad workers then, too, who complained or were afraid of getting tired, afraid of the hardship.

"But we worked so hard then! I remember the Korean War. 'Oppose America, Aid Korea!' 'Protect our homes and defend our country!' We workers made such an effort. We gave extra money to the government for planes and bombs. Workers didn't pay attention to the hours. We went all out. And 1958. 'The high tide of socialist construction!' Workers were excited then, too."

Yang Wanfen added, "For seven days we didn't sleep. We just kept working."

Si Zhaoding went on, "And in 1960, all the problems. No raw materials. We stopped production. Soviet-China relations broke off. We had to give back money to the Soviet Union in goods, like silk. Then workers also worked like crazy. Zhenfu didn't ask the government for wages. We swept the floor, planted mulberry trees, picked tea leaves. We made our wages that way."

Though nostalgic, this paean to themselves also contains a faint trace of ironic self-deprecation. To speak of "zeal," for example, is already to mark a distance between the innocence of then and the cynicism of now. The post-Mao regime periodically pleads with the populace to "raise their zeal" for the accumulation of national wealth in an unselfish manner—that is, for the state. But zeal is a scarce sentiment these days, for people hold a more skeptical view of state power. Moreover, all the political campaigns they mention have been reevaluated: many view the anti-American politics of that era as reflecting a history best forgotten; all believe that the Great Leap Forward ("the high tide of socialist construction") was an unmitigated disaster; the break with the Soviet Union marks a certain socialist rigidity. Ironic questions underlie their nostalgic commentary: Why did we bother to sacrifice? Exactly what was it all for?

Nostalgia is not an innocent sentiment. Indeed, it is not just a sentiment, for it also exists as a strategy of representation. Most social theorists perceive nostalgia critically, as a way of redeeming an idealized past that naturalizes contemporary relations of domination. Susan Stewart, in her reflective essays collected in *On Longing* (1993), deftly traces nostalgia as a representational practice. She points out that it persists as a longing, structured through narrative, for the authenticity of absolute presence and the origin of lived experience; it reflects a wish to close the gap between experience and its mediation in language. Nostalgia is of necessity inauthentic, Stewart argues, because as narrative it does not partake in the lived experience of the past. It is thus ideological because the past it idealizes exists only in its own narrative, there reproduced as a felt absence. Yet nostalgic narrative also endeavors to bring closure to events, thus forcing a bounded interpretation of their significance. Nostalgia's raison d'être lies in that desire for absolute closure, for both the clarity of beginnings and the certitude of endings. Paradoxically, nostalgia functions only in the absence of such fixity and closure. "The nostalgic," Stewart writes, "dreams of a moment before knowledge and self-consciousness that itself lives on only in the self-consciousness of the nostalgic narrative" (p. 23).

Stewart's meditation attends to the relationship between meaning and materiality or, more specifically, between narrative, sentiment, and temporality. She underscores the troubling and pervasive inability to fix a nonarbitrary relationship between representations and their referents, not only in literary works but in all of cultural life. Nostalgia as a utopian gesture searches for certitude in the face of the potential multivocality of meaning.

The pervasive nostalgia in China for the 1950s as a golden era of socialism bears out much of Stewart's argument. This dominant mode endeavors to capture a protected and pure essence of socialism that precedes the history of its degradation. It erases a range of political tensions that had already manifested themselves in the early 1950s, such as the workers' strikes and political campaigns that prefigured the Cultural Revolution. By invoking the socialist dream, these nostalgic memories implicitly cleave to an essential innocence and goodness attributed to the state. They also hark back to the obedience of citizens and their willingness to believe in the state. Such nostalgia acknowledges how much China has "fallen" from that state of grace. At the same time, it encourages a renewed attachment to the state and its post-Mao projects of modernity. If only "the people" would return to that originary unity with the state and not question its power, China could have modernity within its reach.

This hegemonic nostalgia seeks, as Stewart suggests, a purity of lived socialist experience that will provide ideological closure on the meaning of socialism, then and now.[3] In this sense, she echoes other critics of nostalgia who reveal a diversity in forms of domination. Renato Rosaldo (1989), for example, writes movingly of imperialist nostalgia, peculiar to colonialists who yearn for the very ways of non-western life they have destroyed. Kathleen Stewart (1988) writes ironically of bourgeois modes of nostalgia in decorations of a town square that recapture the rustic.

Socialist nostalgia in China also longs for the very ways of life that the socialist state destroyed. Yet the dream about the 1950s is not uniform. Women workers who came of age then share in the official culture of nostalgia, but they also diverge from it. They remember not just the innocence of socialism but a past when they viewed themselves as heroic political agents, exemplified in their willingness to transgress the conventional boundaries of gender. Indeed, their memories create a contested terrain of nostalgia by unsettling the post-Mao vision of natural, ahistorical femininity. They open rather than close a gap in the representations of the past and, necessarily, of the present, creating a certain distance between themselves as older women workers and the post-Mao state.

To understand how these memories unsettle dominant modes of nostalgia, we will have to move beyond Stewart, who assumes that culture and language are universal and shared. No particular subjects appear in her argument, no situated relations of power. She locates nostalgia within representations but outside of specific, and contested, histories. How, instead, can we come to appreciate the nostalgia of those who were so recently designated as subalterns but have since lost that privileged status granted them by the socialist state?

SPEAKING BITTERNESS

Along with sharing the nostalgia for a landscape of social harmony in the socialist Golden Age, women workers who came of age in the 1950s also spoke about the "bitterness" of their lives during that time. I'll admit that even as I provided an empathetic audience, I thought they complained a lot. They spoke about "eating bitterness" with regard to almost everything in their past. Being a woman then, they said, was "bitter"; doing silk work was "eating bitter food"; life itself, Yu Shifu said, was "bitter, then, very bitter." They emphasized the difficulties in overcoming this bitterness, the lengths they went to in struggling against local male dominance, the amount of bitterness they had accepted over the years as conscientious women workers. These remarks were made in formal interviews but also in informal moments, as we walked around the factory grounds or while they worked. I took their complaints to heart, even as I wondered if they weren't a bit overdone. After all, these women also waxed eloquent about how perfect the 1950s were. How was I to grasp the import of their aggrieved tone?

At first, I assumed their rhetoric of complaint was transparent, that the meaning of what they said could be found simply in the surface content of their speech. Only gradually did I come to think of their speech as speech *acts* and to interpret their complaints as a historically and culturally specific narrative practice. After my first stay in China, I began to reread ethnographic accounts of communist organizing just before and after the socialist revolution. I no longer accepted that the only explanation for the Communist Party's success lay in the obviousness of the need to address exploitation. I had begun to ask a different set of questions about the cultural construction of political convictions. At the same time, innovative uses of narrative analysis in ethnographic writing (Caton 1990; S. Harding 1990; Lavie 1990; K. Stewart 1996; Tsing 1993) led me to ponder the genre of this talk by older women. Eventually, I came to realize that their commentary on the bitterness of their everyday lives reflected a narrative practice known as "speaking bitterness" (*suku*).

Speaking bitterness was a political praxis honed and disseminated by the party in the process of revolution. Party cadres used it as a vital method of teaching peasants and later workers how to speak as socialist subjects of the new nation. Speaking bitterness, in other words, provided a means of interpellation; it led people to conceive of themselves as new kinds of subjects, as subaltern subjects. Gradually I could hear, even in their informal remarks, that older women workers cast their lives in this mode, thereby asserting certain political claims. Given their current marginalization, I began to hear their speaking bitterness as nostalgic. The nostalgia existed in the form of their talk and the way it was spoken.

The secondary literature on China describes speaking bitterness as a political tool of the party during the 1940s and 1950s (Belden 1949; Chan, Madsen, and Unger 1992; Hinton 1966).[4] William Hinton, for example, who worked on a UN project on agricultural development in China in the late 1940s, provides an extended description of this process. He became interested in communist land reform and, with the permission of local Communist Party leaders, observed its workings in one northern village.[5] As he describes it from his copious notes, party organizers from outside the village mobilized those individuals whom they had decided were the most oppressed to speak up about their exploitation in a public gathering. First, they met with these peasants separately and educated them about how to interpret their lives in the socialist terms of class exploitation, replacing concepts of fate or kinship noblesse oblige. (Many poor peasants worked for their wealthier kin.) After teaching them to think of the wealthier peasants who hired them as their enemies and the poorer peasants as their friends, the cadres encouraged them to believe they could overcome their exploitation by speaking out about the bitterness they had suffered and then acting to rectify it. Under party guidance, they rehearsed how to perform their tale of bitterness. At the subsequent public gathering, these peasants would "speak pains to recall pains" (Hinton 1966:157) in the form of public accusations against gentry landlords whom party cadres brought before the crowd. This political performance moved others to speak their pains and thus to create a new form of collective identity. It also paved the way for the collective reappropriation of wealth from the accused elite by creating a new public morality about wealth. Though rehearsed, these performances were far from mechanical. Their novelty and their goal of a thorough rupture with previous social ties made them highly emotional and sometimes violent.[6] Many of the poor peasants who first dared to speak their bitterness assumed leadership of their villages in the new socialist regime.

Speaking bitterness later was performed in urban factories as well, but without either the redistribution of the means of production or the violent confrontations common in the countryside. When I returned to China a second time, I gathered stories about these urban sessions. Yu Shifu described them as rather formal affairs that occurred nearly a year after the revolution, when the new party-state had firm control of the cities. Workers descended from Shanghai to visit each factory in Hangzhou and talk about the oppression they all faced as workers. These sessions taught Yu Shifu how to think of herself as a worker in the socialist way. She learned that she was suffering from something called "exploitation" and that she could overcome this condition by joining the party. Unlike peasants, however, she and other workers did not yell their accusations at capitalist managers, who continued to administer the factories for the new state. Rather, they learned that the way to address their oppressed condition as workers was to support the new state.[7]

The importance of speaking bitterness lies in the conception and construction of China as a modern socialist nation effected through this practice, at once aesthetic and sociopolitical.[8] Speaking bitterness identified which social group stood as the national heroes of a particular political moment, and the party designated which people could use this genre. Moreover, only certain kinds of knowledge could be made into the truth of speaking bitterness—class exploitation but not, for the most part, marriage or domination by one's husband. Speaking bitterness was a highly effective performance. By framing their experiences within this narrative, many peasants and workers came to see themselves as new kinds of persons and to interpret their lives in new ways. Many embraced socialist political convictions by speaking bitterness.[9]

Speaking bitterness did not simply offer one way to understand experience; it was not a mere ideological overlay. Rather, it made experience meaningful by having people perform and thereby signify its truth (S. Harding 1990). Speaking bitterness thus provided the representational means by which the party "map[ped] social vision into subjectivity" (de Lauretis 1984:8), and in so doing created a foundation for the socialist subject. It was a political praxis of signification. Such things said aloud motivated not only the speaking self but also others—who, by acting in dialogic imitation of the speaker, affirmed the speaker's actions.[10]

As a narrative form, speaking bitterness defines subject-positions of identification and desire; such definitions in turn encourage people to conceive of their lives according to this narrative. Speaking bitterness incites desire by offering a historical imagination of overcoming. It furnishes a providential plot, organizing the meaning not just of certain aspects of life but of life in its entirety. It subsumes the contingencies of existence into a progressive story of its overcoming through socialist means. The plot of overcoming life's bitterness is resolved through the party. Speaking bitterness thus exists ultimately as a narrative performance of political *resolution* in which people are called on to claim heroic stature in the eyes of the nation-state. It led many of those designated as subalterns, like Yu Shifu, Chen Shifu, and others of their cohort, to fervently embrace the political, social, and military goals of the party-state.

Benedict Anderson (1991) has perceptively argued that narrative form is a critical cultural component of the imagined nation. Following Walter Benjamin, he concludes that conceptions of simultaneity in the homogeneous, empty time of linear history pervade the structure of the nineteenth-century realist novel and that this form provides a narrative of nation-ness. Speaking bitterness operates in a similar manner. It connects people who have disparate experiences, making those experiences tell a story of the coming together of a socialist nation. However, beyond this formal homology, the cultural specificities in the narrative form more pointedly evoke national identity. Speaking bitterness created the conditions of visibility for a new socialist subject, one whose dilemmas in life might lead to state-sanctioned rewards. Such rewards might range from symbolic praise to concrete manifestations in terms of education, job assignments, and household material goods, as well as accession to state power itself.

But this genre also has a history within the socialist era. While "bitterness" constitutes the grounds for heroism and glory, the specificities of bitterness vary with each political movement. After the socialist revolution, the state codified liberation stories; the party brought out workers and peasants to tell the children and foreigners about the bitterness of life before Liberation. Yu Shifu recalled with pride her contribution to educating people by telling her own story in front of elementary school children. Most scholars thus assume that speaking bitterness refers only to the narrative practices at the moment of revolution.

Yet the legacies of this narrative practice persist in what otherwise seem like disparate styles of speech. One can find its echoes during the Cultural Revolution, though they are not commonly so labeled. Struggle sessions witnessed workers screaming their bitter accusations against managers, and students haranguing their teachers (Liang and Shapiro 1983; Luo 1990). Speaking bitterness reemerges again in the initial years after the Cultural Revolution. As intellectuals poured out their bitterness about the sufferings they had endured, they wrote in a form that came to be known as literature of the wounded, or "scar literature" (Barme and Lee 1979; Honig 1984; Siu and Stern 1983).[11] This genre was followed by Cultural Revolution memoirs speaking bitterness in English to an American audience. Such narratives created intellectuals as victims of oppression who deserved state restitution.[12] In its initial years, the post-Mao state encouraged and used scar stories to bind intellectuals to providing political support for economic reform. The state thus participated again in shaping these narratives into tales of redemption and progress; now it is the intellectuals who seek resolution, which is found when they offer to build the nation out of the ashes of Maoism.[13] As a genre, then, speaking bitterness "speaks" people's lives into a socialist realist form. The stature it confers on those who give it voice moves them from undeserved victimization to public recognition of their heroism in enduring that victimization. Those who speak out about their bitterness implicitly speak to be recognized as socialist subjects of the state. Thus we must attend not just to narrative structure but also to the context of the particular performance.

Women workers in the 1980s and 1990s used an informal mode of speaking bitterness. Unlike intellectuals, they spoke it out of turn, on the sly, since the state no longer designated them as heroes of national development. They spoke their bitterness as a counterpoint to the public discourse about them. Their use of this form out of turn makes it nostalgic.

Let us return to the stories of chapter 1, listening again to their language. They might sound like complaints or patent tales of woe, but if we listen from a different angle we can hear the echoes of a politically significant genre. Recall Yu Shifu's words: "It was very bitter, then. You couldn't produce much in one day." Or those of Si Zhaoding, the head of security: "Country people know how to eat bitterness; that work was a real hardship." Or think of how Chen Shifu told her story: " 'My money is enough for her to study at the university.' Those were [my pa's] words when he was dying. . . . But [my ma] was cheated out of the money by others, because she couldn't read." She tellingly described her apprenticeship under the new socialist regime: "I was so young as an apprentice. I didn't even get the usual 'clothing expense.' . . . I really lost out. But I don't want to haggle over it. It's more important to do good work. . . . In 1956, when I entered the factory, I was a little illiterate person. . . . [W]e didn't have as good conditions then. And women were not as important then."

Their language literally references bitterness. It juxtaposes conditions of victimization with their strength in enduring them. These are tough women. Yet their rhetoric emphasizes hardship. Chen Shifu's language, for example, elaborates the misfortunes that, she implies, never really went away: "I really lost out." These are not tales of the good old days. Nor can we hear them as unmediated voices of the oppressed, even while recognizing that their lives were undeservedly hard. These voices have incorporated the language of particular tales of oppression. They hold, in their story line, an implicit demand for recognition of the sacrifices they endured in the face of victimization. The language of speaking bitterness places the speaker in a position of heroism *in relation to* an implied audience: the state. Chen Shifu forgoes just compensation with the knowledge that it is more important to "do good work." Hardship and sacrifice in labor—these make heroes in the eyes of the state. Or they once did.

Just as speaking bitterness has a recognizable language, so it also contains a conventional plot. Consider again Chen Shifu's story of coming to work in the silk industry, which centers on the downfall of her family's silk workshop and her being cheated out of mastering her father's business because she was only a woman. Her father takes ill; relations grow tense when he brings in an older male cousin to take over the workshop.

Her father dies, and her cousin allows the workshop to sink into ruins. Chen Shifu could have saved it, but she was only the daughter, not allowed to take over. She and her mother lose everything and must enter the factory. In the factory, she must struggle to overcome the bitterness that "women were not as important then." She must fight the conservative consciousness of male weavers to learn the craft of weaving. She succeeds in doing so, but only through constant dedication and sacrifice on her part: "So I really lost out. But I don't want to haggle over it. It's more important to do good work."

Chen Shifu's story follows the classic plot line of speaking bitterness. It begins in oppression and moves to an overcoming of that oppression. Her tale of bitterness is founded in the way her gender prevents her from inheriting the family business and protecting her family from ruin. She then progresses to a new experience of bitterness: learning the skill of weaving in a male-dominated world. She overcomes her bitterness by transgressing the boundaries of gender. Her actions are heroic; she changes her gender identity through labor, which is taken up in the name of socialism. Both rhetoric and plot, then, reveal that the genre of speaking bitterness underlies what otherwise sound like informal complaints or transparent descriptions of a hard life.

Yet stories of bitterness told by these women lack the public attention they once garnered. By speaking this bitterness now, inappropriately, they implicitly expressed a longing for continued recognition that would lend a heroic quality to their identities as women workers. They spoke *as if* they still deserved to be seen as heroic, even though the whole interpretive frame of their actions has been brushed aside as part of the wrongheadedness of Maoism. Nostalgia is palpable in the way the stories jar against everything happening in the world around them: changing gender differentiations that make them appear to be women who misperceive what it really means to be a woman rather than heroically overcoming the need to be merely women; the devaluation of workers that makes their labor appear to be just common drudgery rather than Herculean toil for the nation; the feminization of labor in state-run work units that makes them appear to be marginal to the new story, which declares that China's modernity will fly forward on the exploits of the masculine market. The nostalgia, then, is for the political frame that lent a larger-than-life importance to their laboring activities.

Their speaking bitterness moves imperceptibly between past and present and from nostalgia to resentment. This "migrancy" across time came out strongly in another conversation I had with Chen Shifu. Zhong Lan, a young economics professor from the university, accompanied me on this visit to Zhenfu. The university had assigned her to take care of the logistics of my initial interviews, and she had been scrupulously conscientious in helping me. Zhong Lan prided herself on her long family lineage of elite intellectuals. She and I had argued briefly about workers on the evening before our conversation with Chen Shifu. She had insisted that economic reform made life much better for workers and that, in any case, workers did not really have the capacity to think about the future.

Interested in the question but lacking the opportunity to speak much with workers, Zhong Lan took advantage of this chance to ask Chen Shifu: "Aren't things better for you now with economic reform?" Surprising us both, Chen Shifu launched into a detailed reproach: "No. Things were much better then. We had higher wages then, one hundred yuan a month; now we get eighty-four. Before, we looked after one machine; now we are running after four. The younger ones are no longer willing to become weavers. It's too bitter. They run around chatting, all that *xixihaha* stuff. I don't like to chat; there's no time for that. It influences the quality of production. We older workers, we were conscientious, we did things willingly and took initiative [in our work] in those days. We never stopped working. We were timid and cautious; the younger workers are bold." I asked Chen Shifu why, if older workers were not treated properly, she bothered to work so hard. She replied, "If I am not better than others, I feel embarrassed (*guoyi buqu*)."

The nostalgia in Chen Shifu's speaking bitterness evokes a creative political agent, but one who has been displaced. She is someone who was "conscientious" in her labor, "willingly" did what the state asked of her, and "took initiative" in grappling with the bitterness of silk weaving. The agency is gendered, for the nostalgia is for women who felt inspired to undertake far more than had been expected of them. Chen

Shifu makes a claim, through this nostalgia, that she has a history as a subaltern subject even as the vision of post-Mao modernity attempts to make her *into* history.

As Chen Shifu's depiction implies, older women workers embodied their speaking bitterness in the way they labored on the shop floor. Marked distinctions existed in what I saw of the way workers of different cohorts engaged with their daily work. Recall my encounter with Du Shifu, described in the previous chapter. Her unflagging energy and pride in displaying her knowledge of silk weaving was a performative style that I came to associate with this oldest cohort. Everywhere in the factory, whether in the preparation, weaving, or inspection shop, the oldest workers spent the most time at their looms or rows of spinning machines and cared the most about not having mistakes—broken threads or poorly woven cloth—appear in their work. They were the ones who felt "embarrassed," as Chen Shifu said, if criticized by their supervisors for a problem. The discipline they embraced at work resulted less from overt directives and more from a sense of mutual obligation existing between the state and its designated subalterns.

Older workers felt, too, the most identified with producing a commodity symbolic of Chinese culture. They would elaborate on the beauty and complexity of the patterns for me. Workers who came of age during the Cultural Revolution or in the post-Mao era, by contrast, did not approach their work as if it held the key to their identity. They did not take particular pride in the kind of work they did, and their only problem with criticism from a supervisor was public embarrassment or docked pay.

Studies of transnational political economy often assume that relations of inequality are the material effect of relations of capital, production, and consumption. Culture is brought in to make sense of material life, but it is assumed to be separable from it. This explanatory framework, however, cannot help us understand the performance of quite disparate identities and styles of work among these women workers. Women become women by performing as women in many different circumstances, including in the world of work. That older workers had such a distinctive mode of engagement with their work indicates a discursive performance of their gender identities through labor. Their actions speak loudly, albeit nonverbally, about the "bitterness" that older women workers willingly, conscientiously endured so that they might continue to appear as the heroes of China's modernity.

Older women workers wax nostalgic from the margins of the nation-state. They discursively deploy a genre of speaking bitterness to remember their past in a present context that no longer offers the political reverberations of heroism through gender transgression, suffering, and sacrifice. By speaking and performing the bitterness of their labor as if they still deserved the mantle of heroism, these women made a valiant effort to stem the tide of another gendered modernity as it brushed them aside. But already caught up in it, they are half convinced that maybe being a woman worker is nothing heroic after all, just the end of an unfortunate path they took. If their course was not set by fate, then it was determined by circumstances: they had no choice. One might imagine these older women workers as migrants not across space but across time. They have been pulled, while they look back, into a world where they are anachronistic and "Maoist" rather than brave and tough women.

Their discursive deployment of their past both supports and unsettles the post-Mao imaginary of modernity. The narration of their lives in the genre of speaking bitterness continues to uphold an identification with the state, for their nostalgia draws on an imagined unity of mutual recognition between themselves and the state. While that unity has been lost, an undercurrent remains: a sense that Chinese citizens should continue to identify with a socialist state and look to the state to determine national identity. Younger workers, even party members, rarely claimed to speak for or in the name of the state as Yu Shifu or Du Shifu did with me. Most referred instead to *shangmian*, a vague reference to "the above," where they felt state power resided in relation to them. Older workers expected that since the state had constituted its legitimacy in the name of subalterns, the state should have an obligation to, as Chen Shifu put it, "look after them."

Moreover, their narratives perpetuate the discursive production of "labor" as the foundation of full human subjectivity. Labor, for them, still serves as the ultimate measure of human worth and dignity, the grounds for discerning domination and inequality, and the means by which people should search for their freedom. Older women workers learned to interpret labor as the site where women find identities as something other than "mere" women. The younger cohorts, as will become clear, find precisely this vision of modernity through labor to be the domination worth challenging or escaping.

Still, their nostalgia moves like a sword that cuts more than one way. It serves as a stroke of countermemory to the post-Mao transformations of categories of gender and class. The strategic deployment of speaking bitterness inadvertently opens up the mythical quality of the putatively objective knowledge of post-Mao modernity. Their memories trouble the reconstructions of both a postsocialist essential womanhood and a capitalist fetishism of workers. The gap that they open becomes a place from which to craft a genealogy of specific imaginaries of modernity and the intersecting social categories those visions both reify and dissolve. Class, gender, and political generations overlap and disturb one another in these political contests over history. In the process, they unsettle the essentialization of identities in the post-Mao era that both constitute and divide politicized cohorts of women.

I have encouraged the reader to read these stories of liberation and heroism in two directions at once. They tell a story of the past, a cultural history of multiple discourses on liberation. But they also deploy—and therefore creatively reimagine—that history as part of a contemporary discourse on the politics of gender and modernity. Ethnographic histories reside in this tension between a historicity of knowledge and a knowledge of history. Rather than seek a resolution, I find it more useful to approach the writing of history in anthropology through this tension—to allow each method to find the other's limits. I take this approach to be in the spirit of Gayatri Spivak's method (1987) of critical interruption,[14] which rejects the coherence of modern emancipatory narratives while retaining what still makes political sense in those narratives. After recognizing the multiplicity of political interpretations, such as cultural histories of women's liberation and the politics of nostalgia for those histories, I then use one position to critically interrupt, or find the limits of, the other. To interpret the liberation stories of the oldest cohort of women workers in this manner opens out the stories. We can hear them simultaneously as socialist discourses on gender and histories of feminism, as well as about the cultural construction of class, state power, and socialist nostalgia. Spivak's method of critical interruption encourages us to pay attention to the cultural locations of stories about modernity. The mediations of speaking bitterness, re-collecting history, and disciplining labor gather under the sign of an ever-deferred modernity. Such mediations bind together the practical and the imaginary in overlapping global histories.

In the next section, I turn to the Cultural Revolution cohort of women workers, who vehemently reject the oldest cohort's understandings of what it means to be a woman and a worker. They, too, "critically interrupt" a discourse of liberation and a politics of nostalgia by explicitly challenging authority and passionately yearning for political meaning that fuels those challenges. Their passion tells stories of "other" modernities.

Part Two Unsettling Memories

Desire is the movement of memory.

Isaac Julien, director,
Frantz Fanon:
Black Skin, White Mask

Lunch break

Interlude

Modernity feeds on the idea of overcoming the past. In creating a self-portrait as a triumphal march through time, it gathers up the memories of the past into tidy linear narratives that act as mythical guides to that overcoming. Deferred desires for modernity bestow even greater significance on the mythmaking, as public memories must serve to prove a collectivity's ability to reach modernity. Postsocialist dreams of modernity are no exception. The post-Mao state has mobilized memories of the Maoist era to support its novel forms of power and domination. But what if the past persists as a deep wound that resists the closure required by the myth of progress? What if memories of violence—and a taste of autonomy in the midst of that violence—provide a slippage, an unstable foundation to the postsocialist naturalizations of power in the name of modernity? Such are the memories of the Cultural Revolution.

One could tell a simple story of the Cultural Revolution. One could say that the Cultural Revolution began in 1966 and ended in 1976, with Mao Zedong's death. But then again one could say that the Cultural Revolution occurred between 1966 and 1969, the height of political violence. Or one could say it began as early as 1963 or 1964, with the socialist reeducation movement. It could be described as having torn Chinese society apart in senseless violence, as citizens joined political factions that murdered each other for no reason, or for petty, personal reasons, or because they were misled by Mao and the Gang of Four. Official political culture prefers this last, mythical version, which portrays the masses of people as naively, and therefore innocently, seduced by the machinations of a few. This is socialist realism turned on its head. Within this myth, the passage into the post-Mao regime is made to appear predetermined. Post-Mao modernity offers itself as a future world of harmony and abundance. Such a master narrative brings absolute closure, lending authority to the wisdom of a new regime of modernity. But what of the Maoist idea, so prevalent during the Cultural Revolution, that people have the moral and political responsibility to shape their destiny? And wasn't the Cultural Revolution supposed to be the path toward modernity?

Alternatively, one could trace what appear to be sensible reasons that fueled the revolution, or at least reasons that seem fathomable, pointing out that Mao Zedong believed continuous revolution would lead to communism; that Mao worried about new forms of inequality within the socialist regime; that Mao wanted youth to experience revolution so that they would renew the vigor of socialist dreams. One could say that the violence was bubbling just beneath the surface of society, because the populace seethed with the injustices of the class-status system, the contradictions between "revolutionary consciousness" and the inheritance of class labels, and the continued privileges of intellectuals. Objectivist social science grasps at these narratives; they provide reassuring knowledge and, again, absolute closure. Such explanations also lend belief to the rationality of post-Mao modernity. But what of the endless passion, anger, thrill of challenging authority, contradictions, and messiness in all the struggles that make these rational explications sound just a bit too reasoned to satisfy the hunger for understanding?

One could claim, echoing colonial stereotypes, that Chinese people have a psychological propensity to follow a grand leader. Or that they "cathected" their collective desires onto Mao. But wasn't the problem that no one was listening to any leaders?

One could say that the Cultural Revolution violence directed itself mainly against intellectuals, the "stinking ninth category" of class enemy, whom "the state" accused of retaining their elite privilege and bourgeois ways. At least this is the story told by intellectuals, who have garnered a wide audience in the West with their numerous and eloquent writings about their victimization. These memoirs lend support, if inadvertently, to official discourses that call on intellectuals to heal their wounds by advancing economic reform. But then again, who was "the state" during the Cultural Revolution? Weren't various government factions pulling the state into disarray? Or one could speak of the wild enthusiasm of youth, who believed fervently in challenging the authority of their elders and in "sweeping out the four olds" of feudalism and bourgeois culture—old ideas, culture, customs, and habits of the exploiting classes—to make way for socialist modernity. Conversely, one could speak of the lost years of urban youth, sent down to the countryside to learn from the peasants, only to discover they could never return to the cities. Perhaps the Cultural Revolution was, in the end, just one grand scheme to cope with unemployed youth. But then again, wasn't the Cultural Revolution a maelstrom of violence with no design? Wasn't that why Mao called in the army, to quell the urban combat?

And what of the strife in the factories, among workers? Is there a simpler story here? Could their reasons be more transparent than those of intellectual youth? Perhaps it was, after all, a matter of dissatisfaction about inequalities in the wage system, with "unskilled" workers resentful of the more highly paid "skilled" workers. Or perhaps, as a few told me about Hangzhou, the young men who had lost their family's silk workshops to nationalization resented the loss. Or perhaps workers resented the contradictions between their rhetorical position as proletarian leaders of the new China and their daily life as subordinates to the same old capitalist managers, like Lou Shengzhi, retained to stabilize economic production. Or perhaps workers joined in because, as intellectuals like to say of them, their emotions quickly got the better of them and then they didn't know how to control their violence.

I could describe the basic history of the Cultural Revolution in Hangzhou, culled from the memories of those who lived through it. Or should I say the memories of those "involved" in it? But isn't that what the memories of the Cultural Revolution sift through and try to resolve—the level of involvement and responsibility? I could say that the Cultural Revolution in Hangzhou was much as in other cities—students in middle schools and universities began to challenge their teachers, inspired by actions in Beijing; workers followed suit, dividing themselves into the "radical" faction and the "conservative" faction. The division was based, as one person put it, on how much violence one was willing to commit. Or perhaps it really was based on the divisions in class backgrounds. Hangzhou's largest silk factory, built Soviet-style, shut down on numerous occasions for nearly five years as workers with guns battled it out, spilling over into the streets. Students and workers in the "radical" faction assumed leadership of the schools and factories. Zhenfu and the other factories opened and closed intermittently. Political struggle sessions against managers replaced production. Then students and workers traveled around the country (*chuanlian*) to learn from each other's revolutionary experiences. The army entered Hangzhou in 1970, quelling the violence, reorganizing the factories, and sending youth off to the countryside. And perhaps I should also mention that many people, at least in the factories, were reluctant to relive that history by retelling the stories, that they continued to work side by side, and that factory leadership discouraged discussion of the matter among themselves, not only with the foreigner.

Such are the stories that might be told of the Cultural Revolution. They objectify, clean up, make the past something one can hold on to while maintaining a comforting sense of the rationality of it all. Certainly the dominant versions of the Cultural Revolution ease the way for post-Mao reform. But the memories of the Cultural Revolution I encountered cannot be so easily contained. These memories tell other stories that challenge self-contained narratives. They are not "truer" recollections of the past, but narrative representations that construct knowledge about the past.[1] As such, they create a politics of memory that leave open the closures that official political culture, intellectuals' memoirs, and the social science literature attempt to impart to the Cultural Revolution. They bring to the fore the conflicts between forgetting and remembering, as both are entangled in state projects.[2] Moreover, they implicitly raise doubts about the myths that undergird modernity: myths of automatic historical progress and the absolute need for state authority to rectify the past. They force us to recognize instead disjunctures in forms of modern power. Finally, they confront anthropologists with the need to find an alternative to virile, self-assured writings about violence that can too easily lead to fascination with the violence itself. For these memories also guide us to places that, in the end, refuse to submit to interpretation: landscapes without words to describe the wounds or the melancholia accompanying a loss of all belief, transient places that never can be definitely mapped. And perhaps violence is not the whole story.

The following three chapters offer different memories of the Cultural Revolution. I begin with a brief and painful story of a memory that appeared fleetingly to create a moment of danger. I then turn to what I call the "politics of authority" that the Cultural Revolution cohort retains from that period. Finally, I examine the yearnings of the members of that cohort for a life they retrospectively envision they have lost. Their politics along with their yearnings add yet another layer to the cultural practices of a postsocialist modernity.

4 She

Walter Benjamin once wrote, in a now well-known phrase, that "To articulate the past historically does not mean to recognize it 'the way it really was.' . . . It means to seize hold of a memory as it flashes up at a moment of danger" (1968:255). Benjamin, a Jewish man living through the rise of fascism in Europe, knew full well the fragility of historical memory and understood the importance of history to projects of domination fostered in the name of modernity. He searched, as a result, for storytellers who would break through the monolithic structure and mythical qualities of History.

This chapter addresses the quality of historical memory in relation to the Cultural Revolution, focusing on one woman's life in contemporary China. Her story helps me to break through a certain theoretical as well as lived silence about memory in its relation to the quotidian, to capture how memories of violence exist just under the surface of the everyday. While acknowledging the hegemony of state representations in China, and the power of narrative form to create history, we should turn our analytic gaze to perhaps a more marginal, yet nonetheless critical, arena of history and memory for which we have not yet found adequate language: how memories of violence persist in the silence of apparently untroubled lives, to be blurted out in odd moments, and then to disappear again, seemingly without a ripple. In portraying the fragmented nature of memories of violence, we move one step toward challenging the power of master narratives to organize memory into teleological

159

tales. Then, perhaps, we will be in a better position to fracture the illusory seamlessness of modernity.

The Cultural Revolution has become the "other" of the current regime of modernity. Party leaders create their own image and sense of legitimacy through continually re-creating—and claiming to transcend—this historical other. Thus, mention of the Cultural Revolution was pervasive in the public culture of the 1980s as well as the 1990s, though in some places its icons had by then turned into historical kitsch.

Yet the Cultural Revolution looks very different when approached from local, marginal places, through the lives of people who have no public access to the tools for writing History. In the silk factories of Hangzhou, as in most other work units in China, those who viciously fought one another then in opposing factions have continued to work side by side. There exists in these places what I at first found to be a puzzling silence about the Cultural Revolution, a silence that supports the appearance of normality in the everyday. The story I am about to tell is one woman's simultaneous participation in, yet challenge to, that normality.

She approached me while I was taking a walk after lunch around the grounds of the factory. Who had access to the foreigner was a touchy issue in those first few weeks of my stay at Zhenfu. It was wrapped up with policing the cultural and political borders between insiders and outsiders, with worrying whether I would find their management reforms up to western standards, and with maintaining the status distinction between who was and was not allowed to approach a foreigner, as well as claims to the power of representing reality to me.

But she seemed unaware of these problems, eagerly approaching me as if we were old friends. She slipped her arm in mine and proceeded to talk excitedly about how correct it was that Chinese people and American people were now going to be friends, that there had never really existed any good reason not to be friends, and so on. She was referring, of course, to the official policies overturning the Cultural Revolution. During the Cultural Revolution, anyone with ties to the West was accused of having bourgeois leanings. But this was the mid-1980s, nearly seven years after the new regime had overthrown the Cultural Revolution's so-called Gang of Four, and the reform faction in favor of suturing China into the global economy had ascended to state power. The issue of an appropriate political stance toward the West was an important one through which the state created itself in opposition to the Cultural Revolution.

For some reason, the people with whom I had been strolling left and she and I continued on. She confided that she had a cousin in America with whom she had just resumed contact, implying that she was more open-minded than many around the factory. She took me up to her office and, since she seemed so forthcoming, I began to interview her about her responsibilities at the factory in her capacity as a middle-level bureaucrat. She shared her office with another cadre in charge of party work, and soon I found her carrying on a conversation on two levels, verbally responding one way while penciling other answers to my questions. The interview gradually ground to a halt, as I realized she would not be forthcoming with this other person sitting in the room. It was winter, my second winter in Hangzhou, and our conversation turned in a desultory manner to the safe subject of the weather. She quickly discovered that I still had much to learn about how to survive a winter in a city without any heating, and before I knew it, off we went out of the factory on our bicycles to find the materials to make silk-padded long underwear. She cheerfully linked her arm in mine as we walked downtown, reiterating her earlier praise of Deng Xiaoping's great accomplishment in opening China to the West. If this had been ten years ago, she said, she would have been in lots of trouble for being seen with me. I warmed to her, for few indeed had transgressed the political boundary that limited trust between insiders and outsiders or, on a simpler level, had shown so much concern for my personal needs.

Later, with the long underwear almost done, she insisted that I come to her home that evening to finish sewing it off. Because I already had some sense of her unease around party cadres, I was completely unprepared when her husband arrived home to learn that he was a high-level officer in the Public Security Bureau. My only experience of that bureau was of having to report there periodically, for one of its functions was to keep track of foreigners and their activities. I knew that he had to be a party member. He spoke energetically, if somewhat nervously, along the same lines she had expressed earlier—of how correct it was to make friends with foreigners, how it was fine to do that now, and so on. Though his statements sounded less heartfelt than hers, a bit more like formal, rhetorical recitations, he seemed to mean it. And she explained that his job was immaterial, that relationships between people outside of work were another matter.

While he prepared dinner—he did all the food shopping, cooking, and cleaning, she told me—she spoke of how her life within the factory might be completely unchallenging, but outside of the factory she was studying at night school to obtain the equivalent of a college diploma. Her story echoed many popular tales about intellectuals striving to make up for the ten lost years. But I knew very little of her background. Her story mainly served to reinforce the sense of hopefulness she seemed determined to nourish.

After dinner, and after her husband had returned to work, the tenor of our conversation shifted. She told me that the party cadre with whom she shared an office informed her that if the foreigner asked to visit anyone's home, that person was to discuss it with the party secretary first. When she asked him how he knew that, he replied that party members had had a meeting before the foreigner had come to their factory. "But since I wasn't at that meeting," she laughed, "I don't know that rule." Then her tone changed. Whereas only moments before she was an excited chronicler of life's possibilities, suddenly, or so it seemed to me, she broke into tears about her experiences in the Cultural Revolution. "I've been through too much," she sighed. "I don't think we should repeat the mistakes of the past. I ate a lot of bitterness during the Cultural Revolution. No one really knows."

Her words came in a rush: "One night, in the middle of the night, five or six men who worked at Zhenfu came to get me in a truck. They hauled me out of the house and put me on the truck and put my head in a cangue [a wooden yoke]. Then they beat me, hard." Tears were streaming down her face now, her voice was choked. "They beat me really hard. I was pregnant then."

Only a few hours before, in response to my question about why she only had one child, she had replied that one was enough, it was too difficult to raise more children. The government had instituted a stringent one-child policy, but many young women in the cities preferred to have a single child and her story had sounded plausible, though she was from an older generation. My question now to confirm that she had a miscarriage as a result of the beatings was almost superfluous.

"They chose those of us who had dared to criticize them," she continued. "Some of us had dared to speak out and those of us who were smart of course also had sharp words. We couldn't bear the sight of their beating up others."

Where was her husband when all this happened, I wanted to know. (Many stories existed of spouses arrested or implicated for their ties to those criticized and I thought perhaps he was already in trouble.) He was on the other side, she said, in the other faction. The revolutionary faction at Zhenfu indeed contacted him after they detained her in the factory's makeshift prison and he told them that he agreed with their actions. I could not bring myself to ask how she had stayed with her husband after that, for I knew the complicated fault lines that Cultural Revolutionary politics had wreaked through family lives. And though the day's activities had brought us close, I still did not know her well enough to avoid feeling the powerful voyeurism of an anthropologist doing fieldwork rather than the concern of a friend.

As I listened to her story, I felt as if an earthquake had rent apart the normal rhythm of her life. What was apparently a seamless surface had shattered for a moment, as memories of violence, like hot lava, cracked and shifted the pieces of her life before they settled back in. This momentary fragmentation recalls Benjamin's evocation of history as a fragment of ruins (1977). Benjamin was moved to use allegory as a method of interpreting these ruins, of piling up the fragments so as to disturb the myth of time's homogeneity that master narratives build. It was his way of "brush[ing] history against the grain" (1968:257) so that it might retain some of the inchoate qualities of memory. Allegory might allow fragments to remain enigmatic hieroglyphs and thus might enable a subversion of modernity's monolithic story.

The next day, when we met in the factory to continue our interview from the previous day, she was strangely guarded. We sat at the little desk Zhenfu had provided me, in the main reception office, next to Yu Shifu, who also seemed a bit nervous. She again resorted to writing cryptic messages to me. In a moment when we were left alone, she hurriedly explained that she had been criticized by her office mate, who as it happened was an important party cadre in the factory, for spending too much time with the foreigner. There was more to the story, things I pieced together only later about who was and who wasn't a party member and therefore the degrees of closeness to the foreigner that could be hoped for. The cadres apparently had a keen appreciation of the possibilities she held for disrupting the myths of History.

That was the last time we spoke. For the next six months, I assiduously avoided her, as she did me. I saw her in passing, and noticed her daily interactions with factory coworkers, but we never showed any signs of recognition. Years have passed since this incident and only now am I beginning to break through my self-imposed silence surrounding it. I believe that, at first, my hesitation arose from the remarkably tense fallout of an otherwise minor incident. A friendship cut short by fears of certain party cadres' disapproval. My desire to protect.[1] And my ambivalence about my own participation in silencing her because I wished to avoid jeopardizing my research.

But now, in hindsight, I think I was held back equally by the uncertainty of how to comprehend the ways in which memories of violence live just below the surface of the quotidian—how to tell a story about the Cultural Revolution that does not reproduce the state's discourse on it and thereby support its own claims to legitimacy. It is the silence of which Amitav Ghosh has so eloquently written in *The Shadow Lines* (1988), where he grapples with how to write about the violence of riots between Hindus and Muslims in a form that disrupts nationalist discourses: "when we try to speak of events of which we do not know the meaning, we must lose ourselves in the silence that lies in the gap between words and the world. This is a silence that is proof against any conceivable act of scorn or courage; it lies beyond defiance—for what means have we to defy the mere absence of meaning?" (p. 214).

It would be easy enough to analyze her story in terms of the power of state representations. Her discursive construction of her experience resembles the official version of the Cultural Revolution as a time of senseless violence. And she eloquently used the mode of Cultural Revolution scar literature, which lends so much support to the current regime. Moreover, her tale reflects the narrative form of "speaking bitterness," which, as I argued in the previous chapter, remains a genre through which people fashion themselves as socialist subjects.

But while her story replicates a version of the master narrative, it also disrupts it by the very fact of its lack of resolution. Open, unresolved memories work against the grain of dominant stories of the Cultural Revolution, which according to the state's current vision of modernity must have narrative closure. Having a bad memory of the Cultural Revolution has been a badge of honor, but only if that memory includes an ending that draws a clear border between then and now. To keep memories in the present tense, to insist that they continue to be unspeakable and unlivable in the everyday, is untenable. It renders a person dangerous. Rather than seizing hold of a memory that flashes up in a moment of danger, she has created a moment of danger when this memory flashes up. For she refuses to stitch together the fragments into a tale of progress and redemption.

If we were to lift her story out of its quotidian context, if its signification were to be overly dramatized, we would risk recouping its violence in our representations and thereby reinforcing the state's hegemony over memories of violence in our narratives. In representing such memories, we cannot avoid these paradoxes of writing in these power-laden situations. But our goal should be to disrupt modernist narratives that organize memory by reading allegorically the fragments of a storyteller's life.

5 The Politics of Authority

What becomes of the political agency and imagination of those who form their identity in one political moment, only to have that period thoroughly denounced and reviled? This chapter and the next address the lives of those workers who, after developing their passionate ideas and engaged practices of power and authority during the Cultural Revolution, found themselves marginalized in the post-Mao era as embodying the antithesis of the modern subject. On the one hand, these women and men were not the main *jijifenzi*, or "activists," of the deadly factions that fought one another during the height of the ugliest violence. Nor, on the other hand, were they the targets of attack, like She, whose unsettling memories I explored in the previous chapter. Rather, they comprise the more ordinary ranks of those for whom the radical questioning of authority as well as the politicization of everyday life became the commonsense knowledge that ineluctably shaped their aspirations, insights, and actions.

I call that knowledge the "politics of authority." In this chapter I trace its contours, arguing that despite their wholehearted rejection of Maoism, workers whose class status and gender identity were initially formed during the Cultural Revolution even now reiterate certain fundamental elements of those politics through the way they perform at work. Their actions both call forth and challenge disciplinary measures by the state. The politics of authority, moreover, reflect a distinctive interpretation of power that distinguishes these workers as a cohort from either older women workers, who felt liberated by Liberation, or younger women, who entered the factory in the 1980s. These politics informed a specifically Maoist vision for reaching modernity that differed markedly from both the project of the early 1950s and the post-Mao imaginary. This modernity entailed the saturation of the citizenry with political self-consciousness. In contrast with the discursive regime of the 1950s, which made "labor" the site for achieving modern subjectivity, the Cultural Revolution made "politics" itself the mode by which people imagined and talked about how China would, at last, become a modern nation.

Yet even while enacting their "reiterated performances" (Butler 1993) as political actors who confront authority, members of the Cultural Revolution cohort yearn to be anything other than who and what they represent. The constitutive paradox of this cohort lies precisely in a jarring mixture of confrontation and abjection. Its productive and dislocating tension creates the cultural space in which they grapple with the dilemmas and desires of post-Mao modernity. I explore this paradox by addressing first their politics in this chapter and then their yearnings in the next. One must remember, however, that for this cohort, the two coexist inseparably and inescapably. Taken together, the two chapters raise questions about zones of creativity and constraint in the midst of radical social transformations. Aside from rethinking the "afterlife" of subjectivities produced in the Cultural Revolution, this chapter also reflects on recent efforts in cultural studies to theorize the potential of subaltern subjects to maneuver in social fields saturated with power.

"Agency" and contestation have become central concerns of anthropology and cultural studies, as a preoccupation with power and history has forced new conceptualizations of culture. The notion of culture produced by colonialism—and recycled in neocolonialist politics of development—assumes that while a set of routinized and recurrent actions ("customs and traditions") characterizes third world others, actions that define the world belong to post-Enlightenment Europe and the United States. Such a distinction underlies definitions of modernity. It underlies, too, the deferrals by which certain nations are cast as having the kind of agency ill-suited for modernity. This question of agency is compounded for socialist countries such as China. Here the cold war rhetoric of the United States persists, generating the following neo-orientalist view: Chinese culture and politics exist in a symbiotic relationship that constrains Chinese people from ever becoming free, determining agents of modernity.

In order to subvert liberal humanist notions of free will that define modernity, we must reexamine the relationship between social inequalities and cultural meanings. The concept of subalternity is central to this inquiry. In contrast to theories of resistance that assume the oppressed develop their agency from within their collective consciousness, subalternity draws attention to the way notions of agency are themselves culturally construed.[1] Rather than describe marginalized peoples as standing outside of and against power, subalternity poses the challenging question of how practices are always lodged within fields of power and knowledge. The concept of subalternity highlights contingent processes of creating meaning, including the meanings of social inequality itself. In doing so, it opens up the relationship between power and culture. Power becomes not that which manipulates culture but that which gains efficacy and force through culture—in rhetorical strategies, discursive practices, and narrative modes. Yet if one can no longer indulge in a description of an agonistic relationship between oppression and resistance, how can the possibilities for subaltern practices to make a difference in the world be understood?

In addressing that question, this chapter does not rely on abstract philosophical generalizations about subalternity, which threaten to slide back into universalist pretensions. Rather, the answers suggested lie in the historical specificities of subaltern formation in the Cultural Revolution. One of my primary claims, reiterated here, is that since the socialist revolution, the formation and reformation of cohorts through an endlessly deferred search for modernity plays a central role in casting subaltern identities and the contours of subaltern practice. In the intersection of cohort identity with the multiple axes of gender and class we find unexpected transgressions and "room for maneuver" (Chambers 1991).

Cultural Revolution politics stressed the centrality of youth to revolutionary modernity. Youth, Mao said, would bring a renewed socialism to the country: they held a special capacity to challenge the feudalistic ways and bourgeois values of older generations, as well as their misuse of socialist power. But youth, according to Mao, also needed to relive the glories and hardships of revolution to strengthen their commitment to the nation. They would thereby further Mao's project of "continuous revolution" by which China would advance to the heights of modern progress. The Cultural Revolution thus brought into existence a group whose members distinguished themselves from their "elders" on the basis of the idea that age and politics coincide. That is, the Cultural Revolution cohort was discursively formed *as* a cohort in the process of becoming subjects of an imagined modernity.

The post-Mao search for a modernity envisioned as the polar opposite of that offered by the Cultural Revolution has meant a reformation of this cohort. Public culture portrays Cultural Revolution youth as alternately a "lost generation" deserving of sympathy and an unruly generation in need of discipline. Those so cast have suffered bitter reminders that the self-sacrifices they had initially thought meaningful, because wrought in the eschatological light of principled commitments, held no such ultimate significance. At the same time, they yearned for a political world in which their notions of power and authority had the commonsense ring of the hegemonic rather than placing them in the marginalized space of the disaffected.

I do not assume homogeneity among this or any other cohort. This chapter and the next trace multiple positions, paradoxes, ambivalences, and dilemmas that have developed out of a common historical experience. I deliberately focus on several individuals who are exemplars of diverse possibilities. The stories I tell display an overlapping analysis of the politics of authority and a shared narrative of a "lost generation," but that narrative is expressed in distinct ways—an angry explosion, a despairing refusal to act as a figure of authority, the embrace of technical expertise, romantic underground activity, and other, more mundane actions.

My focus here is the formation of a cohort's political imagination. Political agency, I argue, develops through cohort-distinctive interpretations of power and authority. Yet the Cultural Revolution cohort must *reconstruct* themselves on the other side of a formative historical period.

They were not so much victims of history's dislocations as unwilling participants in their own displacement. Their politics and yearnings reveal the multiple layerings of modernity that can coexist and jostle one another in the same historical moment.

AN ANGRY EXPLOSION

It was a cold, wintry day, much like any other in Hangzhou in the middle of January. Everyone at Zhenfu wore several layers of cotton-padded jackets and sweaters. Some hugged glass bottles filled with hot water to warm their hands. Others rubbed their hands back and forth against one another in a futile effort to stop the interminable itching brought on by chilblains. The discomfort of the weather had not, however, stopped the numerous conversations flowing throughout the factory about the new wage and bonus system.

As described more fully in chapter 2, the state had introduced economic reform to dismantle the commune system in the countryside in the late 1970s but had approached major urban areas more hesitantly. Urban reforms had only begun in the mid-1980s, just as I arrived in China. They comprised a variety of measures to turn state-run enterprises into profitably run companies less dependent on state financing, including a reversion of power from party cadres to technical managers, an increase in the autonomy of factory directors in matters of hiring and firing, and the institution of a multitude of commercial, or "free," markets for the distribution of goods and services. The reforms also introduced new wage and bonus systems with their attendant disciplinary rules and punishments that created new forms of hierarchy. These, central government officials hoped, would create more productive workers who would enable China to realize its goals of greater wealth, modernity, and a powerful position within global economies. These reforms also had the effect of radically restructuring urban life.

The changes, while dramatic, were introduced piecemeal so that workers would not rise up en masse, as feared by some. Certain party cadres insisted strenuously on the need for workers to rid themselves of those "Cultural Revolution habits" and learn how to be more "productive." Yet they, too, had a certain air of hesitancy when confronted with workers' complaints. None at Zhenfu refused to hear out any particular worker's saga. None seemed prepared to abandon completely the tenet that, they frequently told me, distinguished socialism from capitalism: socialism takes care of everyone and does not abandon anyone to his or her own resources. And none was ready to act like the type of imperious capitalist manager praised in all the papers for his singular (and seemingly miraculous) ability to create that fanciful phenomenon: the efficient, obedient workforce.

A range of responses appeared among workers: some stood awash in confusion, unclear as to the exact nature of the changes; others were precisely aware of the new differences in their wages relative to those of other workers. Some were expectant, cautiously hopeful that the new system would bring improvements in their lives. Others were cynical, pointing out that basic conditions of work remained the same, and that, in any case, nothing could make working in the silk industry anything but onerous. A few workers vocally supported the new hierarchy of wages, agreeing with the idea that some workers were just lazier than others. Many, however, seethed at how the new system represented inequity and the "nature" of workers. This anger, it seemed to me, simmered at a consistent but low level. I assumed it was nowhere near the point of explosion.

But on this day, much like any other, an explosion did occur. I was in the factory reception office, writing notes at my desk. I happened to step out of the office just as a group of workers, with a determined air, squeezed their way into the small Labor and Wages office. I recognized most of them as workers from the dining canteen. Curious and puzzled, those of us who saw them quickly stepped up to the windows of the office to watch and listen. Several others crowded in around us, as we all strained to hear the conversation inside.

The dining hall workers proceeded to berate the section head vociferously. Zhenfu's factory director, Zhang Changzhang, had obviously been alerted, for he soon squeezed into the office, too. To my surprise, rather than being intimidated by his presence—for he was a remote figure to most workers—the dining hall crew turned on him as well. The tension was electric, as most of those standing outside the window wondered where this action would lead. Nothing like it had happened since the Cultural Revolution; the confrontation had an eerie and unsettling resonance with the struggles of that none-too-distant past.

The workers were irate about the implications of the position-wage system. Under the new system, whose criterion for pay was no longer seniority but job position, service work would be placed in the lowest category and receive the lowest wages. This new position-wage system erased not only the Cultural Revolution politics that had refused such differentiations, but the entire system of seniority that had defined labor valuation in China since the revolution. In the name of "productivity," a new cultural valuation of tasks had been introduced, creating and reinforcing specific representations of gender, of the youthfulness of bodies, and of the "bitterness" of work. For example, because the bitterness of having to bear ultimate responsibility made workers shun weaving, the Silk Industry Bureau used wage differentials to entice them back.

Yet dining hall workers believed that their work was equally "bitter" and deserved recognition as such; they were angered that the hard work they performed would, in the future, be deemed less productive. Indeed, their work was bitter because of its servile status. Service work held a certain notoriety: during the Cultural Revolution it was attacked as a vivid reflection of bourgeois capitalism. This socialist morality reinforced a long-held disdain for commerce. In the post-Mao period, the lack of enthusiasm of those assigned to such labor was read as a holdover of Cultural Revolution politics. Newspapers abounded with stories for public edification that ridiculed waitresses who threw the plates down on the table and department store clerks who idly chatted and ignored customers. As foreigners in China exchanged such stories, they gave a knowing shake of the head at the "backwardness" of China and its long, impossible road toward modernity.[2]

The dining hall workers, almost all men, found themselves caught by yet another change in the meaning of labor. As we have seen, the silk industry as a whole, since the late 1950s, had slowly lost status as it became cast as unskilled "women's work." This had been an uneven

process—not inevitable, but nonetheless overdetermined by government industrialization policies and transnational markets in textiles.
These men had entered the silk industry during the Cultural Revolution,
when any sort of job in an urban factory was a high attainment for an
urban youth—in stark contrast to being sent down to the countryside.
Now they found themselves "burdened" with the onus of being positioned within a women's industry and thus feminized in relation to men
who were going to work in the "masculine" endeavors of the market
economy.

The fury that spilled over into this startling explosion was fueled by
these multiple layers of labor's meanings. But what made everyone most
uneasy as they watched the argument wind through the long afternoon
was how closely their actions resembled those taken during the Cultural
Revolution. These workers had stalked off their jobs in search of political
restitution. And they refused to return to work, even though their shift
was not yet over. Late in the afternoon, the vituperative shouting finally
wound down. The dining hall workers gained nothing immediate by
their action. Its impact would be felt, however, in the halting and wary
way in which the state textile bureau brought capitalism into state-run
industries.

COHORT POLITICS

The dining hall workers were not alone in displaying active defiance.
Throughout the factory, groups of brazen young women and men stood
out: male weavers who dragged out their cigarette breaks and who
spoke fearlessly to their superiors about the degradations of their work,
transport workers who lounged about outside their shop in a deliberate
pose of rest. In the weft prep shop, a group of young women, I gradually
came to realize, had an informal clique. They tended to occupy a small
table just off the shop floor, where they took overly long breaks. Xiao Ma,
the shift leader, would yell at them for sitting too long. That only earned
their yelling back at her. Their tongues, others said, were too sharp.

At first glance, these actions—consistent, if unspectacular and limited—might not appear that distinctive. They could be viewed as conventional forms of "everyday resistance." One making such an argument could point out that these workers were quite explicit and direct. They aggravated authority. They brought trouble, because they appeared not to care about getting into trouble. Their actions might thus reflect a willed intentionality and self-originating determination to confront the oppression that arises from unequal relations of production. Workers' challenges to authority might be taken as evidence that subaltern classes in China have the capacity to develop a sovereign consciousness of their "class interest." The hesitant but determined introduction of capitalist modernity by the state could be seen as accompanied by an ideology whose mystifying effect is partially subverted by such class consciousness. Perhaps these quotidian practices support James Scott's influential theories (1985) about "weapons of the weak," in which foot-dragging and the like provide the only means available to the oppressed for confronting the power that holds them down. Moreover, according to Scott, the oppressed rely on a self-constituted analysis of their own oppression, based on the irreducible autonomy of their experience. Or perhaps these workers engage in tactics of indirect subversion in the practice of everyday life, such as those described by de Certeau (1984). It is tempting, indeed, to conclude that they exhibit the very subaltern consciousness that has so eluded and vexed theorists who care about power and inequality.

What is most striking about these active forms of refusal, however, is that only certain workers engage in them: those who came of age in the Cultural Revolution. The dining hall crew, the male weavers with their endlessly long cigarette breaks and no-holds-barred way of talking to their supervisors, the weft prep workers who refuse to move from their table—these women and men entered the factory just as the Cultural Revolution erupted. In their actions, one discerns not so much a pervasive subaltern consciousness as a distinctive imagination about the political world formed in that era. That political imagination is a politics of authority.

High political consciousness during the Cultural Revolution often became equated with a refusal to participate in production. This defiance alternated with an emphasis on worker creativity. A politically active worker was recognized by her or his zeal during political struggles, rather than by her labor in the production of commodities. Workers actively confronted managerial authority during speak bitterness sessions. They humiliated managers, verbally and physically. These struggle sessions, combined with factional fighting among workers and disruptions in regional supply networks, resulted in workers taking a measure of control in organizing their own daily movements.

Leaving the shop floor was a peripatetic statement of political rights to challenge managerial authority. Walking away from one's work position to engage in politics put one at the forefront of the radical faction. Moreover, people did not believe these actions to be inherently gendered: that is, participants did not view the politics of authority to belong specifically to men or to women. They did not assume that one gender or the other would more easily enact those politics, nor conversely that by taking up those politics, someone expressed her or his gender identity. Nor did they interpret these politics as gendered heroic accomplishments, whether of masculine men or of women transgressing gender boundaries. Maoist representations of the socialist woman had by that time become powerful enough and widely enough accepted to preclude the necessity of arguing for or against appropriate femininity.[3]

I spoke with no one at Zhenfu who continued to believe in the overarching precepts of the Cultural Revolution.[4] Like most others, the workers whom I knew had come to the troubling conclusion that Maoism, in which they had so passionately believed, was a dangerous and destructive fantasy. They neither revere Mao nor particularly support the collectivist ideologies of Maoism. Nonetheless, they continue to hold on to specific ideas and practices concerning power developed during that period. Perhaps their most basic received notion of power is that the dilemmas they face stem from authority. Put another way, they believe that authority is the most problematic feature of social life. This notion of power has certain corollaries. Authority is structural—animated, to be sure, by the multiple interpersonal connections known as *guanxi* through which it operates, but originating nonetheless in the class status system, the party bureaucracy, and unequal relations of labor.

If authority is structural, it resides in the most minute sinews of daily life, persisting as something inescapable and therefore essential to grapple with. Indeed, the Cultural Revolution cohort embraces as common sense the belief that struggle against improper authority is the singularly most important activity in life, lending significance to all other activities. It makes whatever occupies one worth doing. This struggle exists not in a separate domain but as the animating feature of one's engagement with the world. Thus this cohort's politics of authority include the belief that workers have the ability to speak back to power, as well as the imperative to recognize political gaps through which socialist subjects can maneuver. Perhaps most significantly, their questioning of authority occurs by way of perceiving politics as a dialectical relationship: authority exists on one side of a social relationship, and insubordination stands as its opposite force, in the face of which it pushes or stops.

These politics of authority, then, bespeak a form of oppositionality of a very distinctive sort. They form what one might hesitantly call subaltern class politics, but not of the kind that stands outside of history and power. Those who embrace these politics live not in a relation of external opposition to power, even though that kind of external relation is assumed in their politics. Rather, power is immanent in the politics themselves. They originate not from a self-determining consciousness but from a determinate period in history. They do not reflect a priori class interests. The analysis of oppression they signal is produced within, rather than apart from, the hegemony that prevailed during the Cultural Revolution.

Thus one cannot read or deduce them from the "material" relations of production. "Materiality" is perhaps Marx's most abused and misused concept. He did not use the term to refer to the objects of labor or its products, or to the labor process as a thing "in itself" or to capital as a congealed social agent. Nor did he envision the factory, minus its human inhabitants, as providing the "material" conditions of life. Instead, by materiality he meant the social relationships that simultaneously produce and are produced by concrete activities. For Marx, the most important concrete activities were those of labor, broadly conceived and structured through determinate social divisions (1967 [1867–94]). As

Donald Donham (1990) has argued, these labor activities always already bring cultural representations of such things as gender, sexuality, and age with them. That is, class is culturally constructed in the very process of its making. Class and gender involve fantasies of respect as much as engagement with, say, silk looms. Thus, we must finally abandon the dualism through which we view the world, with a material order on the one hand and a separate sphere of meaning or culture on the other (T. Mitchell 1990:546).[5] These workers of the Cultural Revolution cohort developed their politics of authority in the specificities of factory labor, but the latter neither provided an a priori consciousness for them nor fully established the meaning of their experiences.

A DESPAIRING REFUSAL

To further illuminate how the politics of authority pervade everyday life, I turn to the story of one shift leader in Zhenfu's Number 1 prep shop. Xiao Bao is difficult to write about. These days, anthropology's portraits of "ordinary" people more often than not tend toward exemplars of quiet heroism, articulate storytellers, powerful healers, or eccentric shamans. Ethnographies offer them to us as emblems of hope and inspiration in the face of overwhelming predicaments in the world today. Xiao Bao resembles none of these figures. Yet hers is a story of passion—not the passion of ecstasy, but the anger that resides in depression that is the other extreme of elation. Her story speaks of the passion of despair.[6] The discomfort of writing, and perhaps reading, about someone like Xiao Bao underscores the difficulty of embracing a subjectivity that is painful to bear.

Cavernous like the weaving shop, but with more light allowed to stream through, the newly expanded Number 1 weft prep shop stands off to the east side of Zhenfu's main entrance. The door, in winter, remains covered over with a double layer of thick quilts to keep out the drafts. A faded, torn poster with Maoist slogans hangs anachronistically just inside the door. Thin rectangular fluorescent lights drop from the ceiling over row after row of worn, steely green spinning machines with their double layers of small oblong bobbins and wooden hexagonal bobbins that my fancy took for cat's cradles. The shop reminded me of a forest, but one that had been replanted so that each tree stood in measured distance from one another. Workers disappeared inside this unenchanted mechanical forest, their white-capped heads just barely detectable as they moved up and down the length of spindles under their assigned charge. But the larger-than-life production board hung at the back of the shop, in the place where Mao's portrait used to stand, made the women metonymically visible. The board listed each woman's name, along with her monthly production output.

Except for the five or six men who repaired the machines, only women worked in this shop: between fifty and sixty on each of the three daily shifts. I once asked some of the men in the weaving shop if they would go do weft prep work. They laughed at my ridiculous suggestion, saying they would be embarrassed to do it. It went without saying—the unquestionable sign of all hegemonies—that such work would impugn their masculinity. Yet the preparation of the warp thread, the stationary thread laid flat over the loom, was all done by men. Such is the arbitrariness of gendered activities.

In this, the weft prep shop, women fluffed out, spun, twisted, combined, and respun the weft thread, which is the thread that spurts back and forth across the loom, weaving over and under the warp threads. As in all the workshops, the machines never stop their spinning. Twenty-four hours a day, as the three shifts move in and out of the shop, each taking up where the previous one left off, the machines hum. In the prep shop, at least, the rhythmic clanking allowed for conversation without ear-blasting shouts. A certain calm prevailed, at least outwardly. The shop was spared the urgency conveyed by the noise and motion of the weaving looms. Spinning bobbins could be left for longer periods of time without a break in one thread stopping the entire machine.

The weft prep shop served as my "home" within Zhenfu, and the B shift was my shift. Yang Zhuren and I had agreed in our initial negotiations over my presence in the factory that I would least disrupt the production process by spending my time in the prep rather than the weaving shop. Later, I roamed from shop to shop more informally.

My first three days at Zhenfu were spent in interviews with Yang Zhuren and the head of the Number 1 shop. On the fourth day, Tang Shan, whom Yang Zhuren entrusted with my research requests, led me over to the shop for my first full workday. We went up to the second floor, which had just opened up that summer with a small group of women from the countryside. One woman sat alone at a little table at the far end of the vast room. Tang Shan introduced me to Xiao Bao, the assistant shift leader, and then left us alone. Xiao Bao was dressed like all the other women workers: in a white apron with small pockets to hold scissors, covering several layers of jackets and sweaters and pants, and in cloth arm guards worn from the wrist to the elbow, held together with elastic at each end to keep her clothes clean of dust and grease. The only difference was that her hair, which barely brushed against her shoulders, was free of the cap the others were required to wear.

Xiao Bao sat listlessly at her table, which was cluttered with a large notebook, an abacus, and a few cases of spools filled with silk thread. Unlike most others at Zhenfu, who were always bursting with questions for me about my purpose in coming to China and to this factory, what I thought of China, and so on, Xiao Bao showed little curiosity in my presence. We began a desultory conversation about her work. More accurately, Xiao Bao answered my questions, but—unlike Du Shifu, who overwhelmed me with her knowledge of silk production—she displayed a decided lack of enthusiasm. Her answers exuded the same weary air as her entire body. Her job, she explained with extreme brevity, was *shoufa*—measuring and recording the number of spindles each worker produced at the end of the shift. She had worked in the factory for over ten years. She first learned the position of combining the silk threads. Then she became one of the workers who learned all the positions and rotated around them. She was also assistant shift leader.

Xiao Bao said nothing of what this last aspect of her work entailed, but surely it had something to do with supervising the women working on her floor, all of whom were newly arrived from the countryside and just learning the job. One of Xiao Bao's superiors, the shop supervisor, Xia Zhuren, later filled me in, giving her version of the position. Apart from ensuring that workers filled their production quotas, shift leaders had to enforce the new disciplinary rules that docked workers for leaving their work position, for talking with other workers, and for a variety of other offenses. Also, the shift leader should set herself as an example through constant activity, even substituting in empty work positions whenever backup workers remained unavailable. Xiao Bao, much to her superiors' frustration, refused these responsibilities of authority.

Xiao Bao agreed to teach me the basic skill of prep work, *dajie*. *Dajie* entails retying broken silk threads so that the knot remains invisible. As I began my first clumsy efforts, a young woman plunked herself down on one of the empty stools by Xiao Bao to chat. Colorful and energetic, with bright pink earrings and long, painted fingernails, she informed Xiao Bao, her supervisor, that she was having health problems and had found a replacement for the day. Xiao Bao assented, without the least display of authority. I asked the young woman how long she had worked at Zhenfu. "Six years. I was a 'child laborer,' " she avowed sardonically, alluding to the recent newspaper reports that pretended to be scandalized at the "discovery" of the use of young children in the factories of Zhejiang province. "They told me I would learn a skill if I came to work here. Hah, some skill!" And she left. Rather than picking up where we had left off, Xiao Bao suddenly heaved a deep sigh: "I would have gone to college if not for the Cultural Revolution. Now my life is over. There's no hope for me." Xiao Bao was then thirty-one years old.

In the ensuing days and weeks, I sat with Xiao Bao, making half-hearted attempts to learn *dajie*. But I began to realize that my major task was keeping her company. I noted with growing wonder that Xiao Bao never left her table. The table was positioned well back from the densely packed reeling machines, far enough away to make it virtually impossible for anyone seated there to spy the workers in their midst. But Xiao Bao displayed a startling inattention to the labor of the workers under her supervision. They were all "peasant" women, whom urban-born workers portrayed as incapable of the "nimbleness" of finger said to be required of silk work. "Peasants really lack quality" was a common refrain I heard not just at Zhenfu but throughout the silk industry.[7] But Xiao Bao refused to enact what she envisioned as harassment of these women, to turn them into self-disciplined knot-making cogs. Rather than enforce disciplinary measures, she flouted them. Xiao Bao brought oranges and other treats to lure these peasant workers from their positions to chat away the hours with her. They enlivened for her the otherwise endless hours of an uninviting job in a life whose future was painted in shades of gray.

When not entertaining the women on her shift, Xiao Bao's resigned manner returned. "I asked many times to change jobs, to let me leave the factory. But they won't. This work, if your head aches just a little you can't do it. It's too bitter, it 'eats up energy.' " Then she told me a story: "There is one guy in the factory, he refused to come to work. They went and talked with him at his home, they tried to talk him into coming back. But he refused. He's making good money on the outside, in the free market. His wife works here, I know her. They went and talked with her, but she said, 'What can I do?' " Xiao Bao sighed enviously, "We can't do that," meaning that women did not have the same courage as men to just walk away from a secure job in a state-run work unit and risk themselves on the market.

Surprisingly, Xiao Bao envied the peasant women workers as well. These women were unlikely objects of envy, given their precarious status in the cities, but Xiao Bao longed for what she interpreted as their freedom to leave the factory. Recruiting women from the countryside to work in Hangzhou's silk industry remained a rather surreptitious affair. It ran against a long-held government policy that, from 1958 on, drew a strict distinction between city and country. The state's economic and social plans, ranging from industrial to birth quotas, rested on this urban-rural division, which certainly had existed before socialism but which was given a new importance with it.[8] Yet the silk industry had become desperate for women's labor. Since the early 1980s, when the Labor Bureau stopped assigning jobs to high school graduates, allowing them the "freedom" to test into the factories of their "choice," fewer and fewer urban youth were willing to work in the silk factories, with their two-day rotating shifts and tedious, intensive labor. The Labor Bureau consequently looked the other way as silk factories implored workers to encourage their relatives to come in from the countryside. The factories took no responsibility for offering housing to these peasant women—

most lived with their relatives—or benefits, rations, or, most important, urban resident status. Without that status, they could receive none of the social entitlements urban dwellers took for granted but country dwellers had never enjoyed. Still, several of these women confided in me that they believed the factory's quietly whispered promise to resolve their residence problem if they stayed. Given their circumstances it was striking that Xiao Bao felt such envy.

One day, Xiao Ma, the shift leader, stood in front of Xiao Bao's spot, yelling at one of the workers for breaking too many threads. The worker yelled back that the raw material was defective. When Xiao Ma left, I remarked to Xiao Bao that it must be difficult for older workers to listen to a young shift leader like Xiao Ma. Xiao Bao remarked, "Workers used to consider people's face. But now they don't think about that anymore. It's hard to talk with them. But these are all peasant contract labor. They get to leave after five years. Us, we have no future anymore. We have to stay here."

Only much later did I recognize the politics informing Xiao Bao's depressed defiance. Her actions resonate with the politics of authority of the dining hall workers and others of the Cultural Revolution cohort scattered throughout Zhenfu, albeit in a despairing rather than angry mode. Xiao Bao's coming of age at Zhenfu during the Cultural Revolution was not dissimilar from that of the others in her cohort. She entered the factory in the early 1970s, after having witnessed the most virulent period of Cultural Revolution politics in middle school. A child of workers who had both spent their lives at Zhenfu, Xiao Bao began work when the struggles of the Cultural Revolution may have been subsiding but had by no means disappeared. Perhaps she was slightly more adept at these politics than others. Or perhaps she created guanxi, or connections, with the party secretary for her shop. In any case, Xiao Bao found herself appointed the prep shop's branch secretary of the party's youth league, a position she held until she had passed the age for youth league membership. Others told me that Xiao Bao had shown a real flair for writing catchy political slogans.

Most telling in her present behavior is her refusal to embrace her position of authority. If, for the Cultural Revolution cohort, the meaning of one's own position lies in its opposition to political authority, and if

political authority represents that against which one should struggle—
indeed, if struggle against authority is singularly important, making all
other activities meaningful—then it becomes unthinkable to embody
that authority. Once, while I sat at her table, the shop supervisor, assistant supervisor, and union representative all pressured Xiao Bao to add
to her job a newly created disciplinary task of counting the number of
broken threads at each worker's position to pressure workers to become
more attentive. Perhaps they had hoped my presence would embarrass
Xiao Bao into a desire to impress the foreigner with her diligence. She
refused, fueling their frustration with her. She remarked to me later that
if she accepted, she would have trouble maintaining her face with the
other workers.

Xiao Bao's actions reflect yet another facet of the politics of authority:
the creation of what one might call "liberated spaces." Xiao Bao's table
exemplified just such an inviolable space. In the small area surrounding
the table, Xiao Bao had carved out a place where she could enact her
challenges to authority, transforming it from its original purpose. It was
a place from which her superiors had difficulty dislodging her.

The overt defiance and painful yearning that mark the complexity of
the Cultural Revolution cohort are nowhere more vividly exemplified
than in Xiao Bao. She embodies the multiple desires and ambivalences
of her peers, albeit in a more depressed manner than most. Her politics
of authority make her refuse to assume authority. Her small gestures
vividly recalled the recent past. More meaningful to her than any form
of labor, her embodied politics of refusal offered her the only space left
where she could express that part of her subjectivity formed in the
Cultural Revolution. Here, I tell only part of her story—the politics.
These always coexist with other desires, which I address in the following
chapter.

HOW COHORTS ACT AT CROSS-PURPOSES

A consideration of the cultural boundaries between cohorts leads us to
a more complex interpretation of the multiplicities of politics, agency,
and identity among subalterns. Neither the oldest cohort, of the 1950s

nationalization period, nor the youngest cohort entering the silk factories in the late 1980s and 1990s engage in the politics of authority. These politics, which characterize the Cultural Revolution cohort, do not "arise" out of their working lives in the same way for all workers.

As I argued in earlier chapters, women workers of the 1950s embraced the revolutionary discourse of gender liberation because it enabled them to extricate themselves from the degrading cultural meanings of working inappropriately on the "outside," rather than "inside" family social space. Identifying the essence of a liberated womanhood with labor, for them, led to an exhilarating freedom from previous gender identifications. Under the socialist regime, the realm of labor became inextricable from their self-enactment as liberated women, as women who did not have to act like women. When confronted with their marginalization in the 1980s, this oldest cohort wrapped themselves in nostalgia for their lost heroism. Their response was to perform as the heroic worker-citizen by engaging even more intensely in their job tasks.

Given that the party-state created the conditions and representations of their liberated identity, this cohort viewed authority as the site from which they would receive—and deserved to receive—recognition, confirmation, solicitous treatment, a reflection of their social value. Authority was supposed to mirror back to them the kind of socialist subject they sought to become. Working intensely would prove that. In addition, they believed that the "higher ups" should honor them as elders; the desired special solicitude should take the form of less onerous job tasks in their last few years preceding retirement.

Those women entering Zhenfu in the mid-to-late 1980s and early 1990s, as will become clear in chapter 7, also have a distinctive conceptualization of themselves as women workers. Their main concern was a search for an interiority outside of the dominant categories of identification based in labor. Struggling over their job was not a meaningful activity to them. They embraced a politics of indifference about authority and labor rather than a politics either of challenge or nostalgia. Their struggle was rather to free themselves from the strictures of Maoist gender relations and body politics.

Thus, while the Cultural Revolution cohort of workers views state authority as structurally antagonistic and oppositional, the oldest cohort of workers conceives of state authority as being in a hierarchical relationship that is ideally nonantagonistic and mutually interdependent. Members of the oldest cohort desire to win approval from the state by becoming socialist heroes in their work. Each group, then, enacts its strikingly different view of power: the Cultural Revolution cohort by refusing to do jobs well and the oldest cohort by working with commitment. The youngest cohort finds such struggles over labor meaningless. Its members do not confront authority on the job, for they find their greatest challenge elsewhere: in how to be a post-Mao woman, one defined not through concrete activities in labor but through a feminine interiority.

Moreover, the exertions by members of one cohort to overcome what they interpret as their form of marginalization or oppression are either unimportant to women in another cohort or reproduce precisely those effects that the others believe responsible for the major problem they face. Those in the oldest cohort will never gain the respect they feel they deserve if the Cultural Revolution cohort keeps, as they see it, giving a bad name to workers by refusing to work. Women in the Cultural Revolution cohort will never get authority off their backs if the oldest cohort remains, in their view, "model workers," and if the youngest workers also appear to obey the new disciplinary measures. These cohorts thus each *displace* each other's understanding of how power shapes their lives.

The displacements lay in a multitude of gestures, words, looks, rhetorical strategies, and narratives: in the subtleties of how workers remained grouped together with those of their cohort and refused most interactions with workers of other cohorts; in the actions of Cultural Revolution workers when they yelled back at their frustrated shift leaders, who came from the oldest as well as youngest cohorts; in the complaints of those in the oldest cohort to their superiors about how well they worked but how they weren't rewarded properly because those "other" workers fooled around all the time; in the stories older workers told me in which they contrasted their heroic laboring with the "laziness" of the Cultural Revolution workers; in the looks of disgust Cultural Revolution workers threw toward the older workers when they went to the "higher ups" to ask for favors; and in the palpable irritation Cultural Revolution workers felt for older and younger workers alike when they bent to the new production demands without protest.

Such complex relationships should warn us against easy generalizations about "workers," "women," or "women workers"—and perforce "modernity"—as coherent, homogeneous categories. These workers have lived through a process of ongoing transformation in the very meanings and practices of class, politics, femininity, and masculinity. Cohort differentiations, finally, lead us to rethink the contours of modern power.

Concern with power and resistance remains critical in a world overrun by capitalist insatiability, authoritarian regimes, and militant violence. For we must continue to imagine spaces of possibility in such a world. To do so requires that we devise more supple theories of resistance, however. The troubling assumptions that underlie most contemporary discussions of resistance do not suffice for theorizing the complexities of power. These assumptions include the idea that subjects can stand outside of power and move directly against it, that a binary division exists between power on the one side and a resistant agency on the other, that agency is acultural and ahistorical, and that power works outside of culture rather than within it. Such theories, we should note, were themselves produced at a particular moment of modernity's global intersections, when European and U.S. radicals were inspired by the politics of Maoist youth.

My interpretation of the cultural borders that differentiate cohorts suggests another way to think about resistance and modern power. Dominant discourses have led cohorts of subalterns in China to have quite distinct engagements with power. Liberation discourses produced nongendered women who embraced a regime of labor that led them to overturn local patriarchies; in becoming enthusiastic subjects of that regime they inadvertently participated in creating a new cultural logic of domination. The Cultural Revolution hegemony of continuous revolution produced subjects whose belief in the politics of authority leads them to flaunt their opposition to the very regime that older workers are desperate to uphold. The post-Mao discourses of modernity cast all these workers to the side: the two older cohorts rely on their specific interpretations of power to grapple with that marginality and, in the process, expose the historical contingency of the post-Mao modern imaginary. The youngest cohort enacts the multiple and contradictory desires engendered by post-Mao reform, at times exceeding the grasp of the latest form of power configured in the name of modernity.

Poststructuralist theories about discourse have opened up new and profound ways of analyzing the agency of subjects who always maneuver within fields of power.[9] I have drawn on these theories in my argument about cohort formation. But the differences among subalterns in China force us to expand theories of discourse in order to elaborate on the operations of power. If discursive power in China is visible through its constitution of subaltern cohorts, then one must address the further question of how cohorts represent power in differential ways. One finds, in post-Mao China, not a unitary discursive regime of gender or of class or even of modernity, but a multiplicity of representations about power that coexist with one another but also conflict with each other. Subaltern cohorts stand next to one another in the same social space of the factory shop floor. They all contend with the dominant post-Mao imaginary of modernity. Nonetheless, they find themselves construing the workings of power in quite distinctive fashion—and in a manner that displaces one another's implicit agendas. Foucault's insight that power and knowledge constitute one another (1980) must not obscure his other insight: that modern power manifests itself in historically and culturally specific practices. Thus, agency and resistance take a multiplicity of forms because people who live through the same moment of modernity might nonetheless, because of their past engagements with diverse regimes of power, "see" the current regime in disparate ways. Attention to just such heterogeneities reveals the historical contingencies of modern imaginaries.

6 Yearnings

Those long, drawn-out years
Those years, so confused;
What was true, what was illusion,
It's so hard to say.
Tragedy, Joy, Separation, Reunion
I've been through them all.
To keep on, to persist
What's it all for?

Down the long expanse of humanity
Searching high and low,
Yearning for a genuine life.
Who can tell me,
Am I right or am I wrong?
I've asked everyone at every turn.

Forgetting all the old wrongs,
What's left are true feelings spoken anew
In thousands of homes all over the world.
The stories are few,
Like a single song of a common life.
The past, the future, I'm rethinking it all.

> Theme song from soap opera *Yearnings*

Yearnings is a heart-wrenching television serial that played to rapt audiences in China over several months during the winter of 1991.[1] I had just returned to Hangzhou after an absence of five years, and everywhere I turned, it seemed, people I knew were engrossed in the program. I could hear the strains of its theme song all over Hangzhou; during the day at Zhenfu I listened as workers vociferously argued about how to interpret the latest episode, while in the evenings friends invited me over so we could watch the show together.

Yearnings tells a melodramatic tale about the intertwined lives, loves, and tragedies of two families, one of intellectual background, the other of working-class background, as their joys and sorrows unfold over the decades from the Cultural Revolution through the late 1980s. *Yearnings* examines lives devastated by the Cultural Revolution. How does one face the deep sorrow of lost possibilities? How does one evaluate the passion with which people pursued the violent politics of the Cultural Revolution? Most of all, what does one do with that passion for meaningful engagement when, in its aftermath, one's life appears as if lacking a frame of greater significance? These were the implicit, gnawing questions, it seemed to me, that fed *Yearnings*'s explosion of popularity.

The Cultural Revolution generation haunts the contemporary landscape. At times, they appear in popular representations such as *Yearnings* to be a "lost generation," a characterization that elicits sympathy while effacing questions of politics. But the politics of authority this cohort embodies also lead to apprehension about the potential trouble they pose. The vision of modernity with which they came of age incorporated a theory of progress that underscored the importance of insistent insubordination to hierarchy and authority. This form of politics has become completely unacceptable in post-Mao China. Its mode and style of resistance also appear anachronistic to many, especially to the youngest cohort, who have come of age during a time awash in the excitement of market-inspired desires. They aspire to move beyond such intimate involvement with the state. Progress, for them, refers to the ability to attain personal satisfactions without having anything to do with politics. The post-Mao state fosters this version of progress in the name of modernity.

The normative stories of victimization by the Cultural Revolution that, within demarcated boundaries, receive official approbation never quite succeed in controlling the instabilities that might erupt from this generation. The melancholic repetition of Cultural Revolution stories indicates that the closure the state would like to bring to that history is incomplete. For narratives of loss produce not just despair but anger. Hence, alongside stories about a lost generation, there is much commentary about the need for this cohort to undergo discipline. Unlike those in the oldest cohort, who experience the marginalization of their heroic exploits through labor, members of this cohort find themselves more specifically in the category of the abject. Judith Butler theorizes abjection as transpiring in

> those "unlivable" and "uninhabitable" zones of social life which are nevertheless densely populated by those who do not enjoy the status of the subject, but whose living under the sign of the "unlivable" is required to circumscribe the domain of the subject. . . . This zone of uninhabitability . . . will constitute that site of dreaded identification against which—and by virtue of which—the domain of the subject will circumscribe its own claim to autonomy and to life. (1993:3)

The Cultural Revolution generation represents the abjection that underlies the specter of post-Mao visions of modernity. One proves oneself a modern subject in the post-Mao era by expunging what the Cultural Revolution generation has come to represent. Or, to put it another way, the normalization of post-Mao subjects occurs when this generation is made into abjected figures. They stand in for what one might call "the Maoist difference." Unlike social groups whose alterity lies in their culture, race, or sexual desire, this group represents the radical difference of political epochs (or, if you like, political epics). However, the Cultural Revolution cohort can never be fully obliterated; as with other alterities, they form the constitutive inner limit of the post-Mao social order. Yet their presence perpetually threatens to disrupt the dominant narrative of the Maoist era that sustains the post-Mao imaginary of modernity. Their abjection traces the wavering edges of that imaginary.[2]

This abjection, together with their passion for meaningful engagement, generated a yearning among this cohort that was palpable: it pulsated through Zhenfu. I always found myself overwhelmed by how quickly people of the Cultural Revolution generation poured forth their life stories to me. Tang Shan; Xiao Bao; Xiao Ting, the prep shop's assistant supervisor; Huang Lin, one of the textile engineers; and many others rushed to assure me, the first time I met them, that apart from the daily activities they happened to engage in, they were not really workers and I should not consider them as such. They described their various intellectual capabilities, which went well beyond what their current work tasks might reflect. They spoke repeatedly of how they most certainly would have gone to college had the distorting hand of history not intervened. An exemplary incident occurred in the workers' dining canteen. On one of the first days I walked into the dining hall, a young cook greeted me warmly as he took my order. Seeing my foreign face, he excitedly blurted out a few phrases in Japanese to me. Momentarily taken aback—I do not understand a word of Japanese, though I recognize its sounds and cadence—I quickly realized that he was not naively confusing foreign appearances but displaying cosmopolitan knowledge that he hoped to share with me. Some weeks later, when I had come to know both him and his wife, the union representative in the prep shop, he explained his desire to maintain at least a veneer of learning despite the Cultural Revolution.

This chapter explores that passion for meaningful engagement felt by those who came of age in the Cultural Revolution. It produced a yearning on the part of members of a cohort who felt, in retrospect, that as a result of their past they had lost possibilities rather than gained them. Their yearnings constituted a "structure of feeling" (R. Williams 1977) generated from the discourses of modernization that marginalized them. Though shared, the yearning did not have homogeneous effects. Nor did it always remain contained within dominant discourses about the past and future of China's modernity. This yearning could as easily unsettle authority as support it. I present three different stories of yearning among the Cultural Revolution cohort: the first tells of an earnest embrace of the party and its future possibilities, the second describes a parody of authority by a depressed worker, and the last relates a romantic engagement in a new set of oppositional politics. The final story brings us to an exploration of how unsettling memories can lead to a redemption of political passion.

AN EARNEST PARTY MEMBER

Because she had been assigned to take care of my needs while I remained at Zhenfu, Tang Shan and I met on my first day there. Tang Shan's position as youth league secretary for the entire factory was highly prestigious. It generated a certain envy among other workers her age. They whispered about her engagement to the party secretary's son and nodded knowingly about her rapid rise to power. However, in the wider social landscape, at least in Tang Shan's eyes, her position in a silk factory reflected a comedown. In our first conversation, before I knew much of anything about her, Tang Shan felt the need to explain why she had ended up in the factory: she happened to graduate from high school and take the college entrance examination in 1978. In normal years, she assured me, she most certainly would have passed the exam and gone on to college, though the competition is stiff and the number of entrants few. But 1978 was not a normal year. It happened to be one of the three years (1977–79) when the government allowed all of those who had missed their chance at an education during the Cultural Revolution the opportunity to take the exams again. With so much competition, Tang Shan explained, the cutoff score for the few who gained the privilege of entering college was much higher than would be the case later. With disappointment still audible in her voice, Tang Shan said she had missed the cutoff score by a mere twenty points. Though Tang Shan did not get sent to the countryside like many urban youth, and indeed went through high school after the formal end of the Cultural Revolution, her view that the Cultural Revolution played a formative role in cutting off her future led her to view herself as part of the Cultural Revolution generation.

"The south, especially Zhejiang," Tang Shan went on, "is a lot more competitive than the north. People are smarter in the south. Zhejiang used to send more *xiucai* candidates to the imperial exams than any other area of the country." Tang Shan felt she was capable of becoming an intellectual due to not only her southern roots, but also her family's class background. Her mother was an elementary school teacher and her father an editor at the local radio station. One could see, she implied, that with such an intellectual class inheritance she most certainly should have had no trouble attaining the status of intellectual.

Gradually, over the months at Zhenfu, Tang Shan narrated a story of herself as someone who, despite her life's big failure, had the determination to prove herself worthy of the status I silently called "an intellectual but for." Tang Shan entered Zhenfu shortly after her failure to gain admission into college. She settled for Zhenfu, she said, because she preferred to find a job to support herself rather than become a "waiting for work" (i.e., unemployed) youth with no purpose in life. She worked for several years in the Number 3 prep shop, spinning silk yarn. Then management "plucked her up" to work as a cadre in one of the administrative offices, the Labor and Wages Section. Such a move off the shop floor and into one of the few coveted office jobs is spectacular, rare, and closely watched. Tang Shan interpreted it as proof of her intellectual capabilities. Shortly before I arrived, she found herself promoted again, this time to the post of youth league secretary. Tang Shan implied the promotion recognized her as one of the few in the factory who was more of an intellectual than a worker. Others were less generous. They whispered that *guanxi*, or connections, had led to Tang Shan's meteoric rise. Much later, I asked Tang Shan about her fiancé. She told me proudly that he served as an undercover policeman, but she never once mentioned his influential mother.

One day I found Tang Shan sitting dejectedly by herself in the dining canteen. I asked what was bothering her. She confessed that despite the prestige of her new position, she disliked doing party work. "It's too difficult now," she explained. "It involves so much 'thought work.' You have to go to people's homes at all hours of the day and night and talk with them. But people's thoughts are so much more complex than in the past. They are too difficult to handle. Not like in the past. Now everyone has their own thoughts. You have to study psychology to do this work, and even then talking someone into a particular kind of thinking is not rewarding, it doesn't lead anywhere. It's not a skill."

Unexpectedly, Tang Shan asked to go back to her previous position in the Labor and Wages Section. Zhenfu's party secretary—Tang Shan's mother-in-law—reluctantly agreed. Despite this retreat from party work, Tang Shan was one of the few people of her cohort who earnestly supported the party. By the mid-1980s, the term most frequently associated with the party was "corruption." The vast majority of those I met viewed the party with cynicism. Every week, it seemed, the newspapers described the party leadership's determination to clean up party corruption. They held highly publicized self-cleansing campaigns, projecting an image of the party as still dedicated to serving the people. But "the people" whom I knew grumbled loudly about how party cadres used their power to amass wealth in the market, which they turned back into power and then back into wealth again.

Tang Shan stood out as one of the few who defended the party out of principle and not expediency. She believed that China's future could lie only with the party if China were to avoid the chaos of Eastern Europe. After the famous 1989 demonstrations of students and citizens against the government, a movement largely fueled by anger about corruption, Tang Shan again stood out as the lone voice at Zhenfu who criticized the demonstrators. Unlike other party and nonparty members alike, she blamed the demonstrators for their own downfall and defended the need for law and order.

Tang Shan drew pleasure from including me in her imaginings about political order. She teased me about my "plain and simple" dress, choosing to interpret it as a sign that I shared a broader party morality. She heard my criticisms of the United States as sanctioning official critiques of western culture. At times, she drew me in as her "sister" who needed further education about the importance of state authority, though she had none of the innocent sincerity of Yu Shifu.

Tang Shan was not alone in defending the party. Xiao Ting, the assistant supervisor of the prep shop, for example, held a similar set of beliefs. She narrated a virtually identical story to me: because of the Cultural Revolution, she missed the cutoff score for college by a few points and had little choice left but to enter the factory. She had worked diligently, however, believing both that the party was good and that she could rise to the best of her abilities. But these two women were in the minority of those people whose life trajectory had been radically altered by the Cultural Revolution. Rather than make a politics of insubordination to authority the meaningful framework of their lives, as have many of their cohort, Tang Shan and Xiao Ting wrapped themselves in the insignias of power. Yet they, too, believed in the significance of holding political convictions. They fervently embraced a dominant discourse that hailed the power of the state as providing a steady beacon for China's course toward modernity. Their belief that state power is indomitable satisfied their yearning for meaningful engagement, forestalling the possible plunge into the abyss—hovering at the edges of post-Mao reforms—of a life empty of ultimate significance.

The cultural construction of class that Tang Shan and others crafted in the factory was of a piece with her support for the party. Those at Zhenfu from the Cultural Revolution cohort did not define their class identity by the actual labor in which they engaged. Instead, they imagined a future never to be secured that they could make real only in narration. That imagination was as real to them as their position within Zhenfu. They, like others, conceived a paradoxical world: though it would be without class labels or even class tensions, they would form its privileged elite. Theirs was a post-Mao vision of the modern social world in which people move about, gain wealth, and become elites by way of individual, inherent talents. History, in this world, returns to its putatively linear path; the palpable burden of abjection dissipates in the comfortable separation between the state and its citizens. Class disappears along with it. Yet their desires to maintain meaningful political convictions drove this cohort, at times, to unsettle that vision in their biting commentary, sarcastic refusals, or, for Tang Shan and Xiao Ting, defensive postures.

I had come to respect the imagined class trajectory of Tang Shan and others. Only once did I by chance witness Tang Shan being forced to pierce those webs of class imaginings. In the winter of 1991, when I had returned to Zhenfu, Yang Zhuren invited me to meet his daughter-in-law, who was on her way to the United States to study chemistry. She hoped to ask me a few questions and brush up on her English. As I sat with the young woman in Zhenfu's reception room, Tang Shan came in to find me. She seemed to shrink before my eyes. Tang Shan introduced herself to Yang Zhuren's daughter-in-law apologetically, referring to herself as a mere worker. She mentioned quietly that "we workers" have a difficult time going abroad. It was a painful moment.

A PARODY THROUGH DEPRESSION

While Tang Shan tried to normalize herself using the legitimating authority of the party, others in the Cultural Revolution cohort dealt with their abjection and yearning by exaggerating them. I turn briefly again to Xiao Bao, whom I discussed in the previous chapter, because she offers a striking bridge between Tang Shan and the story that follows. On the one hand, Xiao Bao certainly did not embrace the political power of the state. Nor, on the other hand, did she cast herself as a staunch oppositional figure, as did my friend in the next story. Yet her depressed yearning led to an unintended parody of official power. Recall that Xiao Bao, like Tang Shan, fashioned herself as an "intellectual but for" the Cultural Revolution. She sighed on numerous occasions over her lost chance to attend college. In her lament about being stuck in the factory, she "forgets" that finding a position in an urban factory had been a highly sought after privilege just a few years earlier. She also reinterpreted her brief, prestigious position as youth league secretary for her shop as taking the time that she otherwise would have spent studying for the college entrance exams in the late 1970s. Like Tang Shan's, hers was an interpretive move that struggled with official representations of her generation.

Recall as well that Xiao Bao spent a great deal of her time virtually immobile at her table on the shop floor. In refusing to act in the ways expected of a shift leader, she displayed both her implicit commitment to a politics of subverting authority and her deep desire not to view herself as a worker. Xiao Bao clung to a profound grievance, the sense that she deserved an office position. The prep shop office had ten people working in it, almost all of them workers who had moved off the shop floor. In addition to the supervisor, assistant supervisor, party secretary, and union representative, the office included a number of workers who kept various records—of work schedules, workers who took time off, the use of equipment, and wage calculations. To Xiao Bao, her desire did not seem beyond the realm of possibility. She told me stories of two lost opportunities to move into office work. Once, early on, the prep shop's party secretary had taken a liking to her, she averred. He wanted to pull her into one of the coveted office positions. But then he retired and someone else, who had better connections, got the job meant for her. In the second instance, the position was taken by a woman in her shop who, she related, had a powerful father in another factory. He convinced Zhenfu's party secretary to let his daughter move off the shop floor and into the prep shop office. Xiao Bao remarked disparagingly that the woman was hardly known as particularly intelligent.

I realize in hindsight that Xiao Bao's yearning to have the trappings of an office position critically informed her politics of space. Her refusal to leave her table thus had multiple meanings. One, as I argued in the previous chapter, was her creation of a "liberated" space apart from authority. But another lay in the way Xiao Bao in effect enacted her desire to locate herself in the office by turning her shop floor space mimetically into that office. Xiao Bao and others well knew that an office job meant more comfort—one could sit and rest all day, and it often entailed only a partial day's work. She knew that the young woman who had recently moved into the office even used her time there to study for her degree. Xiao Bao similarly sat at her "desk" doing a minimal amount of work. Her mimicry of office life, performed on the shop floor, daringly made this knowledge visible. It refused the delicacy of not speaking about what everyone knew. It had the effect of parodying official bureaucracy as represented in the shop office. And it destabilized what should have been a representational understanding of how space marks hierarchy.

The effect was electric. No one else on her shift drew as much criticism from the office staff as Xiao Bao. Her superiors frequently remarked to me and to one another about her behavior. They searched for explanations in her recent adjustment to motherhood, in her "attitude," in her "energy." Yet they could not budge her.

A ROMANCE WITH REVOLUTION

The yearnings of the Cultural Revolution cohort to overcome their abjection led to diverse positionings. An earnest embrace and a mimetic parody of authority exemplified two modes of yearning. But the paradoxical combination of the passion embedded in a politics of authority and the desire to embody a reimagined history could also result in a continued romance with revolution. For some, their unsettling memories could turn into new forms of redemptive political convictions. SJX was one such person. More than anyone else whom I met in China, SJX willingly engaged with me in philosophical discussions about power and inequality. More than anyone else's, his politics forced a revision in my own, as together we romanticized about how to change the world.

Our initial encounter was fortuitous. I had been at Zhenfu for about a month when I went onto the day shift in one of the weaving shops. At the far end of the shop floor in an inconspicuous room, young women engaged in *yaoyu* work—rereeling the already reeled silk thread onto small weft spools for the looms. I wandered in, curious; the women who crowded around me to chat returned that curiosity. One young woman, Hu Min, boldly and with much good humor refused to answer my questions about boyfriends, marriage, and children, questions that people often asked me and one another on first meeting, as if to inquire, Who are your kinship networks? How can I place you? While the other young women giggled with embarrassment, Hu Min bluntly but laughingly protested that she wasn't even married yet and I shouldn't be so inquisitive. But then she excitedly said that she had a boyfriend who was studying English and maybe he could practice with me. Wasting no time, she promptly left not just the shop floor but the factory to bring him back. A lanky fellow with curled hair, her boyfriend had put on a brown western suit to meet me. His lapel sported a red pin on which was written the Confucian precept *Tianxia weigong* (the whole world is as one community). He worked in a local paper factory, he said, and today was his day off. Sitting on cartons in the *yaoyu* room, we proceeded to make a pass at some English phrases, while he self-consciously protested that he didn't really have much time to study. "You know," he said, suddenly very serious, "they really don't like us workers to study because they think we are not working hard then. So I just use my free time at home and study as a pastime."

A week later he returned. Not too long into our English session, sitting once again in the *yaoyu* room, I responded, in answer to his question, that I was doing research in China in sociology. (Whenever I said "anthropology," people assumed I meant the study of fossil bones. If I said "cultural anthropology," they wondered why I was not with the national minorities.) He grew animated and said he was eager to help. Reverting to Chinese, he launched into the latest political scandal: the government had delayed an issue of the new journal *Democracy and Law*. "There's still no freedom here," he declared. "There's law, but it's all controlled by the party. There should be private law, but there really isn't any. It's all controlled by the party." Glancing nervously around to see who might have heard, I abruptly cut short the conversation, out of concern for his political safety. No one else had dared to criticize the party so openly to me in such a public place. Talking with a foreigner about such political matters could be especially suspect.

That was the last time we met in the factory. Both of us, however, were eager to learn from one another. We began to have surreptitious assignations almost every week. His desire to speak about dangerous political subjects and my desire for open conversation lent a sense of pleasurable risk to our encounters. We whispered secrets about how to bring about radical change. We mirrored for one another the importance of our political desires. We created a space of mutual recognition, even as we challenged one another's most basic interpretations about the workings of power.

Our implicit, unspoken pact was that we should keep our friendship from gaining attention. We chose different spots for each meeting—a certain corner by the West Lake; in front of the Friendship Store, a shop for foreign tourists; an intersection in the crowded district near his home. We rode our bicycles slowly, pretending not to know one another, or we acted as if we had just struck up a conversation in passing. We waited until we had found the most isolated area in one of the numerous gardens surrounding the lake before launching into our discussions.

Together, the two of us conceived a romantic vision of the potential danger—and exciting promise—of our conversations. With one exception, I refused, at first, to write down anything we had said for fear that public security might search my notes if they became curious about our connection. It was a healthy paranoia; it also lent a greater sense of subversiveness to our friendship. Our mutual romance with politics made it difficult to separate the need for secrecy from our desire to make our politics appear more important by acting as if secrecy were essential to them. Later, I took to referring to him in my notes as SJX, his initials romanized.[3]

SJX wove stories of his life that conjured up images of his brave participation in political protests, his yearnings for the lost glories of his family, his eagerness to discuss politics with a foreigner, the masculinity of his heroics, and the complexities of his identification and nonidentification as a worker. I present the fragments here, not to tell a coherent story about him but to show the complex paradoxes of negotiating one's "right to historicity" in terms of narratives of progress in a postsocialist world.

January 3, 1986

January in Hangzhou. Rainy and damp and still too cold for the flowering trees around West Lake to bloom. Liu Lao had paged through his agricultural calendar just the previous Sunday, and warned me not to expect the weather to turn until after Chinese New Year's. But the sun made unpredictable appearances every few days, giving us false hope of an early spring.

SJX and I had decided to meet. The sun happened to come out that afternoon, and we rode off to West Lake in search of a place on the far side, away from the relentless tourist crowds. But even there, young lovers locked in intimate embraces occupied all the benches. They were oblivious to our presence. We finally settled on some large stones near the water.

"Your friend [i.e., girlfriend] told me that practicing English had given you encouragement to begin studying again," I commented in an offhand manner, just to start up the conversation. I thought my remark rather innocuous.

"Yes, I had basically given up on studying. I feel that my life is over." The

intense emotion in SJX's rejoinder took me aback. I had not expected him to
plunge immediately into such depths.

"But you are young," I responded awkwardly, having supposed that we
would discuss "politics" and not his "personal life."

"You don't understand," he replied. "I used to work in the propaganda
section of my factory." Thinking of the propaganda cadre at Zhenfu who had
sliced through my relationship with She, I was startled: "You don't seem like
someone who would do that kind of work."

"Yes, well I used to work there. You see," he launched into his story, "our
factory is very famous. It is an old factory, from before Liberation. At that
time, the products from our factory were famous abroad. A relative of mine
was the laoban *[i.e., the owner] of this factory, so from the time I was little I*
had 'feelings' (ganqing) toward this factory. When I first went to work there,
they put me in the propaganda section. Of course, at that time I should have
gone to college. I tested into several colleges, a drama school, an arts college,
but though I passed the test they would not take me, because of my parents."

SJX joins his story with the pervasive narrative of yearnings, a narrative
so taken for granted that he need not explain it even to the foreigner.
But unlike Xiao Bao, he tells a story that yearns not just for the lost glory
of the future but also for the lost glory of the past. SJX had briefly mentioned in a previous conversation that his parents had been cadres in
Shanghai, but during the Cultural Revolution they had been "sent
down," first to Hangzhou—seen as a backwater by comparison—and
then to the countryside. In 1984, the post-Mao government restored them
to cadre status and allowed their return to Shanghai. Here he crafts a
genealogy for his family that claims an extraordinarily elite status, beginning well before Liberation, which itself preceded his telling of the
story by some sixty years. Later conversations will embellish upon this
genealogy.

In post-Mao China, the repudiation of Maoism had generated a great
deal of wistful regret for pre-Liberation times. Assumptions about everything from the higher quality of manufacturing to better education to
the greater ability to achieve national glory prior to socialism abounded,
along with nostalgia for the prominence and honor of elite statuses that

many now "remembered." SJX wove his family stories through these dominant narratives about history. His memories bespeak a yearning for a family eliteness that he had never experienced. His "feelings" for the factory resonate with an almost biological connection. Yet his telling of these tales was not just a retrospective sigh. The telling itself was a performance that made that lost glory momentarily real in the present. These fantasies of glory forsaken were as significant as his everyday activities in defining his identity.

"You know, in China, if one person in a family does something wrong, then the whole family and all the relatives must suffer the consequences. This is feudal thinking from the past. It's such a pity. Our generation, our lives have been sacrificed. So after I couldn't go to school, I went into the factory. They had me work in the propaganda section. But I could not stand it after a while. It was all lies. You know, this TQC [i.e., Total Quality Control, a managerial technique to improve productivity]. Our factory is supposed to be a model for the success of its application here in China. But it's all lies. They just write down on paper, but really nothing has changed. You know these reforms — it's just a lot of noise and blowing wind, but there hasn't been any real reform. In your country, the laoban *has to make his factory successful, because it affects him. But here it is different. Those cadres don't care; it doesn't change their lives whether the factory changes or not, so they would rather not change. I couldn't stand the hypocrisy any longer. I felt it was against my conscience to put my name to those false reports. So I asked them just to make me a worker."*

"That must have seemed strange to them, to ask to step down from cadre to worker."

"Yes, you know of course cadres get preferential treatment. We are the first to get gas cooking equipment and housing. They already had housing assigned for me. I gave them back their gas and didn't want their housing. So now my life is over; if I didn't have my hobbies, my life would be completely without meaning."

SJX models himself on an amalgam of stories: parables of honorable and upright officials of the Confucian imperium, willing to risk their posi-

tions and wealth in adopting a righteous stance against the emperor—
tales that were popular in post-Mao China. Echoes of other fables overlay the Confucian ones: stories of the truly dedicated socialist exemplar
who believes in honesty, selflessness, and the greater good of the
whole—fantasies that were often the fodder of cynical amusement in
post-Mao China. SJX held utter contempt for the party and often rebuked
socialism. Still he maintains a certain socialist idealism. His is a romantic
self-portrait, drawn with serious commitment.

*I felt awkward in the face of SJX's dramatic pronouncements. "Who do you
talk with about these things?"*

*"Yes, you know my friend [i.e., his girlfriend], she is very good to me, but
she doesn't understand. Workers think only of the short-term, getting enough
money."*

*"You are still young," I insisted again, thinking that at age twenty-nine
he still had much ahead of him. "You could still study."*

*"Yes, we have relatives in Hong Kong who said I could go there and live
with them. But my father didn't want his child to go so far away. He has
already suffered enough. I couldn't make him suffer more. He was a manager
of a factory right at Liberation. Then in 1951, he was criticized. Because his
brother is an official in Taiwan. He was put into jail. Of all the people who
were put into jail then, he was the only one who came out alive. Originally,
we had a big house in Shanghai; the government, if they had returned the
money to us, it would have been enough for me to study in the United States.
But they made a policy that those who were rehabilitated after 1982 don't get
anything back, because our government just doesn't have the money. Really,
if it weren't for my hobbies, I would have no interest in life."*

For SJX, as for some others of his cohort, this yearning for an imagined
elite family past and the lost opportunity to become an intellectual is
about "placing" (Kingsolver 1992) himself in a national history. His narrative is a quest for his rights to historicity in the face of the dominant
interpretation of the Cultural Revolution, which portrays that era as
having erased people's histories rather than developed them. The yearning of SJX also informed his refusal to identify as a worker. SJX views

his girlfriend as embodying all the stereotypes of workers. He accepts the abjection of the "worker," that "dreaded identification" against which he imagines his own autonomy. He thus momentarily staves off the possibility that he, too, might get thrown into that category from time to time.

January 19, 1986
January 28, 1986
February 7, 1986

No field notes on these encounters with SJX. During these conversations I learned about his continued underground activities. I can remember the dialogues: SJX, in tones mixed with bravado and earnestness, revealing his active involvement in the Democracy Wall Movement. This popular movement of 1978–79 began in Beijing and spread quickly to other cities. It erupted with attacks on the Communist Party, demands for human rights, and, most significantly, calls for socialist democracy. Mass meetings, demonstrations, and poster writing proliferated, as an unofficial press flourished around what became known as democracy walls. Those who participated in this loosely organized social movement largely conceived of themselves as an opposition from within socialism. At first, the central government attempted to interpret it as support for the new Deng Xiaoping regime. But after five months, they found it enough of a threat to bring it to an abrupt end, imprisoning the most outspoken with jail sentences of twenty years. Since then, any open discussion about the protests or those in prison because of the protests is officially forbidden. Apart from those arrested, no one has publicly proclaimed their involvement; such an announcement is tantamount to declaring oneself an enemy of "the people," that is, an enemy of the state.

I can hear SJX speaking about being part of a network that passed around underground literature, painstakingly copying it out by hand before passing it along. I can visualize the idealism written across his face as he spoke.

But, in fact, I made no record of these conversations. I thought it was too dangerous to do so. In retrospect, I saw him through his eyes; I reflected his own view of the importance of his political passions.

SJX's continued political activism did not preclude his getting caught up in the narrative of yearning. Conversely, for SJX yearning did not erase his fervent belief in the importance of being an interlocutor of power, even though he thoroughly rejected the overt politics of the Cultural Revolution. SJX, as did others in this cohort, grappled with how to act beyond taken-for-granted beliefs, how to frame their passion for political meaning. Carrying forward his politics also meant placing himself in the narrative of progress for modernizing his nation.

February 9, 1986

Chinese New Year's. Everyone was supposed to have a holiday for three days, but the silk factories forced most workers to work overtime. SJX invited me to dinner at his house for the first of the three evenings of celebration, even though he had to work the early shift that day. SJX lived quite close to Zhenfu. I wanted to avoid having anyone there catch sight of me or entertain even the slightest suspicion of my friendship with SJX. I rode a circuitous route through the narrow alleys nearby to avoid passing in front of the factory gates.

SJX's living arrangements were extraordinary. While most young people live with their parents until they marry, thereupon receiving housing from the husband's work unit, SJX lived by himself in one of the old one-story, two-room houses that still crowded against one another in the city's working-class district. The house had belonged to his parents, after they were sent down to Hangzhou. Housing is held in perpetuity by families with only minimal rent. His parents passed it on to SJX, who preferred to remain in Hangzhou rather than return with them to Shanghai. His place was neat and sparse, with coal stove, bed, desk, and television, along with a guitar, a calendar advertising a blond western woman, and a small handcrafted diamond-shaped portrait of a young girl's face. "One of his classmates made that for him when they were young, and he still keeps it," his girlfriend Hu Min remarked, upon following my eyes around the room. Once SJX had confided his reluctance to marry, even though he was engaged to Hu Min. There was another woman, he said, to whom he still felt devoted. Was this the same woman? I wondered. A former classmate of his, she had gone on to graduate from college and was now working in Beijing. She had everything SJX dreamed about for himself. When she married, he had said, then he would marry. But as far as he knew she didn't have a boyfriend yet. SJX, despite my questions, never elaborated on why they never got together; I could only surmise that he no longer matched

her status, since he had failed to become an intellectual. SJX easily inter-
twined a romance of politics with the politics of romance.

The three of us sat down to a veritable banquet SJX had prepared: chicken,
eel, yellow fish, fish soup, green pepper and pork, West Lake fish, vegetables,
and champagne. Hu Min joked: "In the past, in 1968, we used to have signs
and slogans saying, 'Down with American imperialism.' Now here we are be-
ing friends." We briefly pondered the ironies of national political histories.

After dinner, we listened to a tape of the popular Taiwan singer Deng Li-
jun and to disco music that SJX played in my honor. He began to ask me
questions about my research. I spoke of my interest in social inequalities.

"It's best not to have a communist system, but to have a free system like in
the U.S." This was SJX.

"But you have to understand that our freedom is attached to our money. If
you have money, you have freedom. If not, not."

"But here we can't do anything. I admire Ronald Reagan. He believes in
freedom."

I gulped. "Yes, if I had to live in your system, I'm not sure I could do it.
But I do think that Marxism describes our society correctly."

Astonishment: "You have studied Marx?" This was not the first time I
had met this reaction. Few could imagine how or why those living in the
heart of capitalism would bother to read Marx. "So you know about the law
of surplus value?"

"Yes, I have read many of Marx's works. I think he has a great sense of
humor."

SJX continued to stare at me in amazement.

The irony of our astonishment at one another's political convictions
pushed both of us, in the ensuing year, to reexamine our cherished political fantasies. Our cross-talk, humorous in retrospect, captured how
each of us strained past the political othering contained in the binary
opposition of socialism and capitalism. It mirrored the way political passions had moved each to idealize the other side of the divide as the place
of insight from which to craft subversive fantasies. Gradually, we came
to appreciate the other's angle of vision into the mythmaking capacities
of the forms of power each of us knew best. We located ourselves on the

borders of our respective systems, attempting to open up well-patrolled closures of dominant modes of thought.

Marxism had offered me an abiding insight into the fetishisms of social inequality. As I listened to SJX, however, I gained a much greater appreciation for the challenge of analyzing the complexities of power, including the power of the state. He made me see more fully than before how a socialist system can contain its own reification of knowledge about social desires, and how our search for the path to democratic freedoms would undoubtedly take a quite unexpected route that bypassed classical forms of socialism altogether. For his part, he tempered some of his more grandiose fantasies of the United States as the space of unlimited freedom. I hope I also conveyed the difference between capitalist endeavors and democratic action.

Much later, SJX accompanied me back across town to where I lived. I refused to let him ride all the way up to the gate where the guard could see him. In response to my caution, he avowed his bravery: "My friend's [i.e., girl-friend's] older brother is a party member and he warned me the other day not to speak too openly with foreigners. But I told him that even if she [i.e., I, as an American] were a spy, I would talk with her. I still haven't told my father about having a foreign friend, because he might worry about my getting into trouble. And he might get upset, remembering back to his American friend Alice from World War II days." SJX had told me in one of our early encounters that just like him, his father had made an American friend. She was a nurse, stationed in Shanghai at the end of World War II. SJX did not know all the details about their relationship, but he implied it had romantic overtones. Just like many anthropologists, Alice left China and lost touch with his father.

The foreigner plays a crucial role in antistate politics. Speaking with a foreigner about politics enhanced SJX's performance of himself as politically fearless. Relations with foreigners, with outsiders, provide a site of ambiguous struggle: the state encourages certain kinds of interaction, such as joint ventures, while forbidding or discouraging others—romance and politics. Talking with a foreigner, for everyone I met in China, was as much a political decision as a personal one. For SJX, romancing his politics meant envisioning himself as a dashing male hero in an international arena, a phantasmatic identity that he inherited from the time before socialism. Because I enjoyed our romance of politics, I was reluctant to articulate to SJX a critique of his infatuation with heterosexual romance.

February 17, 1986

Rainy and dark. I rode my bicycle over to SJX's home; or rather, he met me at the main intersection near Zhenfu and his home, because I am still unfamiliar with the twists and turns of the narrow alleys lacing through that part of the city. As always, our conversations coursed through his family genealogy and politics. I asked him about his studies of Marxist theory, picking up on our last conversation. He sighed and told me that "from very little I was by myself. I lived with my father's friends," because his parents had been sent to the countryside. Filling in the bits and pieces he had told me before, SJX said that he was self-taught, that he had been accepted into the Beijing Drama Institute but then rejected because of his parents' class status, and that he had become a worker because he was unwilling to pai ma pi, or ingratiate himself. "I know that is the only way to get ahead in China, but I'm not willing to do it. That is why I have come down to this level [i.e., of being a worker]." He had tried to leave the factory to work for a foreign hotel, but the factory had demanded ¥50,000 in "training fees" and 300 tons of coal before they would release him.

"There's nothing I can do." Then, after a pause, "I would like people to be jealous of me."[4]

"Why?"

"That would mean I had accomplished something. If I had gone to college, maybe I would be studying overseas by now. My father studied overseas in Japan, he went to college there, but he didn't finish. He used to work for a Japanese boss. My father liked him very much. He was the person who gave us our house on Nanjing Road [a famous commercial street in Shanghai]. But then the Anti-Japanese War broke out. My father's older brothers were fighting against the Japanese. They made him come home. They said that is no way to act, studying in Japan. So he came home. My father came home and joined the Communist Party."

"If your father was in the CCP, then why did they give him so much trouble?"

"Because his older brothers were very high up in the Guomindang [the nationalist government or GMD, supported by the United States] and they accused my father of being a spy. You know the mountains where the GMD trained their generals? My father's older brothers were there. Only the very top generals of Chiang Kai-shek were allowed there. He had another brother who is a general in the CCP. If it hadn't been for him, my father would have been in even worse trouble. Now, his brothers write to him. But my father is afraid to write back. So I write for him."

"Do you think there is anything good to socialism?" I asked. This question, seemingly abrupt, was motivated by his family narrative.

"Just speaking theoretically, not about China, yes I do. Because there isn't supposed to be any exploitation. They say capitalist countries have exploitation. But we're not supposed to. But take, for example, my factory. A few years ago, the factory made a profit, but workers' wages actually dropped. The workers' money went to the factory. Isn't this exploitation? I think the system of public ownership is good. But in a capitalist system a few capitalists own all the wealth. Here, we have a few leaders who control everything. What's the difference? I'm not sure I see any difference."

Though I thought otherwise, I hesitated in that moment to pierce through the emotional tone of his memories.

March 3, 1986

Rode with SJX to the Bai Causeway over West Lake to see if the peach blossoms had come out. I mentioned reading a book of poetry collected from the Democracy Wall Movement. He said I should look for his poems, published under a pseudonym. He told me his pen name. "Once," he said, "there was a woman at my factory. She really liked me. In fact, she started to fall in love with me. She admired my political values and encouraged me to keep doing what I was doing. She already had a fiancé but she said he didn't share the same values. Then, as she began to care about me more, she became afraid for me, and started to encourage me not to do those things anymore." He laughed and shook his head at this irony, as if to say that women in love are so contradictory. His daring political will, he implied, would not be dragged down by such feminine fears.

His daring political will, however, depended on creating stories about admiring and fearful women. While SJX imagined himself as an upright and passionate political radical, his vision of his political courage rested, in part, on a specific set of gender politics: the construction of his masculinity. In the post-Mao period—in everyday talk, literature, mass media, karaoke bars, and the business of making money—one encounters a pervasive rejection of the gender politics that had associated political bravery and modernity with women transgressing gender boundaries or women making gender irrelevant. Instead, the goal is to have men discover their masculinity. This goal defines the gendered bravery of pursuing the future of modernity. Popular and oppositional discourses encouraged a search for a masculinity that men discovered they had lost or, some feared, perhaps never had (see Louie 1991; Wang 1989).[5] They blamed the state for what they were only just discovering, or rather inventing: their castration.[6] Their desire for a hypermasculinity characterized by forthright sexual feelings and a tough, indomitable spirit is initiated in relation to political opposition to the state and fantasies of becoming successful capitalists.[7] Men seen as effeminate, embodying the cultural qualities previously admired in intellectuals—aesthetic refinement and emotional delicacy—are represented as ineffectual political and economic subjects. These representations of masculinity have often played themselves out indirectly over the bodies of women.[8] Male writers in search of a Chinese masculinity have mapped women's bodies as the grounds on which they can find themselves as men—and transcend Maoist gender politics. The politics of this masculinity gestures toward a devastating critique of the state, but it does so through a partial erasure of women's agency (R. Chow 1991b). SJX contributed to this erasure.

January 8, 1991

Five years later, SJX and I met again. Our meeting took place just one and a half years after the Tiananmen demonstrations, which had spread to Hangzhou and other cities throughout China. SJX had succeeded in leaving the factory. He had a job, as he had hoped, as security guard at one of the fancy hotels for foreigners. We strolled in the Botanical Gardens, where we climbed to an old pagoda at the top of a hill. He berated me for my lax letter writing.

Then he launched in: "I was planning to go to the United States. But then last year's events erupted. I participated, so now I have a police record and can't go. I really have guts! I participated in 1979 and now ten years later again. You would probably be frightened to death to hear what I did in the demonstrations. But I felt brave, and wanted to participate.

"I was one of the leaders. The demonstrations started in Hangzhou in the middle of May, about May 14. I went to join in, at Wulin Square. We decided to march to the provincial government. When I turned around, there were people as far as I could see. It was very moving. We demonstrated every day for about a month, even after June 4 [when the army attacked students and citizens in Beijing, ending the demonstrations there]. I organized people watching on the streets to join in. And I stood up and spoke into the microphone and wrote a big banner saying, 'The people support the students.' A reporter on TV interviewed me.

"All the government officials in Hangzhou sympathized, but when the orders came down to carry out punishments, they had no choice. They came to look for me. They came to talk to me every day for ten months. That was considered good treatment. They could have put me in jail for five years. But I didn't do anything chaotic (luan) *like turning over cars or burning anything or talking to foreign journalists.*

"Those police who questioned me, now we have come to know each other quite well. If I have a problem at the hotel, I just call them. So now we are on good terms! China is like that. Their thinking is confused, too."

These stories of passion and yearning return us to issues involving the relationship of ethnographic dialogue, cultural critique, and social transformation. Hearing their stories helped to move my thinking toward global processes that affect not only subaltern women and men in China but also my own research and writing about them. Storytelling about political desires blends here with the politics of narrative as individuals of this Cultural Revolution cohort and I negotiated the meaning of political passions. The way they constructed their political "voices" both supports and disrupts the flow of legitimate knowledge and authority. It also points to the specificities of imagined modernities and the kinds of subjects compelled by its multiplicities. The interconnectedness of gender, class, and political histories is especially telling here in the way that political passion and yearnings are intertwined. The shared yearning for political meaning nonetheless sought diverse resolutions, all produced by the collision of their past with the post-Mao imaginary of modernity. As we turn to the youngest cohort, whose members have come of age squarely within the post-Mao search for the horizon of modernity, we will find quite a different set of identities and desires.

Part Three Space and Subjectivity

The flow of Huang Daquan's eloquence continued una-
bated: ". . . As far as traditional architecture is concerned,
our ancestors fully understood the miracles that can be
worked with a boundary wall. There were more than a
dozen different kinds of boundary wall. . . . And each had
its own particular functional and aesthetic value. Most in-
genious of all was the dragon wall with open windows:
that could not only create a division between motion and
stillness, it could also create stillness within motion, or
motion within stillness. It could encompass people, while
giving them boundless scope for the eye. It would be true
to say that without a boundary wall, there can be no such
thing as a coherent group of buildings. A deep courtyard
must have a high boundary wall, or where's your deep
courtyard?"

> Lu Wenfu, "The Boundary Wall,"
> in *The Gourmet and Other
> Stories of Modern China*

Three generations of silk workers in one family

7 Allegories of Postsocialism

The previous chapters addressed distinctive visions of modernity formed in the 1949 and Cultural Revolutions. These projects imagined, respectively, that gender transgressions in labor and continuous revolutionary challenges to authority were the fundamental acts necessary to acquire a modern subjectivity. Throughout, I have traced how distinctive cohorts unsettle power when they bring historical memories of these political projects to bear as they experience the post-Mao imaginary of modernity. When we turn in this chapter to the current period and to the youngest cohort, which came of age in the 1980s and 1990s, we can readily see the disjunctures that distinguish this most recent project of modernity from previous ones.

In post-Mao China, networks of overlapping power shape a complex social terrain in which official discourse intersects with capitalist market dynamics and a vibrant oppositional intellectual culture. In this context, gender has become highly visible as a category of analysis and a subject of controversy.[1] There has been an explosion of public discussion in China on the marking, defining, and inhabiting of feminine and masculine identities. This commentary doubles as a debate on the socialist state and the means and mode of reaching modernity. The naturalization of gender forms the central motif in what I call the postsocialist allegory of modernity.

This allegory tells a story of how communism repressed human nature.[2] Because such repression, like all repressions, produces the very obsessions, perversions, and fetishisms it hopes to forestall, communism failed. Maoism deferred China's ability to reach modernity, so this allegory goes, by impeding Chinese people's ability to express their natural humanity that, all along, lay beneath the cultural politics of socialism. Of course, in this allegory that "natural" humanity is gendered. Indeed, it becomes "obvious" that Maoist notions of women's liberation through transgressions of gendered divisions in labor were actually an unnatural attempt to change innate femininity. The allegory is an emancipatory story, holding out the promise that people can unshackle their innate human selves by emancipating themselves from the socialist state. To the extent that the state recedes, people will be free to "have" their human natures.

One encounters this allegory in a multitude of public spaces—employment policies, government discussions about social benefits and family planning, television shows, stories in popular magazines, films, and novels—as well as in heated arguments about women's appropriate place in society, sexuality, and relations with the West. Much oppositional critique of the state by intellectuals, mainly male intellectuals, is founded on the idea of naturalizing a gendered human self. This postsocialist allegory is evident, for example, in the recent film *To Live*, by internationally acclaimed director Zhang Yimou. *To Live* describes the trials and tribulations of one poor couple as they attempt to hold their family together through political storm after political storm. They wish only to live for their family. It is a simple, human, and universal desire. In one telling scene just after the socialist revolution, the husband explains to his son why their lives will get better and better:

> "Our family is like a little chicken. When it grows up, it becomes a goose. And that will turn into a sheep. And the sheep will turn into an ox."
> "And after the ox?" asks the little boy.
> "After the ox is communism," replies the father.

But communism destroys their all-too-human desire. The couple loses first their son, who dies in the naive programs of the Great Leap Forward (1958–60)—the Maoist grandiose leap into creating a truly communal society—and then their daughter, who dies in childbirth as a result of the inane and deadly struggles in the Cultural Revolution. In the end, we see the couple painfully gathering the remaining threads of family, with only the grandson left them. The grandson has a box of tiny chicks. And the grandfather begins, "When the chick grows up, it becomes a goose . . . " And when the boy asks, "And after the ox?" his grandfather remains silent.

To Live plays out the allegory of postsocialist modernity, creating a tragic spectacle of the natural human desires that have always lain beneath the depredations of communism. This rendering of human nature takes specific gendered and familial forms: it is anchored in sexual difference, conjugal love, and the nuclear family. All along, according to this allegory, women have merely wished to express their natural femininity in motherhood and wedded love while men have needed to find their rightful masculinity in economic exploits outside of the state sector, in virile sexual expression, and in the mastery of political power.

My aim here is to disrupt this powerful allegory, as I elucidate how it actively invents post-Mao gender identities and new forms of gender inequality. What is taken for the emergence of human nature reveals precisely the manner in which postsocialist power operates. Indeed, the shifting meanings of family relations signal that such nature is invented, not "discovered," as spousal relations become more important than the residual hegemony of filial obligation to parents, and the ideology of romantic love triumphs over the ideology that makes marriage a means to reproduce family status. Moreover, the state, far from receding in this process, actively involves itself in naturalizing femininity and masculinity. At the local level, in factories such as Zhenfu, state cadres have adopted a variety of practices that shape the trajectory of women's lives—especially the lives of those in the youngest cohort—in the direction of naturalized femininity. Even as "nature" provides the grounds upon which many hope to move beyond socialism into modernity, it also provides the state with a source of legitimation. The state represents itself as enabling "natural" social relationships to come forth from the repression of Maoism. Moreover, local cadres are as committed as anyone else to the idea that China will reach modernity not simply by producing economic wealth but by producing the kinds of people who can embrace the attributes that appear to constitute modern selves.

The latter project addresses not only the Maoist past but also the orientalism of the West. One of the lingering colonial stereotypes of China depicts the Chinese people as not having "individual" selves. Their individuality is assumed to have been stifled first by traditional Chinese culture, with its extended kinship orientation, and then by communism, with its group orientation. And without individuality, it is said, Chinese people cannot become modern. The postsocialist allegory speaks back to this stereotype in its embrace of what, on the surface, appears to be a universal human nature. The excitement of this project for local cadres as well as for many others lies in this sense of moving into a global imaginary of modernity.[3]

Yet this terrain is heterogeneous. The gender and sexual politics of this postsocialist allegory have elicited much tense negotiation in post-Mao China. Chinese feminists both in China and the United States have pointedly argued that new forms of gender inequality have been ushered in, even as they, too, feel that greater emphasis on gender identity is important in order for feminism to proceed. For example, certain Chinese feminists have embraced "difference" from men as the way to advance the cause of Chinese women against what they perceive as the "sameness" instituted by the state (see Barlow 1997; Dai 1995; X. Li 1994; L. Liu 1993). That is, they have created meanings for the category "woman" that hold the state at a distance. Their notion of difference, however, is not necessarily predicated on any view of its naturalness. Rather, they describe the social, literary, and discursive histories that have made gender difference meaningful.[4] Moreover, their point is that new forms of women's subordination created through this hegemonic difference uphold postsocialism.

Still, even as the state reaches out to construct appropriate natural selves for women, women often exceed the boundaries of those selves. The multiple discourses on gender in the post-Mao era are powerful not simply because they repress desires but because they induce a positive interest in matters of love, sex, and marriage. For young women workers, such a positive interest moves them beyond any meaningful engagement with "labor," which to them represents mere drudgery and is unimaginable as a realm of heroic acts. Post-Mao femininity also moves them beyond a politics of authority, which to them appears caught up in the same dynamic of power as the state displays. In the place of "labor" or "politics," the post-Mao imaginary of modernity makes "bodies"—their fecundity, their management, their interiority, their sexual pleasures— the site for constructing modern subjects. Of course, these women workers must continue to labor diligently in the silk factories. But the imaginary of post-Mao modernity, in residing so fundamentally in the knowledge of sexual difference, produces the conditions that lead women workers to displace previous meanings of labor and authority. The pleasures and dangers of exploring one's gender identity thus make this imaginary an arena that, while saturated with power, nonetheless contains contradiction and paradox. It is also an arena of differential power, one that constitutes new forms of gender inequality, even as—or precisely in the way—it provides excitement to young women.

In this chapter, I address the microtechnologies of practices at Zhenfu that induced in women a positive desire for marriage and family. They were not solely responsible for encouraging young women to become preoccupied with love and marriage. The plethora of popular magazines for women filled with romance stories, fashion tips, and increasingly explicit discussions of sex; the soap operas on television; and the romance novels from Hong Kong and Taiwan that throbbed with the heartache of women searching for love—and the way that this popular culture exemplified the commodification of desire in the market economy—all played a crucial role. For this reason, I have offered quotations from these sources as epigraphs to each section. Yet, my emphasis on the state is meant to disrupt assumptions about the naturalness of these desires as I trace the complexity of how power operates in post-Mao China to construct gender difference in everyday life.

A FUR COAT AND THE LUXURY OF MOTHERHOOD

Ten years ago, I was a young high school graduate. . . . Before long, I brought my "three big conditions" into the course of love. These three conditions were good looks that were worthy of people's notice; a good job that brought pride when you mentioned it; and diligence, someone who liked to manage family matters. A lot of young girls had the first two conditions; but the third was my own. Because in my youth I was a tomboy. I hustled about, I was bold, I was extravagant with money, I was utterly ignorant about housework. Would it ever work if someone like me with this kind of "moral character" didn't find a man who was attentive and capable?[5]

It was the winter of 1991 and I had returned to China to renew old ties and find out what had changed in the intervening years in the lives of the women workers I had known. I called Zhenfu factory and, loaded down with gifts, went to a lunch they had quickly organized in my honor. Many of the workers and cadres I had known attended the lunch. But one conspicuous absence was Xiao Ma. Xiao Ma, they said, was on maternity leave.

When I knew her last, Xiao Ma had been the youngest shift supervisor in the factory, a mere twenty-three years old. Her supervisors considered her to be a conscientious worker. They hoped to mold her into a leader. I had spent a great deal of time with Xiao Ma on the B shift in the Number 1 prep shop, where she worked along with Xiao Bao. I often followed her on her rounds as she fixed production problems or yelled at workers to get back to their positions. I knew Xiao Ma disliked her job. She was quite diligent, but she felt uncomfortable supervising workers much more senior than she, especially those from the Cultural Revolution cohort; for them, ignoring her authority was a meaningful political project. She didn't have the skill, she said, of "talking" to people, of convincing them to work with polished words rather than yelling at them. "I don't have the temperament to be a shift leader," she once protested to me. "You always have to be careful of how you talk to people. To the older generation, you can't just use the language of orders to talk with them. You must use words that sound a little better. Someone who is older, she can give orders to the younger people, but I can't do that with older people. To be shift leader, you always have to be thinking of how to say things, how to talk to people. I'm not good at that. You always have to be worrying about how to handle relationships between people. I'm not good at that."

Xiao Ma also had made it clear that she had little interest in marriage. Several of her friends who had entered the factory around the same time as she did were beginning to marry. But she seemed to feel little pressure. Older workers teased Xiao Ma about "life's big event," and she usually brushed them off with an uncomfortable silence.

I spent a week at Zhenfu before I saw Xiao Ma. She burst into the reception room and threw her arms around me. Xiao Ma looked stunning: she was wrapped in a glorious fur coat, with one of Zhenfu's colorful silk scarves draped fashionably around her neck and her hair swept up. She was full of the high energy, laughter, and rapid-fire talk I remembered. She asked me about my life but before we could get to hers, she heard her baby crying. She had left him, she said, with his (paternal) grandfather. I didn't understand at first, not knowing whom Xiao Ma had married. As was often the case, I was enlightened later, by someone else: her father-in-law was a cadre in the office that handles workers registered for the militia. Since there were virtually no such workers anymore, her father-in-law made an ideal baby-sitter.

With baby in tow, she took me to meet her husband, who, as it turned out, worked at Zhenfu as well, in the transport section, driving trucks. While he went out, we sat in the transport shed and talked. I asked how she had met her husband. Given Xiao Ma's utter lack of interest in marriage, I assumed that, as often happened, someone else in the factory had served as her matchmaker when Xiao Ma could no longer put off "life's big event." In addition, the fact that her husband was also from Zhenfu suggested to me that she had made the best of a bad situation. I knew that few workers in the silk industry, women or men, wanted to marry someone else from the silk industry. The rotating shift system was too disruptive of family life; moreover, silk work had an ever-decreasing social status in China's working-class world; electronics or the tourist hotels held more allure.

To my surprise, Xiao Ma talked excitedly of her marriage as being the happy result of her own choosing and as demonstrating the compatibility of two people based not on social status but on their individual personalities. "We had seen each other at several meetings [in the factory], but hadn't really known each other," she began. "I was looking for someone who was not going to be as strong as me, because, you know, I have a pretty fierce character (*xingge*)," she laughed. "I'm not good at admitting when I'm wrong, even though I am wrong sometimes. So I needed someone who wasn't as fierce as me. So that's what I looked for." Then she added, "He's not very good-looking. But that's fine."

As unexpected to me as her newfound pleasure in marriage was Xiao Ma's luxuriance in motherhood. She had been on extended maternity leave for nearly a year. Workers get three months of maternity leave; with special permission, they can take six months of breast-feeding leave.[6] Given that the silk industry was desperate for labor, the pressure to return to the factory was usually keen. I wondered if there had been complications with the birth.

But Xiao Ma never mentioned such problems. She was visibly pleased with her new status as mother, not least because it enabled her to stay out of the factory. She commented not on the details of childbirth but on the bitterness of silk work. In an ironic reversal of the party-inspired mode of speaking bitterness, Xiao Ma made labor the cause of that bitterness rather than the means of its alleviation. Xiao Ma's superiors, as I said, viewed her as a diligent and conscientious worker. But she told me how her attitude began to change just before her marriage. "This three-shift–four-rotation system is really too much! After you left, then the two prep shops joined together again. Then I really had to run around a lot [as shift leader of the two]. It was too exhausting! I told . . . it was Xia [the shop supervisor] then who was there. I told her that my foot was bad and I couldn't do it anymore. She said I wasn't willing to eat bitterness. Wasn't willing to eat bitterness! So, I just stopped going to the meetings. There would be a meeting, and the next day she would come and say, 'Why didn't you arrange for such and such a kind of prep work?' And I would say, 'I didn't know about it. I wasn't at the meeting.' " Here, Xiao Ma exaggerated a look of innocence, rolling her eyes up to the ceiling as if to say she didn't know anything. "After a few times of this, she gave up and said, 'Okay, okay, I'll arrange to give you a different kind of work.' So then she gave me intake/outtake. But it was still three-shift–four-rotations."

Xiao Ma then proceeded to detail how she passed the days in seeming self-indulgence now that she was a mother: shopping for food in the morning, preparing lunch, feeding her husband and child, and then preparing for dinner. But what, I wanted to know, did she plan about returning to the factory? She confided that she had no plans to return when her leave ran out. "What if someone from the factory pressures you to go back?" I asked. Once again she rolled her eyes in mock innocence. "I guess I won't show up and then they will just have to take my name off the factory rolls. Then I won't belong to the factory anymore."

"But what will you do?" I persisted, knowing that abandoning the lifetime security of a state-run factory job also meant giving up all forms of social welfare, including at that time food rations, child supplements, health care coverage, and retirement benefits, in addition to the basic socialist security of a guaranteed wage.

"Stay home as long as possible," she replied.

How did Xiao Ma transform from a hardworking, albeit harassed shift leader to a woman luxuriating in marriage and motherhood? How did she become a woman who found herself excited by domesticity but thought socialist labor not only unfulfilling but a hindrance to her feminine desires? The allegory of postsocialist modernity offers one explanation: Xiao Ma has finally been set free to express the natural femininity that socialism had repressed. The rhetorical strength of such an allegory rests on the ahistorical essence that it posits at the root of female identity, an essence that exists both beneath and beyond political culture. It constitutes the figure of woman as the sexed subject, opposite not just the modern, humanist man but also the Maoist woman (see Barlow 1994). This essential woman makes the Maoist woman worker look ridiculous and unnatural. In being so gendered, modernity becomes a universal tale beyond cultural difference. Such a tale fails to consider the discursive power of socialism that produced, and did not just repress, other gender identities and practices.

Another possibility would be a political economic interpretation that divides socioeconomic life from its symbolic meaning. In separating the "material" from its representations, such an explanation might empha-size estrangement in the socialist labor process.[7] Xiao Ma thus freed herself from alienating labor, if only to embrace another type of unful-filling labor. Gender, while culturally constituted, is seen as a determin-ing structure in social divisions of labor; Xiao Ma thus "chose" her op-tions within a world of structured choices. This argument leads us, at least, to view the social world *as* socially made. It also reminds us that labor is one of the issues at hand. Yet this argument would still naturalize "labor" as the place where humanity, ultimately, finds its significance—whether in the oppression of labor that alienates individuals from their humanity or in the possibility of self-fulfillment in nonalienating labor. Such an approach therefore fails to take into account how representa-tions of labor have developed historically. Moreover, this argument treats gender as a social construction that remains unchanged through-out the socialist and postsocialist periods.

Finally, a story of cultural essence might be told, emphasizing how Chinese culture had emerged from the ashes of socialism. Xiao Ma's desires for family, in this view, demonstrate that Chinese people were, all along, truly rooted in kinship, the trope that singularly represents essential Chinese culture in the classical anthropology of China. As with caste in India, anthropologists—but also popular writers of all sorts—have invoked kinship to explain all manner of life in China, from eco-nomic motivation to religious practice. More recently, apologists have praised the Chinese family for lending strength to the growth of trans-national capitalism in Asia.[8] Lurking behind this essentialist trope lies the stereotype that Chinese people are "group-oriented"—a mentality seen as impeding Chinese people's ability to have modern selves because it blocks the expression of individual desire. We thus return to colonial conceptions that make Chinese culture the bar to a full-blown modernity. It reduces kinship to genealogy rather than tracing a complex genealogy of the concept of "kinship." Allen Chun (1985, 1996), for example, argues that our received view of "Chinese kinship," especially the emphasis on descent, is an invented tradition of British colonialists as well as an im-portation of the British anthropology on Africa into sinology.

"Family" is an important symbolic institution, and not only in China: wrenching debates over "traditional" family values and gay marriages in the United States make that quite clear. Such debates reveal family as a contested cultural domain rather than something essential that underlies culture. Feminist scholars of kinship in China have also disrupted the colonial view by raising questions about power relations in kinship networks. They have traced the class and gender inequalities in kinship, the ability of women to maneuver within patriarchal families, and the specific regional practices that challenge an overarching view of a singular "Chinese" kinship system (Judd 1989; Mann 1994; Silber 1994; R. Watson 1985; R. Watson and Ebrey 1991; M. Wolf 1972). I here follow their lead in pointing to the political differences revealed as distinct cohorts of women create and contest historically varied meanings of family and the relationships between family and work.

The enthusiasm Xiao Ma and her cohort have acquired for conjugal love, marriage, and motherhood—and the way they contrast these activities with labor, making the two opposing sites of fulfillment—does not reflect ahistorical expressions of a modern self. Rather, these sentiments and practices have developed in the post-Mao era in numerous overlapping discourses: of local state practices in the silk industry, official political culture, popular and intellectual discussions that herald sexuality as the realm of freedom from the state, and a market economy that has begun to commodify a multitude of desires. The wide-ranging public discussion in China about love, sex, and marriage is certainly preoccupied, in part, with overcoming western stereotypes and thus presents the "modernity" of these gender identities as universal. But far from existing outside of or despite the state, the discourses of gender identities are produced and deployed by the state. Local cadres have a positive interest in cultivating these new forms of femininity in their women workers. They, too, want their workers to have the proper conceptions of their bodies and desires. Yet this interest creates a certain fracture in post-Mao work life. To the extent that local cadres succeed in ensuring that women workers have a post-Mao modern subjectivity, they necessarily fail to convince these same women to remain committed to laboring for the state.

BUT WHY MARRY?

> As for the benefits of cosmetology, it improves the skin, prevents aging, raises self-confidence in social situations, and shows respect for one's spouse.[9]
>
> More than 250 new cosmetic products were put on the market in Beijing during the Sixth Five-Year Plan. . . . The import of foreign advanced technology and facilities has helped the Beijing Liyun Daily Use Chemistry Corporation turn out Huazi shampoo with equipment imported from Japan. Huazi is popular because it is safe for hair and skin but helps to hold the hair style. Its annual production now tops 4 million bottles and sells well all over the country.[10]

A commitment to marriage and having children was certainly not unique to Xiao Ma's cohort. I met no woman at Zhenfu, at other silk factories, or at the university who was over the age of thirty and not married. Occasionally, people quietly told stories of one or two women who had never married. They assumed these women had something terribly wrong with them. Those sympathetic to them said that even if these women had no problems before, they must surely suffer severe mental stress because of the gossip about them. Such stories reminded me of the increasingly powerful discourse of the Christian Right on "family values" in the United States, in which unmarried women, single mothers, and lesbians are portrayed as unnatural women who disturb the social order and cause the nation's decline.

But while women from different cohorts accepted marriage and family as a fundamental aspect of life for all women, they nonetheless appeared to have quite distinctive interpretations and experiences of the meaning of family. The oldest cohort of women workers, as we have seen, came of age within a cultural landscape of gender that contrasted "inside" and "outside," relying on a dichotomy that was not homologous with an opposition between family and work. The place of women inside the appropriate social sphere defined women as "proper" women, but their inside activities were not construed as solely dedicated to motherhood or caring for a family. Labor in silk-producing households was also appropriate for women.

Women of the oldest cohort, without any sense of shame or regret, readily described how they were sent out to live away from their mothers for long periods of time and how they often did the same with their own children. They viewed these actions as the most appropriate way to care for children in a world of extended kinship. Yu Shifu mentioned, almost in passing, that her mother had gone out to live for several years as a maidservant in another household, leaving Yu Shifu with her (maternal) grandmother. Chen Shifu also spoke quite casually about living in the countryside for several years with her grandparents while her father and mother established their silk workshop in Hangzhou.

Yan Shifu, another older worker, spoke matter-of-factly about sending her own children out for a number of years. She worked at a small collective silk factory not far from Zhenfu. It was an inconspicuous factory, under the aegis of the neighborhood committee rather than the municipal or provincial bureau. Yan Shifu explained that she and others there had developed a special attachment to it, because it had had such a precarious existence but meant so much to the neighborhood. She had gradually worked her way to the position of the assistant director. Because the factory was small, it did not merit many cadres, and Yan Shifu found herself managing all aspects of production and factory life. I asked how she resolved the problem of having to care for her family. "I didn't take care of my family. I let that go," she replied. "Every night I was at the factory. I gave the children to others to take care of." Yan Shifu described her workplace as the child whom she and other older workers have taken pleasure in watching grow up, changing from a broken-down old temple-turned-silk-factory to a thriving collective. As for her "own" children, they were raised by others: the oldest by his (paternal) grandmother and the youngest by someone who was paid to raise him in her household. Both children moved back in with Yan Shifu once they were adolescents. Again, Yan Shifu did not think this situation strange or unusual. Having children raised by extended kin seemed to her behavior that warranted neither cultural condemnation nor commentary on her unnaturalness as a mother. Certainly, women of this cohort never conceived of family as an alternative to socialist labor nor as the site where they would find their most meaningful female identities.

Members of the Cultural Revolution cohort, too, did not treat marriage and family as either the expression of their desires, a reflection of appropriate gender identity, or the solution to the question of how to have a meaningful life. Marriage had presented a problem for some of the women workers who came of age during the Cultural Revolution. But as they saw it, the problem stemmed from politics and not from their inherent character as women. Several of the women lived in the countryside for a number of years, but they refused to marry there. Given patrilineal strictures, they would have had to stay with their husband and his family. Only after managing to find a way back to Hangzhou did they marry, rather late. Others who stayed in the city married late as well, delayed by the difficulty of finding permanent work, which they considered to be absolutely essential before starting a family of their own.

None of the Cultural Revolution women portrayed marriage and family as the fulfillment of their most important desires. Xiao Bao was quite explicit in stating that she had no "feelings" for her baby when he was first born and preferred to leave him with her mother-in-law. She assumed that maternal feelings for her son would grow over the years, and that her mother-in-law, not nature, would help in that direction. She did not feel any need to worry about whether she was womanly; she did not conceive of womanliness as her project. Xiao Bao had just given birth when we first met. The government decreed that new mothers could receive an extra hour each day to feed their child for the first month and a half after birth. Xiao Bao took the time to go home, but she went to her own mother's house and not to her son. As she spoke of her situation to me, she pulled out her child's residence card and showed me his picture. "My child sleeps at his father's mother's house, not mine. I'm indifferent with him, so he doesn't have any feelings for me. I can't even get any milk from my breasts. I hit him and then he cries and wants to go to his grandmother."

Throughout the factory, I found members of the Cultural Revolution cohort sharing a similar disposition: Xiao Ting, assistant head of the prep shop; Huang Lin, one of the textile engineers in the planning office; Tang Shan; and others—they were, as a group, refreshingly lacking in anxiety about the quality of their mothering, even as they took responsibility to arrange for the care of their children. None of them went on and on describing the virtues of their children or the importance of making a good home for their husbands. None of them reveled in the idea that being a woman meant luxuriating in family life.

The disparities in the way these cohorts interpreted the meaning of marriage and family was equally reflected in the different ways they expressed their gentle and persistent concern over the fact that I was not married. Many of the women I knew asked me, at one time or another, whether I was married, why I was not married, when I planned to marry. Some workers persisted in urging me to marry, despite my protests that I was not interested, as they worried that I would otherwise have an incomplete life. Yu Shifu told me I would forever remain a *guniang*, or young girl, if I refused to marry. She feared that I would fail to attain the status of adult woman that would enable me to speak with social authority. Her conviction differed considerably from one that might express horror at my failure to fulfill my essential femininity. Yu Shifu and Jiang Changzhang, Zhenfu's only woman vice director, liked to tease me about bringing back a child for them to hold when I next visited. Tang Shan, too, teased me about the need to buy Zhenfu's quilt covers (lavishly displayed at weddings), four for me and two for my husband. Some agreed with me that, all things considered, it was best not to marry. Others decided that perhaps my "career character" was so strong that it overwhelmed my gender characteristics.

Women workers' concerns for my marital status both overlapped and diverged from those I experienced from others in China. From the moment I first stepped off the train in Hangzhou, my gender and marital status were matters that affected my position. Officials at the university had assumed that a Ph.D. candidate would be a man. Appalled at the discovery that I was a woman, the university's foreign affairs cadre asked me, before I entered his waiting car, whether I was married or had a fiancé. I was naive, at first, about the implications of the question. Their fears, as I later learned, were fed by their understanding that for Americans, sex and marriage were not inextricably bound together. Perhaps they worried that I was one of those "loose" American women who were into "free love." The American movies shown on Chinese television had certainly made that figure popular in China. The stereotype might seem laughable, but they also had it right—many of us from the United States living in China did not believe that sexual expression should be held within the confines of heterosexual, monogamous marriage.

Others voiced the opposite concern—that I might be interested in marriage with a Chinese man. My adviser, a cosmopolitan intellectual who had studied in England prior to the socialist revolution, once stated quite bluntly that he thought it was wrong for Chinese to marry foreigners. I took his comment as advice directed at me. I believe it seemed to him and to others who expressed this view that Chinese people had only recently recuperated from foreign onslaughts; marriage to a foreigner would be but another form of creating instability in their national identity. University officials thus never felt easy about my interactions with male graduate students and faculty. Nor did I spend much time alone with young male workers in the factory. No one, as far as I know, ever imagined the possibility that I might be a lesbian, though I believe that such a surmise would not have calmed their apprehensions. As it was, I moved largely in a female homosocial world of both unmarried and married women, with sporadic interactions with husbands of friends, older male workers like Ding Zhuren, and brave souls like SJX. Although I was always marked as a white foreigner from the United States, people also saw me as a woman not attached to a man.

Women workers, though also concerned with my marital status, showed that concern in subtly different ways. Women of the oldest cohort tended to stress that I would be left without a child to care for me in my old age. As Jiang Changzhang once said to me, "Who will look after you? You will be so lonely." To them, a husband serves the purpose of siring a child who will remain filial in one's old age.

Those who had come of age during the Cultural Revolution generally had a somewhat different attitude. They tended to make gestures of identification with me as they told me tales of their desires not to marry. Xiao Bao once related the following story: she and four other girlfriends had vowed to one another that they would never marry, that they would stick by one another forever. Only after each of her other friends had, one by one, succumbed to marriage did she finally feel she had no choice. Tang Shan, too, confided that she had hoped to put off her marriage until she got her degree from Television University to assuage her painful disappointment at missing the opportunity to attend college.[11] I took their stories as gestures to assure me that in their eyes, I had done something worthy of respect. These women viewed marriage as an inevitability rather than an achievement.

Xiao Ma, in contrast, urged me to marry because, she implied, it was pleasurable in and of itself, a fulfillment of my female identity rather than an obligation. Her cohort of friends in the factory spent a great deal of time talking about what kind of man they wanted to marry. They spoke of men who were tall, men who had a good conscience (liangxin), and men who had wide networks of social connections and knew how to make their way in the world. The men who best matched these characteristics in the 1990s had become entrepreneurs or at least were active in some form of market activity. They were men who had the ability to find scarce goods, who could bring home coveted items to their families, and who had proven their masculinity in these market achievements. Xiao Ma's friends also displayed in public their pleasure at being with men. SJX's girlfriend, Hu Min, was always trying to figure out how to spend more time with SJX, running off from her job surreptitiously to visit him at his home around the corner. This kind of public display was in stark contrast with the behavior of the older cohorts, who became embarrassed at the mention of their husbands or who found discussion of them irrelevant.

AN UNMARRIAGEABLE CASTE

> Their hands are at last brought forcibly together by the section leader, palm to palm. He has never felt more strongly about her body before, nor she his. Their hands touch for a split second, like lightning, and in the midst of everyone's resounding laughter their hands part, and they both turn to escape. But that split second seems so long, long enough for them to experience and savor for a lifetime. It is as though in that split second when they touch, he

realizes that this is the hand of a woman, and she that this is the
hand of a man. . . .

   She is not an imaginative person, and has never been one to use
her head. However, the experience of that night is frequently re-
vived in her body, giving rise to an endless physical yearning. She
does not know what she is yearning for, but feels that her body has
been neglected, that she is surrounded by a desert of loneliness.[12]

The social technologies of the factory that contributed to producing the
feminine desires of Xiao Ma and her cohort begin with a relatively new
development: this youngest cohort in the silk industry has become an
unmarriageable caste. Xiao Ma spoke of her marriage to someone who
worked at Zhenfu as the result of her personal choice, based on personal
compatibility. Yet marriage to someone in the silk industry has become
the least desirable option for young people in Hangzhou. The young,
unmarried people in the silk factories with whom I spoke, both men and
women, all said they hoped not to marry someone doing that kind of
work.

   This aversion to marriage with a silk worker is a recent phenomenon.
In the story I have told throughout this book about the silk industry, the
desirability and gendering of silk work did not follow predictable paths.
Prior to the socialist revolution, silk weaving was a highly sought after,
secretive, masculine trade. Men wove the silk largely in households; they
needed a wife both to help with the trade and to produce a son to whom
the skill could be passed on by his father. Working-class women marrying into these silk workshops viewed themselves as marrying up. After the silk industry was nationalized in the mid-1950s, these families
moved into state-run factories as a family. The women and men already
located in the factories but not yet married at the time of the revolution
saw their marital circumstances change dramatically. Men attracted
wives because they could find them highly desirable jobs. Ding Zhuren,
for example, brought his wife into his weaving shop. The women in the
factories also were highly desirable marital partners because of their
revolutionary class label. They succeeded in marrying up by marrying
party cadres, army personnel, engineers, teachers, and the like. Yu Shifu,

for example, married an army radiologist, while Du Shifu married an engineering designer and Chen Shifu an accountant.

Up through the 1980s, the silk industry continued to be largely a family affair. Long, generational strands of inherited positions characterize the silk industry. The manner in which socialist work units, as I argued in chapter 2, functioned both metaphorically and literally as family facilitated this arrangement. Inheritance of positions took on added importance during and after the Cultural Revolution, when families tried to keep their children from being sent to the countryside or helped them return to the city by obtaining a permanent work position for them. With that position, their children could retain their urban residence card. Yu Shifu's daughter worked at Zhenfu, as did the son of the shift leader in the weaving shop, Zheng Shifu. Ting, the assistant supervisor of the prep shop, ended up at Zhenfu because her parents worked there, as did Xiao Bao, Xiao Ma, and countless others of the younger two cohorts. The Cultural Revolution cohort of women still managed to marry up: Xiao Bao married a cadre in the Seafood Bureau; Tang Shan married a public security officer; and Huang Lin, a worker who herself had managed to return to a college established by the municipal silk bureau and become an engineer, married an engineering professor.

Only in the mid-1980s did young workers in the silk industry become, for the first time, a highly undesirable marital group. They were then forced to turn more toward one another as prospective marriage partners. A number of transformations combined to create this marital dilemma. One was the shift in the status of the silk industry itself, which in the decade's early years abruptly changed from representing Hangzhou's most advanced industry and the city's pride to being one of the most "backward" of enterprises. According to popular stereotype, workers in Hangzhou's silk industry did not have sufficient intelligence, well-placed social connections, or initiative to acquire more "skilled" working-class jobs. Second, their very product—silk—became a sign of their industry's backwardness. The elaborate silk quilt covers for which Zhenfu is famous, and which are used in traditional marriage ceremonies, had come to represent Chinese "tradition" and thus precisely the opposite of what would make China modern. As one of China's main exports, silk had also come to symbolize China's place in the global economy as dependent rather than hegemonic. Third, the silk industry had become "women's work" in the 1980s, making it more difficult for both women and men in the silk industry to marry. The men's association with a women's industry feminized them. They had difficulty projecting the kind of masculinity young women now sought, the masculinity most associated with market exploits. Women's association with this particular women's industry, while seemingly appropriate, also devalued them, as men sought women working in more prestigious jobs that did not of necessity subordinate family life to the rhythms of work. Finally, the status of subaltern had lost its glory in the post-Mao era. Neither laboring in the name of the state nor challenging authority in the name of a truer form of socialism was a project that made sense any longer. Working within the state-run economy had lost its attraction, as that sector began to be perceived as a hindrance that kept people from reaching their full potential or from pursuing the wealth and excitement they could fantasize obtaining in the market economy.

The profusion of representations in both official and popular culture depicting the need for women to define themselves through their desirability to husbands rather than their relationship to their sons made Xiao Ma and her cohort of women silk workers suffer the dilemma of their unmarriageability with particular intensity. Marriage still might enhance the status of their families and even that of the factory insofar as it operated like a family, but these young women no longer conceived of marriage primarily in such terms. And they had decidedly rejected the portrayal of marriage as a weighty matter of political culture, which was dominant during the Cultural Revolution. Rather, they as well as others felt marriage to be one of the most important means by which women could fulfill and express their basic feminine needs and desires: that is, a woman's human nature. As they attempted to free themselves from the socialist modernity of their seniors, they also viewed marriage as the site of fluid and multiple possibilities: pleasure, freedom from the state, and, most broadly, the place from which China, at long last, would become recognized as modern.

China needs women to marry appropriately, then, if the nation is to reach modernity. It is for this reason, I believe, that Zhenfu's cadres worried about the predicament of their unmarried women workers as much as, if not more than, these young women workers did themselves. At least in retrospect, I realize that factory cadres were actively concerned with the issue of women workers' marriageability. There were two sites that clearly deployed the microtechnologies of producing feminine subjectivities. One is the state-controlled workers' union; the other, the birth-planning office.

THE UNION AS MARRIAGE BROKER

When the heat of their feelings finally burst through the restraints of reason, they seemed like a newly married couple wallowing in their temporary love nest, offering themselves to one another, searching one another, possessing one another. . . .

He took her head to his chest and caressed her hair. "I never used to believe in love at first sight; now I believe it. There's never been a woman who has made me feel such earth-shattering feelings." . . .

He walked to the window, leaving his broad back to her. "I have a wife, and a son. I thought of telling you several times, but I couldn't confess." . . .

"You don't have to be so uptight. I'm not going to make you take responsibility for anything. Okay, I know you have a wife. What I want to tell you is that I also have a husband. . . . My whole life I've been very cautious, I never thought I would do something criminal." . . .

"You've used the wrong word; love is no crime," he shouted.

"I'm not blaming you, and I don't regret anything I've done. In other people's eyes, we have transgressed, because we both have spouses. But what is marriage? Maybe it can lock up a life, but it can't lock up feelings. True feelings between people is the most precious thing; I'm not willing to betray those feelings, because they are the purest emotions, they carry no utilitarian value, and they are egalitarian. Of course, you and I don't have a future, we just have the present."[13]

During the time I spent at Zhenfu, I did not attend closely to the implications of the effects of the workers' union on workers' daily lives. The union had formerly been a powerful organ. During the Cultural Revolution, it had operated as the power base from which the radical faction took control of the factories. In part for that reason, the post-Mao state thrust it aside. Following the attitude of many in the factory, I too dismissed the union as so much leftover socialist bureaucracy, superfluous to the real business of reform. I noted the running commentary of union representatives on marriage, as well as the leisure activities they organized for women workers to meet men, but I brushed it off as idle conversation and busywork used to fill the empty time on their hands. Only after I had left China did I ponder the relationship between subtle, seemingly insignificant or degraded practices and the establishment of new regimes of subjectification. Only then did I turn my attention to the union's activities as one critical means through which the state silk industry turned women workers' attention to marriage and motherhood. My notes are fragmentary in this regard; what follows pieces them together with my memory of one union representative, one of Xiao Ma's superiors in Zhenfu's prep shop.

Dai Hongyun had worked in the prep shop since 1969, when she went to work at Zhenfu at the height of the Cultural Revolution. In her late thirties when I first knew her, she had become the shop's union representative just as economic reform was getting underway. Hongyun, as Xiao Bao told it, had been the shift leader before she used connections to move up into that position. (Remember that Xiao Bao kept a close eye on everyone who managed to get a coveted office job off the shop floor.) Hongyun had a different story: her headaches convinced her superiors that she was incapable of doing any more prep work. Hongyun was supposed to help with general production problems as well as union activity, but she seemed to spend most of her energy engaging people about their personal lives and those of their coworkers. Not infrequently, she came up to Xiao Bao's place on the shop floor to while away the time. Far from presenting herself as an officious representative of the state, Hongyun had the demeanor of a harmless gadfly.

At the first production meeting of the prep shop that I attended, amid the lively banter, Hongyun kept up a running commentary in my ear about each woman's marital circumstances. Pointing to one of the assistant shift leaders, she remarked nonchalantly (in a not very soft whisper): "That one over there is already twenty-eight years old and not yet married. I heard that she's looking for a foreigner for a husband, to go abroad," she finished in a tone of incredulity. Then she proceeded to point to the other three shift leaders, including Xiao Ma, letting me know that they, too, were not married. "How do they find boyfriends?" I asked casually. "Me. That's my work," Hongyun promptly replied with combined pride and self-consciousness. "I'm supposed to introduce them. I've had two successes so far."

Hongyun's work as a marriage broker was far from episodic or isolated or outside of her duties. She held a key position in the factory devoted to normalizing young women's desires for marriage. She cajoled, encouraged, and endlessly, it seemed, talked with women about their need to marry. She often teased Xiao Ma. Once, as I sat next to Xiao Ma at her shop floor desk, Hongyun commented loudly that Xiao Ma was getting on in years and it was time to start looking. Perhaps she hoped my presence would make a difference. Xiao Ma was uncomfortable but sat silent and literally shrugged off the concern.

Hongyun not only insistently pressured Xiao Ma and others so that they would develop a positive desire to marry, she also took active interest in their marrying appropriately. A woman had to maneuver past the dangers of expressing female sexuality with the wrong object of desire, at the wrong time in her life, or without the intention of marriage. In particular, foreigners and the sons of high-level cadres were two categories to be avoided. The popular press frequently recounted the dangers such men posed to women. Stories about the latter type usually took the form of morality tales about rape. One local case much discussed among my friends in Hangzhou involved the son of a top-ranking official in Shanghai who, the story went, had lured countless unmarried women to his bed with the promise of marriage. He was eventually executed in a highly publicized manner. Such stories implicitly portrayed the degeneracy of those who had profited from the old Maoist system. Or, to put it another way, official commentary attributed any decadence in the post-Mao era to Maoism and the perversions of power it had spawned.[14]

Stories about women's sexual affairs with foreigners were equally condemnatory. As Hongyun implied in her comments above, for a factory worker the desire for a foreign husband reflected a dream that was not only illusory but dangerous. One controversial and much discussed story in the media told of a young woman who had let herself be played with by two foreigners (nationality unmarked), believing the first one when he said he wanted to marry her and then finding herself lured into an affair with the second one as well. The court in China sentenced her to three years in prison for lascivious behavior, but her lawyer defended her on the grounds that even if her behavior was wrong, she nonetheless acted out of innocence rather than immoral sexual desire. The decision was reversed (*Baokan Wenzhai*, 1 March 1986, p. 4).

These morality tales reveal concern with the dependence of national identity on sex and reproduction. They express anxiety about the ease with which women, through uncontrolled desire, can disturb the sanctity of national borders. Casual sexual involvement of women with male foreigners wounds national pride. Marriage with foreigners injures national status, for women marry out and move to their husband's home. Women thus are the weak link in the national armor. When they succumb to desire, they open China up to penetration, plunder of national resources, and lack of control over its/their bodily territory. Women's bodies get "occupied" by—but also become preoccupied with—foreign desires. Echoes of China's semicolonial past, combined with the deferred desires for a recognized location in a shifting neocolonial world, resonate in these morality tales. Exerting control over women's bodies seems a logical strategy for a state that wishes to do battle on the masculine territory of global capitalism. Thus, the stories speak of how certain categories of desire represent sexuality gone awry, sexuality that poses a danger for women—so that women's desires must be contained for their own sake—but also sexuality that might disturb the social order. Women must not confuse "inside" and "outside," thus weakening the boundaries of the nation, nor should they perpetuate the sins of Maoism by taking inappropriate advantage of privilege gained in the old socialist system. Both types of tales display anxiety about the inability to reach modernity, even as foreigners, who are presumed to have unlimited sexual needs, represent the source of modernity.

Many of my friends assured me that if the woman in the second story had fooled around with two Chinese men she would not have been brought to court. Indeed, for many, this story also revealed the changing and uncertain role of the state in regulating public morality. During the Cultural Revolution, they might have expected a woman to receive punishment for any kind of sexually inappropriate behavior. But in the post-Mao era, the state represents itself as willing to allow people a private life free of political intervention. The state has cultivated, with some ambivalence, a discursive space for the "personal" to appear as if it were devoid of power. Yet in China just as in the United States, there is intense political negotiation over how to draw the boundaries of that category. One arena of negotiation involves the extent of official intervention in behavior considered immoral according to dominant norms. In the United States, similar debates rage over legislating access to birth control, sex education, new reproductive technologies, abortion, and pornography, as well as the controversies over cases of sexual harassment, civil rights for lesbians and gay men, and sodomy laws.

In these matters of proper and illicit desire, Hongyun had to determine the limits of appropriate and inappropriate state intervention. Hongyun gave permission to marry—or denied it. She, like the other factory cadres, could decide whether a woman merited punishment or empathy for inappropriate sexual behavior. Zhenfu was desperate for workers and would not readily mete out punishment that would make the factory lose labor power. Yet local cadres were still responsible for establishing morally upright models of behavior. The state's gaze on women acquired a new intensity with its focus on the appropriate age of marriage, for example, because of its novel post-Mao population control policies. Hongyun encouraged women not to marry too late, but also not too marry too early.

In one of the weekly prep shop meetings, people suddenly discovered that one of the workers on Xiao Ma's shift had skipped work for four days without asking Xiao Ma's permission. Learning this for the first time in the meeting embarrassed Xiao Ma. I turned to Hongyun to ask how that worker could have been so bold. "Since she entered the factory the same year as her shift supervisor [i.e., Xiao Ma], she doesn't feel she has to listen to her or think about her face," she replied. Then she added, as if in explanation of her behavior: "This worker already has a boy-friend, even though she's only twenty-one. She came to me last year for permission to get married, and I refused her. 'What's your hurry?' I told her. 'Having a child is very bitter.' " But Hongyun eventually gave her permission. She decided that since this worker was from the countryside and lacked permanent urban residency, the young woman was not fully under Hongyun's jurisdiction.

Hongyun's advice, cajoling, supervision, and criticism of women workers were normalizing techniques marshaled in the name of the state. By paying such close attention to the details of women's romantic entanglements, Hongyun, as union representative, encouraged women to adopt a feminine desire for marriage, expressed appropriately in terms of object choice and age. Her activities served to create the presumption that women have a vocation *as* women. They represented one small but vital aspect of how the state intimately involved itself in subjecting women to the disciplinary techniques of femininity, marriage, and sexuality. Taken together, they shifted women's attention. Rather than devote oneself to labor or to the politics of authority in order to become a modern woman, one satisfies that desire through preoccupation with marriage and motherhood. Yet a gender identity as a modern feminine woman is not naturally possessed by women, even though "nature" is said to endow women with the capacity to express such an identity. To the contrary, to attain that identity requires conscientious effort. This is achieved not by way of formal "thought sessions," as in the Cultural Revolution, but precisely in the barely noticed and unremarkable activities of someone who represented the state in the guise of a "gossip." Though these activities sometimes entailed constraining women, Hongyun was much more concerned with inducing a positive desire.

In saying that the state normalized women as part of the post-Mao project of modern subject formation, I do not mean that the state had full control over these projects. To the contrary, in crafting marriage, motherhood, and sexuality into concerns of utmost importance for women, official commentary created a new area that demanded constant state attention. Along with popular discussion, it encouraged a responsiveness that had diffuse cultural consequences, including experimentation with desire outside the boundaries of what was considered normal or appropriate. The sheer concentration of effort on regulating sexuality, that is, produced its own elusive object of control—an excitement about sexuality.[15]

The intention of Hongyun and other interested cadres at Zhenfu was to create desires for a feminine identity that would lead to marriage. In conjunction with the explosion of commentary about sex in a multitude of contexts, however, Zhenfu's cadres could also make illicit desire seem attractive. Their endeavors to make women into modern subjects thus had powerful but unpredictable effects. They led to diverse actions by unmarried women workers. Xiao Ma was not one of those, as far as I knew, who indulged in exploring "inappropriate" desire. But she undoubtedly had heard the numerous stories, including those about workers at Zhenfu forced to make public self-criticisms when discovered.

Hongyun's efforts to keep sexuality in line sometimes seemed Sisyphean. Inappropriate sexuality appeared, at least to cadres, to be constantly plaguing the factory, turning up just outside of their control. Hongyun often found out only after the event or, as she saw it, after the damage was done. One day, I ran into Hongyun coming out of a committee meeting on family planning. She explained that in the meeting they had reviewed the past year's work and planned the next year's work. Then she quickly revealed: "We talked about one woman at the factory; her parents wouldn't let her get married. They didn't like her boyfriend. She often went to sleep at her boyfriend's house and after a while, naturally, she got pregnant. Then her parents let her get married, and so did Zhenfu. We didn't make her have an abortion, but she has to write a self-criticism."

Though I had at first too quickly dismissed them as irrelevant to the "real" business of modernity, Hongyun's endeavors as marriage broker were effective in getting young, unmarried women to concern themselves with the need to achieve modern womanhood by attracting a spouse. Far from merely stepping back to allow "natural femininity" to take its course, Hongyun brought the state's positive interests and regulatory powers to bear on the issue of the proper modes of marriage.

Yet we commit a serious error if we fetishize the monolithic power of the Chinese state (see Taussig 1992). First, Hongyun did not simply represent "the state." Local worries about the silk industry's unmarriageable women workers jostled with market-spurred popular representations of romance, beauty, and fashion; state birth-planning policies mingled with official and popular discussion of national identity and the need for China to have "modern" forms of marriage, sex, and motherhood. Hongyun's concerns were thus multiply determined. Second, the positive interest in romance and marriage produced in a multitude of arenas, including Hongyun's purview, could not be fully contained by the normative modes that Hongyun and others sought to institute. Even in commenting negatively on inappropriate desires, Hongyun added to other forces that helped create curiosity and interest in those castigated activities. Some women workers, influenced by these dominant regulatory activities, nonetheless interpreted the need to achieve womanhood in unsanctioned ways—seeking out foreigners, getting pregnant before marriage, and, as with Xiao Ma, ultimately refusing silk labor altogether.

BIRTHING MODERNITY

> For many years now, women's reproductive organs . . . have been "forbidden territory." . . . But today, women live in a time when science and technology are developing rapidly. They should understand and recognize the structure and physiological function of each part of the female organism, in order to discover in a timely manner any abnormalities or illnesses affecting their family planning.
>
> . . . When a couple have met one another through an introduction, the women tend to be "modest." They are unwilling to get examined before marriage. The man just asks a relative who works at the clinic to write out a certificate stating normal health before marriage. Such a sloppy marriage. As a result, on the wedding night, they begin to discover that the woman is a "stone maiden"—congenitally without vagina.[16]

The microtechniques of making marriage and motherhood into achievements for women were not deployed by the union alone. China's birth-planning policy provided another prominent arena for these practices. The novel aspects of the policy put into effect in the early 1980s deserve particular stress (see T. White 1992). This new approach reversed the Maoist practice of supporting large families to increase the laboring potential of the nation. One of the goals of the new policy—the only one commented on in the United States—is to restrict families to one child, though families in the countryside have generally been allowed to have two children.[17] China's birth policy has been the object of intensive scrutiny and fierce criticism in the United States. Restricting families to one child and pressuring women who exceed the limits to get abortions have been vigorously denounced. The U.S. discussion of China's birth policy assumes that the policy is a repressive restraint, preventing what is taken to be a natural desire to reproduce. Such a view, in turn, naturalizes a priori links among nature, gender, and childbearing.

Ironically, this debate over China's birth-planning policy is occurring even as domestic controversies over reproduction have made it increasingly clear that nature and gender are contested cultural domains. Reproduction in the United States has become a contentious site of discourses about race, poverty, religion, sin, government welfare, the social compact, the meaning of family, and capitalist materialism, as well as about women's control over their own bodies. The images drawn on include that of an autonomous fetus birthing itself, thus erasing women from cultural representations of birth, and women as the potential danger fetuses must overcome to succeed in being born healthy (Berlant 1997; Ginsburg and Rapp 1995). Religious and medical authorities present themselves as essential to the process of aiding fetuses to overcome women's physiological obstinacy, lack of education, or moral laxity (Tsing 1990). Feminist voices argue that women's own diverse needs and desires concerning reproduction should be primary.

The use to which China is put in these debates continues a colonial legacy of constituting western modern selves through non-western others. U.S. feminists, whose early criticism of China arose from their concern over women's rights to their own bodies, have had to pause as they find themselves uncomfortable allies of the Christian Right, who join their attack on China to their assault on women's reproductive agency in the United States. Perhaps the most startling and contradictory reminder for me of this change came when I received a phone call from one of the lawyers defending undocumented Chinese immigrants in the infamous *Golden Venture* case. Several hundred Chinese had stowed away on a ship, paying thousands of dollars to gain entry into the United States. Before they could manage to come ashore, however, their ship ran aground off New York City and they were promptly placed in jail. The lawyer defending their right to stay in the United States thought he had a winning case, as a little-known executive order signed by President Bush gave refugee status to those Chinese who could claim they had fled China's birth policies. He hoped I would testify about the policies' draconian and cruel consequences. The lawyer had placed a political paradox before me. I certainly agree with the need to defend those entering the United States against the virulent anti-immigration sentiments that have made cultural citizenship such a pressing issue.[18] Yet I refused his request: I decided I could not condone the neocolonial, Christian demonization of China. The most telling sign of the separation of this attack on China from a concern with women's reproductive agency is that the defendants were all men.

Despite the American portrayal of China's birth policy as a restraint on nature, the policy as instituted at Zhenfu revealed a cultural practice with a quite different aim. Far from restraining women from a "natural" desire to have children, it actively creates "female" natures that will place their primary attention on the mode and manner of giving birth. It encourages women to adopt an intensified focus on their bodies as the locus of their "femaleness." The practices associated with birth planning thus participate in the post-Mao production of modern identities in which women are made to feel their most important goal is fulfilling a biological desire for motherhood. Yet the birth-planning policy reaches beyond gender identity or the materialization of sexed bodies. As Ann Anagnost (1995) has argued, the policy and the popular consciousness it has engendered are concerned with the quality, rather than simply the quantity, of population believed to be necessary to remake China into a modern nation. Birth planning pursues in yet another way the phantasm of modernity. It hopes to produce a physically and intellectually capable population, one that will be robust in the face of competition. But the birth-planning policy's phantasmic search for modernity is not beyond or above gender, either. Rather, modernity is configured through the naturalization of gender.

Curiously, the anthropology of modernity has been largely silent on the role of reproduction. Analysis that relies on Foucault's argument that biopolitics define modernity can offer useful insights into the importance to modern states of regulating the characteristics of a population. However, Foucauldian biopolitics ignore the centrality of gender in the politics of reproduction. Such analysis thus encourages a separation between biopolitics, on the one hand, and gender relations, on the other, as if the former impinges on the latter rather than the two being mutually constitutive. Moreover, Foucault assumed that biopolitics respect national borders, taking an approach that portrays modernity as arising within discrete, homogeneous cultures. Consideration of the cultural politics of reproduction, however, makes possible a different view of modernity—one in which people negotiate the contentious meanings of reproductive practices and the knowledge about femininity and masculinity produced through them, in which such negotiations provide a site of imagination that crosses borders as readily as staying hemmed within them, and which includes instabilities and deferrals as well as fulfillment.

China's birth-planning policy lies at the heart of a gendered biopolitics of post-Mao modernity. It participates in an unequal transnational dialogue, contending with a persistent history of normalizing colonial and now transnational relations of cultural difference. In what follows, I trace the local institution of the birth-planning policy at Zhenfu. My story centers on the activities of one woman, the main cadre in charge of implementing the policy at the factory. It highlights three aspects of the policy: first, how bodies are naturalized as the site of feminine identification; second and paradoxically, how its interventions into birthing reveal "nature" to be a cultural artifact; and finally, how such active interventions make birth the site of a cultural struggle. The hegemony of the policy, while manifest, was not complete. Its reiterations and the manner in which it implicitly decoupled nature from kinship created gaps through which women workers maneuvered.

In this analysis, I join other feminist ethnographers who, in recent years, have moved beyond differentiating the cultural construction of gender from the "natural" facts of sex to examining how "nature" in its various guises is itself culturally constituted (Haraway 1989; Martin 1994; Strathern 1992; Yanagisako and Delaney 1995).[19] This research has been pursued to contest the naturalization of power underlying norms and practices of gender. In China, the relationship between culture and nature in the birth-planning policy does not quite replicate that found in the West, whereby culture is said to act upon nature. The birth-planning policy, while making nature a site of intervention and contention, also crafts nature as that which will finally overcome the "culture" of kinship that colonial representations depict as the critical hindrance to China's arrival at the horizon of modernity.

Zhenfu, like all state-run work units, had a small but vital birth-planning office. The office had only one cadre, a young woman named Li Hua. Unlike many young women at Zhenfu, Li Hua had none of the shyness or circumspection that made some of them run from me in embarrassment. Thirty-one years old at the time I knew her, she had an energy and directness that either evolved from the necessities of her job or made her ideal for it. Li Hua's "Birth-Planning Section" office was located alongside Zhenfu's other main administrative offices. The office had existed before the post-Mao era, but with a much more minor and perfunctory role in regulating marriages. Under the current regime, and with the changing policies about birth, its importance had grown. More workers visited Li Hua than any of the other leaders of the factory. A striking display of her purview could be found in the several large, easily read charts visibly positioned on the wall behind her desk. Like the production charts in the shops that announced the capabilities of each worker to produce silk, Li Hua's charts broadcast the abilities of each female worker to produce babies.

On closer inspection, the charts spoke about more than just births. Women's bodies appeared to be drenched in statistics. The charts set out information, by workshop, on the numbers of workers not yet married, already married and when, divorced or separated, and widowed. They classified women by age at marriage and type of birth control used; they listed abortions and adoptions, as well as the numbers of workers with only one child. And behind every statistic was a story. Li Hua knew, it seemed, the circumstances of virtually all the workers regarding their marital state and compatibility with their spouses. It allowed her, she said, to determine which kind of birth control to dispense and how to manage the quality of births.

Li Hua's work at the factory thus did not just encompass monitoring the number of births or restraining women from giving birth; she had a much broader concern with appropriate marital and sexual activity. In short, her office served as a node for shaping a normative heterosexuality. Yet it was normative heterosexuality inscribed onto women only. Li Hua's charts gathered statistics on women, not men. Ian Hacking (1991) reminds us that what he felicitously calls that "avalanche of numbers" has a history as a moral science; the most notable metaconcepts that underlie statistics are deviancy and normalcy. Li Hua classified women along a number of axes that drew those workers to attend more closely to their bodies as central actors in compelling them toward normative heterosexuality, appropriate marriage, and the capacity for healthy births. Far from allowing women to gravitate naturally to marriage and motherhood or to embrace these activities outside the interest of the state, the office's birth-planning activities encouraged this interest within the state's purview.

Li Hua gathered her information from workshop representatives who made up the factory birth-planning committee. Each workshop had one person, usually the union representative, who gathered information on women workers' marital circumstances. In addition, in order to marry, each worker had to come to Li Hua for permission. She issued a certificate that they could present to the government registry. In this process, age and health served as her main criteria, and again, it was women's ages rather than men's that received the most scrutiny. As Li Hua explained, "If women marry when they are twenty-five years old, then there will be four generations born within one hundred years. If women marry when they are twenty, then there will be five generations. Anyway, it is the custom that men are older and women younger." If one pays attention only to women's ages, one assumes—dangerously so— that the men will not disrupt birth planning.

Health inspections ensured the quality of births. "If there is a serious health problem, I don't let them register [to marry]. I do 'thought work' with them. For example, some male comrades have stones. They can take them out and then have children. Some women have hypoplastic vaginas. The vagina doesn't have an opening. After the operation, they can get married. There are two people here with this problem. One is the shift leader in the Number 2 shop. After they got married, they couldn't have children. Then they found this stone. We didn't put a lot of emphasis on health inspections before. We just started last year."

Li Hua demarcated women into those capable or incapable of giving birth. The most obvious distinction was drawn between women who menstruated and women already at menopause. Li Hua kept statistics only on women who menstruated. Each woman reported the arrival of her period every month in another little office at the back end of Zhenfu called the "Women's Health Office." The office provided a place for cleaning one's vagina to prevent infections while menstruating and of- fered free menstrual pads. Every month, women came in to say they were not pregnant. Conversely, in announcing their period women in- dicated their capacity to become pregnant. They simultaneously regis- tered their appropriate lack and also their maternal capability. Every month, they went through a process of declaring that they were women, normative women. Men, on the other hand, did not report their ejacu- lation activities or their sperm count.

The manner in which Li Hua dispensed birth control also emphasized women's responsibility for marriage and birth. Li Hua chose the appro- priate contraceptive method for each woman based on her marital status, on whether her husband stayed at home regularly or traveled for his work, and on whether she had already given birth or had an abortion. Li Hua handed the contraceptives not to the woman directly but to the birth-planning representative of each shop, who in turn dispensed them to the women in the shop. It was a community affair. According to Li Hua's statistics, of fertile, married women at Zhenfu (unmarried women did not receive birth control), 270 had an IUD inserted, 64 took birth control pills, 9 had a monthly shot of Depo-Provera, 304 either used a diaphragm or gave condoms to their husbands to use, and 122 had their tubes tied. Li Hua placed 95 women in the category of "other": those who lived apart from their husbands because of bad feelings between them (6 couples); those unable to have children, though married; and those who were divorced (5 couples), widowed (7), or had long illnesses (77). Li Hua assumed these women did not lead a sexually active life; they did not receive birth control. There were other women who did not yet need birth control because they were recently married but had not yet had children (93 couples), were currently pregnant (30 women), or had not yet married (352 young women). And there were those who had miscarriages. "A woman in the financial affairs office has had three miscarriages. And another woman in the party office, she's had two miscarriages. We're examining the reason now." Far from simply preventing women from giving birth, the birth-planning policy made women pay close attention to birth. Moreover, it used birth to divide feminine identities along the lines of normalcy and deviancy.

Abortions, to be sure, also formed part of the policy. Abortions are the aspect of China's birth-planning policy that receives the most lurid attention in the United States. Conservative lawmakers and religious political activists depict China's one-child policy, which relies in part on abortion, as yet one more example of how communism denies human life. They effectively use these representations to portray Chinese state policies as the "other" of their own state family-planning policies. Their neocolonial stereotypes of China allow them to claim that they stand for human life, while simultaneously denying women control over their own reproduction and penalizing the poor and women of color in the United States for giving birth.

Yet far from encouraging abortions, birth-planning cadres like Li Hua work to ensure they are only a last resort, relying instead primarily on contraception and "thought work." The city had suggested fining women who needed abortions, but Zhenfu had rejected that approach. Zhenfu did, however, have a quota from the municipal district: they had to maintain the number of abortions at under 3 percent of all women of child-bearing capacity.[20] In the past year, Li Hua had managed to keep

Zhenfu to 3.1 percent. The district awarded them the title of "advanced work unit."

Li Hua divided women into those who needed abortions because of faulty birth control and those who inappropriately got pregnant. The latter group included anyone who became pregnant without using birth control—in other words, anyone who had sex outside the normative mode. Women in the first category were awarded fifteen days of rest, continued to collect their wages, and in addition received money for nutritional foods. Women in the second category received the opposite treatment: loss of pay for the days they rested and no additional money for nutrition. Of the thirty-one abortions Li Hua recorded for Zhenfu during the previous year, four occurred because of a problem with the woman's diaphragm, two because of condom problems, seven because the women failed to use contraceptives while nursing, and eighteen because the women had used no birth control at all.

Anti-abortion rhetoric in the United States casts abortion as a sign of irresponsible sexuality, a decline in civilization, an immoral sin against God, and an act against appropriate femaleness as nurturant. In China, contrary to its fundamentalist Christian portrayal as antilife, abortion is believed to be bound to life, but not to its American critics' view of life. Rather, abortion is tied to the health of the individual body and of the body politic. Li Hua, for example, believed that abortion is bad for the body, that it weakens a woman's health. Women who have an abortion, perhaps because they became pregnant before marriage, might later give birth; Li Hua felt that an abortion would lessen the chances of a subsequent healthy birth. It also posed a high expense for the family, Li Hua said, because after the abortion a woman must eat rich meats and other highly nutritious foods. But abortion was unfortunately necessary, at times, to create a healthy nation. "We want to be like other developed countries," Li Hua explained. "If our population is large, it is dangerous for the economy." Thus women's bodies serve as threshold figures for the national body; they facilitate—or retard—progress toward modernity.

Abortion in China, unlike in the United States, is not that which prevents women from attaining their appropriate feminine identity. Rather, it is of a piece with the various discursive practices that naturalize gender as the ground of modernity. Indeed, contrary to signifying the downfall of civilization, abortion provides one means for attaining it.

Abortion contributed only in small part to this larger cultural transformation; it was one of the various strategies that Li Hua pursued to ensure that women achieved proper motherhood. Adoption, for example, was a means to motherhood that she encouraged if women were unable to give birth. It was an uphill battle. "It's a matter of face. Mothers-in-law blame women [who cannot give birth]. It's feudal thinking; they look down on women. They think you are not really a woman, but a half-man, half-woman." Still, several at Zhenfu had adopted: a woman who worked in the dining refectory and another in the Number 1 weaving shop, Li Hua informed me. Because women's identities have become so fully intertwined with birth, the nature of adoption has changed. Li Hua said that there used to be no problem in knowing who the birth parents of the child were and that the adopted child usually treated her birth parents like relatives. "A woman who worked with me, she knows where her birth mother and father are. And they have good relations. My older sister's husband's younger sister—she's adopted, too. Her family had lived downstairs from her adopted parents. They had four children but couldn't afford to raise them. She still sends presents to her birth parents on New Year's Eve and they send presents to her children." Now, however, in a mimicry of "natural" childbirth, women try to hide that they have adopted a child and they cut off ties with the birth parents.

More fully reflective of a national policy than were the practices displayed in the union's matchmaking, the biotechnologies of the birth-planning policies crafted a pervasive post-Mao modern imaginary. This imaginary focuses intensely on the health, strength, and normality of individuated bodies. They form the basis of a successful modernity. Newly born bodies, untainted by socialism, will become vital resources in building the nation out of the ashes of Maoism. If born properly of healthy parents, without medical complications, and raised properly by mothers who educate their children to reach new intellectual heights, each child will then carry within him- or herself the qualities necessary to create wealth and power for the nation. This individuation of the population rejects and represses previous socialist visions of national strength that stressed the quality of social relations.

At the same time, birth-planning practices inscribe a maternal femininity on women's bodies. They lead women to a close, detailed, and intimate knowledge of the "materiality" of their femaleness. This is not merely an effort to recall women to a femininity apparently evacuated of socialist distortions. Rather than stressing the kinship relations enacted through birth, as one might have found previously, these practices emphasize the birthing itself. Women must know, understand, worry about, and display the operations of their bodies as mechanisms for reproduction. Their capacity to give birth becomes a source of their essential femaleness, but it is also a site fraught with failure, abnormalities, recalcitrance, and lack. While the birth-planning practices assume a family framework, they also destabilize it by making the body and its birthing capacities stand on its own; such self-sufficiency implies that these capacities could be generated in multiple contexts, not just in that of marriage or wider kinship relations. Moreover, while gender in the post-Mao period rests essentially on its concrete embodiment, it also requires a great deal of work for its maintenance and regulation. Such efforts implicitly undercut that which they purport merely to reflect: the naturalness of gender relying on the materiality of bodies. Visions of modernity thus must be continually reiterated to ward off possible destabilization when confronted with the contingent politics of gender.

Insofar as women become implicated in birth—indeed, men's participation in reproduction is almost completely effaced—they birth the modern body politic. In so doing, they are also made into subjects of that modernity. The discourses of birth planning did not have an unquestioned hegemony, however. Li Hua, like Hongyun, found herself having to negotiate the multiple ways that women interpreted the intensification of the state's gaze upon their bodies. Young, unmarried women workers, even as they were shaped by the forms of knowledge that state birth planning produced, reinterpreted and challenged their effects, sometimes acting within them in unexpected ways. Neither the union's matchmaking activities nor the birth-planning policy was intended to make women turn away from labor entirely. Yet that is exactly what Xiao Ma did, as she eagerly became a post-Mao modern woman.

The allegory of postsocialism is enticing: it holds out hope and excitement; it celebrates national strength and private pleasures; it appears to move beyond the regulatory politics of Maoist socialism; it seems to carve out a space separate from the state; and it seeks, finally, to overcome the cultural difference reverberating through the long aftermath of semicolonialism. In disrupting this allegory, I do not mean to deny the pleasures it accords nor the insights it provides into socialism. To challenge the dominations enacted in the name of modernity, however, requires denaturalizing the politics of human nature in the post-Mao era and deconstructing how power, including state power, operates through these politics.

The layered histories of imagining modernity in China should give us pause before universalizing theories of gender. Psychoanalysis is one such theory. U.S. feminists have gravitated toward its insights about subjectivity and desire, as well as its recognition of how far power reaches inside people and how thoroughly domination can affect us. Feminists have turned to psychoanalysis for understanding the depths of power, on the one hand, and the failures of its effectiveness, on the other. Yet the strong influence of psychoanalysis on U.S. feminist theory resembles, in some respects, the allegory of postsocialism. Those who invoke it tend to forget the long history of the invention of the psyche in the West and how that invention, too, played itself off against colonial difference. Psychoanalysis tends to ignore the way its own interpretations create a discourse that inadvertently crafts ahistorical gender difference. Like the erasures by the post-Mao imaginary of the heterogeneities of gender identifications among political cohorts, feminist psychoanalysis remains uneasy with its inability to account for cultural, ethnic, and historical multiplicities. These multiplicities exist among women as well as "within" them. The ways bodies and interior desires have been invented in post-Mao China might usefully suggest to U.S. feminists the need to interrogate the psyche historically and cross-culturally.[21] Just as I have argued that the postsocialist allegory creates new forms of domination even as it opens new possibilities for women, so, too, one might investigate how psychoanalysis participates in logics of dominant assumptions as much as it undermines them.

In tracing the cultural construction of post-Mao gender identities, we also disrupt homogeneous stories about modernity. The disjunctures among the three cohorts of women workers should be evident by now. Class, gender, and political histories intersected to produce diverse projects of modernity. Fulfillment in and transgressions of labor, a politics of authority, and the naturalization of bodies lend specific form to epochal differences in imagining modernity. The coexistence of the three cohorts in the contemporary world and the politics of memory in which the older two cohorts engaged created a disavowed complexity within post-Mao phantasms of modernity. The members of each cohort of women workers saw themselves as overcoming the constraints in the project of their predecessors, even as those in a particular cohort did not all respond in the same way. This sense of overcoming always informs imaginaries of modernity; it leads women at specific political moments to embrace their different gender identities with enthusiasm.

8 Rethinking Modernity

SPACE AND FACTORY DISCIPLINE

Changing representations of urban space provide one of the most telling ways to examine processes of modernity. In China, official institutions in the post-Mao state have self-consciously turned their gaze toward urban design to induce effects of modern power. These spatial practices overlap with other modes of impelling modern subjectivities, addressed in the previous chapters. What do the revolutionary transformations of the past two decades in China tell us about the way spatial discipline participates in imaginings of modernity? How do the various cohorts of subaltern women contend with a post-Mao politics of space? How do their disparate engagements unsettle modern imaginaries?

As elsewhere, such structural designs are most obviously sought in the industrial discipline of urban factory work. The factory, arguably, embodies the icon par excellence of modernity. In this respect, Hangzhou differs little from Kuala Langat, Juarez, or Dakar. Factory managers, urged on by the state, have adopted "capitalist" techniques of scientific management as they intensely pursue that quixotic thing called profit. They have begun to redesign factory architecture in the name of efficiency. They have sought women who will be docile and quick. In Hangzhou's silk industry the emphasis on exports has led to intimate interweavings of factory space into global capitalist markets. The image of fragile but enduring Asian women offering up silk to the world enables that interweaving. All of these transformations have wrought their disciplinary effects on Hangzhou's workers. This globalization of factory space might lend itself to the initial conclusion that modernity, as a universally compelling phenomenon, produces unified, stable, and identical effects of power.

Indeed, the idea that spatial relations can everywhere shape the same modern subjectivities has led scholars on a journey in search of cross-cultural panopticons.[1] Foucault transformed the panopticon, that visionary architectural plan of Benthamite utilitarianism, into a metonym of the modern disciplinary gaze (see Foucault 1979). Intended as a design for prisons, the panopticon is a circular building with a guard tower in the center. The peripheral building contains individual cells structured such that the inmates remain observable at all times but can themselves see neither their fellow inmates nor the person in the guard tower. According to Foucault, the panopticon furnishes the perfected apparatus of discipline by means of a hierarchized, continuous, and functional surveillance independent of any person who might exercise it—a gaze that never stops gazing. It produces subjects who assume responsibility for self-discipline, because the power of the gaze is visible to but unverifiable by them. The power created through this architectural structure is thus pervasive, anonymous, and productive rather than repressive. It fosters a regulated population. Foucault argued that this modern "disciplinary regime," which began in the eighteenth century, marked a turn in European history. Since that time, individuals have increasingly become subjects and objects of surveillance and knowledge by various institutions (e.g., prisons, medical clinics, schools) as well as by the disciplines of the human social sciences (see Dreyfus and Rabinow 1982; Foucault 1973, 1975, 1980).

Nowadays, even in the midst of global flows and flexible accumulation, one continues to come upon this project of panoptic modernity virtually everywhere. Contemporary nation-states adopt visions and methods for creating "efficient," "productive," and "functional" social orders from the crisscrossed terrain of transnational flows. Architectural plans for a "rational" urban life, assembly-line techniques for producing mass consumption goods within regimes of flexible accumulation, increasing surveillance of bodies through new reproductive technologies, sophisticated military methods of torture, satellite communications technology, literary narratives and mass media, plastic surgery to make

Asian women look western—these form the transnational cornucopia from which "citizens of the world" (to paraphrase Kant) are seemingly created.[2]

The panoptic gaze, however, needs to be captured in its historical and cultural specificities.[3] In a space as seemingly global as an urban factory geared toward export, spatial productions of modern subjectivities collide with polysemous histories of past spatial relations. For space—and the authority to construe it—is a contested domain because of its recognized connections to power. In China, these polysemous histories are located in several sites: in the specific interpretations of scientific management by local factory managers; in architectural histories rooted in the prerevolutionary era as well as in the early years after Liberation (1949); and, finally, in different cohorts' memories of past spatial relations, memories that have taken on a subversive hue in the context of current economic reform. As a result, modernity in China does not neatly replicate a hypothetically transnational—that is, Euro-American—model. We begin, then, with a puzzle: the spatial logic of the factory can be read as conducive to certain disciplinary effects, and the current self-conscious efforts of the state even more so. Why, then, are they only partially effective?

Each cohort brought a specific politics of space to its encounter with the post-Mao gaze. For the two oldest cohorts, their dynamic memories of their shifting relationship to the state led to discrepant cultural struggles over the meaning of space and its implications for how subalternity is experienced at different times. Together with the youngest cohort, they employed their diverse politics of space as another critical means for creating heterogeneous gender identities among women. These divergences reveal gaps in China's successive imaginaries of modernity that provide room for women workers to challenge, exceed, and inflect its seeming transparency. They also highlight the deferred desires that continue to impel China's modernity within antagonistic relationships of cultural difference in a transnational world. For even when the state and factory managers self-consciously claim to borrow at least selected western practices, the impurities and constitutive "outside" of western civilization that Chinese culture has been made to represent—to recall the introduction—turn their modernity into another form.

In what follows, I suggest an approach to spatial disciplining of workers—and thus to arguments about modernity—that takes account of the way history articulates with epistemic structures. That which has been taken as homogeneous and called "modernity," as I have argued throughout, obscures a range of practices. For memories are reordered but not erased by the introduction of newer epistemes.

SPATIAL DISCIPLINING

China's party-state imagines new levels of wealth and power it might attain in global networks of culture and capital. To that end, factory cadres have adopted capitalist techniques to induce dramatically higher levels of "efficiency" and "productivity" in urban factories. They have embraced "scientific management," that quintessential biopowerful technique for producing disciplined workers. In the silk-weaving factories of Hangzhou, state bureaucrats and factory managers yearn for a perfectly ordered, spatially disciplined, and therefore productive workforce. Their visions have been created in opposition to the spatial modes of authority prevalent in the Cultural Revolution. As we saw in previous chapters, during the Cultural Revolution workers often left their work positions to focus on the production of a Maoist political consciousness rather than the production of silk. In its initial years, virtually all workers abandoned their posts to reinvigorate that consciousness through factorywide meetings in which they forced managers to confess crimes of following the capitalist road. The more radical workers, mainly from the younger generation, left the shop floor in pursuit of their political rights; they challenged managerial authority by dragging managers out of their offices and forcing them to do manual labor. Workers continuously moved on and off the shop floor, one moment weaving some cloth or spinning thread, the next moment participating in a political meeting. When not engaged in political struggle, their work regime still involved factorywide political meetings with other workers.

The sign of advanced political consciousness during that time was the refusal to participate in production. A politically "red" worker displayed her or his zeal in political struggles rather than in producing commodities. Leaving the shop floor was thus a statement of the political right to challenge managerial authority. Workers took a measure of control over organizing their own daily movements, mixing the space of the factory with domestic space by doing their laundry, shopping, or washing bicycles at the factory or during work hours. In this manner workers during the Cultural Revolution challenged the meaning of their place, both physically and in terms of social divisions of authority and power.[4] Even after 1973, when managers returned to their offices, they did not punish or pressure workers to produce more silk goods. For then, too, the most important product to come off the shop floor was supposed to be political consciousness.

Just as significant, the labor process during the Cultural Revolution era was structured such that it mattered little at which position any particular worker prepared thread or wove cloth, for workers labored in collective groups. Collectivity remained the hallmark of Maoist production processes. Even when bonuses were restored after the Cultural Revolution, cadres allocated them to groups of workers. The amounts of cloth and yarn were noted, but they were not tied either to individuals or to particular work stations.

The state has rigorously criticized that system as one of the many inefficiencies of the Cultural Revolution. With economic reform, the intensification of production made the individuation of workers a new site of political intervention. The abandonment of the collectivist production of the Cultural Revolution and the objectification of the individual worker through spatial arrangements, measurement, and quantification constitute the same political project. These novel modes of power form a cultural space in which the creation of the individuated subject lies not outside of state rule but within it.[5]

Silk factory managers sought to spatially root each worker in one work space. The Textile Bureau designed the position-wage system (described in chapter 2) for that purpose. Each worker receives wages based on the position on the shop floor she or he occupies; bonuses are calculated by piece rate, again tying individuals to work positions. In the prep shop, the shift leader records each worker's number of filled spindles at the end of the day. Inspection workers sew each worker's name into every side of cloth she or he has woven. Alienated labor it might be; still the identification of individual, product, and position is total. Even when one worker substitutes for another, the spatial ordering of individuals remains such that the cloth or thread from that work station gets recorded under the original worker's name. Management thus spatially ranks and specifies workers so that they can more readily discern anomalies in the working body. Yet these techniques involve not only a spatial disciplining of bodies but a spatial disciplining of consciousness as well. Each worker must identify with a particular workplace and with the thread or cloth produced there.

In the ideal plans of party cadres and factory managers, each worker remains fixed to his or her designated spot on the shop floor, leaving it only for meal breaks and at the end of the shift. As part of this spatial disciplining, each worker should stand at a set interval from the next worker, the distance prescribed by the number of spindles or looms at the work station. The machines are evenly spaced so that the shift leader, shop supervisor, or master teacher can readily perceive production problems when walking up and down the central aisle of the shop floor. To ensure that workers do not leave their positions, management has instituted a number of disciplinary rules—discipline having been lost, they say, during the Cultural Revolution. Workers are not allowed to chat with one another during their work shift. Because of the pounding, deafening noise of the looms and spinning machines, chatting would require leaving one's work space. Nor should workers leave the shop floor to accommodate the kinds of "personal" labor chores they had incorporated into their work during the Cultural Revolution. But conversely, no worker can become unduly attached to any work station. A worker must accept a change in assignment—for example, from twisting the silk threads to sweeping the floor—without protest. Individuation also means interchangeability of the parts.

In rearranging spatial modes of authority in the factory, state cadres have imagined a space of national wealth and modern nationhood: a reformed nation-state. Paradoxically, however, these silk factory spaces have also been constructed as sites of global interconnections. Factory managers proudly told me of their exertions to faithfully mimic western techniques for disciplining workers. During my sojourn in Hangzhou's silk factories, a German manager came to lecture; factory engineers and cadres went to Como, Italy, to study dyeing techniques; and the American best-selling manual of business success, Thomas J. Peters's *In Search of Excellence* (1982), gained wide popularity.

The silk itself, as both a commodity and a cultural artifact, signifies the transnational nature of the factories. But China does not export its own patterns and uses of the silk, which domestically appears mainly in elaborate symbolic designs for wedding quilt covers. Instead, they "blank out" their notions of beauty and utility by producing plain white silk for western designers. Or they weave western desires and tastes into the cloth.[6] In this case, then, one cannot simply conclude that transnational flows consist of an Asian appetite for western culture. For things "Chinese" have become increasingly difficult to distinguish from things "western." These silk factories, though recognizably in China, in effect are no longer solely of China: their sites have been reterritorialized. The place of the factory has shifted underneath workers' feet, even as they remain in "place." In this sense, workers in China, too, can be thought of as transnational.

The intimate microconnections of power that link artifacts to bodies should not obscure the specificities of China's search for the modern. The introduction of western techniques does not erase history, much as this might be factory managers' intent. For their visions of scientific management themselves embody a particular history. In pamphlets written in 1979 and 1980, silk corporation cadres broke down and subdivided the body's movements in space to have a better handle on them. Their inspiration, they told me, came from American Taylorism.[7] One pamphlet includes a section on prep work:

For the task of rewinding pure silk thread that has not been twisted:

1. *Relieving the previous shift:*
   Accomplish the one link, three checks, one do well.
   "One link": Enter the production position fifteen minutes early; link with the previous shift over the production situation

(including the raw material, the batch number, etc.); check the machinery's condition.

"Three checks": Check the last shift's markings for mistakes; check the ring frames for roundness; check the patterns of the thread spinning on the spools for regularity.

"One do well": Do well the markings for dividing the shift.

2. *Making the rounds:*

The path for making the rounds must be rational (*heli*). When inspecting for quality, use hands, eyes, and ears together. Differentiate the weight and tension of the thread. Do the easy first and then the difficult. Stop the spools or the ring frames to fix problems.

The path for making the rounds should follow the shape of the character for "bow"(弓), starting from the head of the first line of spindles to the end of the second line. The second round should still begin from the head of the first line, in proper order, and not return along the path.[8]

Both eyes should look to the left and right at the ring frames and spindles and not stare idly. Concentrate without rushing.

Both hands should be industrious. Accurately lift the thread, accurately correct the tension.

When checking the quality of the filled spools, do not entangle the ends, get grease or sludge on the thread, or cause other defects. If it does not meet quality standards, do not go on to the next production process.

Should the ear hear a strange sound in the machine's operation, immediately take care of it.

Microtechniques of the body these may be; yet these instructions have their specificities in the way that consciousness and literacy come into play. Taylorism in the West treated the body as if it were a machine, so that movement would become rapid and automatic without involving any thought. The novel regimes of flexible accumulation that have re-placed Taylorism continue to make consciousness an aftereffect, as it were, of rapid changes in the body or work environment. Indeed, as Emily Martin (1994) has observed, American corporations are advised to become like biological systems in order to survive in a fluid, shifting world. Here, in contrast, one finds an emphasis on the need for workers' participatory consciousness in their actions rather than on a mere physical reenactment of motions in space or a flexible bodily adaptation to space. The pamphlet recalls recent Maoist history, a time when consciousness was the privileged site of political possibilities and political threats. Cultural Revolution sessions consisted of yelling and beating someone into a conscious realization of their errant ways owing to their class status. But consciousness in this case is not the repository of a unified subject's inner truth. It signifies rather a permeable site reflected through outward actions. With economic reform, Maoist consciousness-raising has continued in the form of "thought work" (*sixiang gongzuo*). Party cadres in the factory now do thought work to bring workers' minds to bear on production. There is no work without thought, and the opposite also holds true.[9]

Perhaps the most striking feature of the pamphlet is its stress on tracing characters as a form of discipline. The characters themselves are significant. Writing, in this instance, is not simply a transparent medium of communication, in which signs represent or mirror reality. Signifiers here rather outline the body's actions, a display of action that both imitates and constitutes the form it signifies.[10]

Body manuals have a rich history in China. This handbook is reminiscent of earlier choreographies, especially prerevolutionary ritual manuals, in which literati conceived of writing as enacting the world (Zito 1997). As Angela Zito has argued, learned men treated writing as a way to discern the pattern of interpenetration between cosmic and social worlds and as a way to keep reproducing that pattern. They viewed writing—together with painting, ritual, and architecture—as one of the significant forms that shape consciousness and human agency. The act of writing lay at the heart of a proper ritual performance, because it was in itself a performative enactment of the world.

It is in this sense that imitating the correct characters with one's body becomes essential to correct silk production. Characters can only be known through the consciousness and perception of the person performing the action. While there seems to be no reason to require literacy of workers, workers must skill their bodies up rather than down, for they need to train their bodies to move in strict accordance with the strokes for "bow." Rationality is often invoked as a key sign of the modernist project (Harvey 1989), but this form of rationality in production does not replicate western notions of de-skilling (Braverman 1974). In our post-Foucauldian haste to chart modernity, it might be useful, then, to remind ourselves, as Weber (1968 [1922]) argued, that rationality has no a priori content and makes sense only in a given cultural context. Scientific management does not lend itself to the free play of signification. In specific material worlds, as people invest categories with meaning they rely on imaginations that are shaped by historical developments.

SPATIAL SUBVERSIONS

These techniques provided the spatial disciplinary measures that party cadres and factory managers put into practice and imagined would come to fruition; indeed, they have partially succeeded. Yet these same factory spaces and the bodies and consciousnesses that are objects of control retained memories of past spatial arrangements that held a different semiotics of production. The spaces that managers rearranged were not blank; the history of earlier eras—the 1950s and the recent Cultural Revolution—still resided in them. Certain workers questioned and contested the new authority of efficiency with memories of previous spatial relations through which they still moved on the shop floor. Through these memories, they created zones of subversion, both subtle and direct.

During the time I spent at Zhenfu, I was struck by three particular sites in which distinct cohorts of workers marked out their identity. The most dramatic, it seemed to me, entailed the reappropriation of public space. In the context of economic reform, resting rather than working formed part of a political assertion about the identity of a good worker. A group of six or seven women on the B shift of Zhenfu's Number 1 prep shop, my home shift, had claimed a comfortable and visible place to take breaks, where it would be clear to all that they were not at their work positions: a small table just off the shop floor, in full view both of the shift leader, Xiao Ma, as she sat at her desk and of the front entrance to the shop. It was the only place to sit down. Their actions were no simple matter of taking long breaks, as they flaunted their presence, sitting and loudly complaining about the new production pressures.

They postured against the authority of efficiency. These women made up the generation who had come of age in the Cultural Revolution. Once, angry about having been penalized for spinning the wrong box of silk yarn, one of the women joked to the others about needing to get back to the old method of hanging signs on people, as they did during the Cultural Revolution, and calling them "capitalist roaders." Theirs was a brazen challenge to the reform attempts to re-form them.

Most of this generation, as I have argued, no longer embraced the specific politics of the Cultural Revolution. They, too, had become disillusioned with its excesses and the sense, as one person put it, that "we had a carrot sitting on our heads and didn't know it."[11] Yet they went to great lengths to retain their political rights to challenge managerial authority—or, perhaps more accurately, their political rights not to have managers challenge them. They remained conscious that work experiences in the factory were political, despite efforts by the state to separate the "economics" of the factory from the "politics" of the state. The Cultural Revolution generation contested efforts by the state to refigure their bodies by retaining their memories of what it had previously meant to be a good worker: to maintain a consciousness of class and therefore of the ability to move on and off the shop floor without being positioned by managerial authority.

Their refusal of spatial disciplining was hardened by the sense I found among several of these women that they might have attained the status of intellectual had the Cultural Revolution not shut down all schools. Through their retrospective claim to the possibility, now lost, of that identity, these women refused the spatial authority of reform that placed them in the category of mere worker by forcing them to remain on the shop floor. This Cultural Revolution cohort thus maintained a recalcitrant presence in the factory. They shared in the abjection of other subaltern workers, but it was precisely their desire not to be made abject that led them to recall the historical meaning of their place in the factory. Members of the Cultural Revolution cohort were decidedly "unfeminine," at least within the allegory of postsocialism. Their talk was loud and tough, their manner rude. They did not offer up Asian fragility for consumption. No submissive behavior here.

A second site, one in which members of the oldest cohort tended to mark out their identity, appeared to me more marginal than the table, yet just as crucial. This was the dense and massive space of the spinning, twisting, and combining machines. For memories also resided in these machines and their alignment. The machines loomed a head taller than workers, so that prep workers disappeared among the rows of spindles. No central vantage point, no panopticon, existed from which to gaze on them. To see what they were up to, management had to walk up and down each and every row, a disciplined disciplining in which they rarely engaged. Older groups of workers gathered periodically amid the thick forest of machinery to rest and chat with one another. Their activities recalled previous practices: these older workers, as part of the so-called conservative faction of the Cultural Revolution, had taken refuge from and refused to participate in the ever more chaotic and vindictive political winds of revolution. They tied their identity to the memory of labor just after Liberation, when silk work was a skill displayed with pride, a skill that women worked hard to attain. These women countered efforts to turn their bodies into ever more efficient producers by insisting that they be recognized for the hard work they had already performed. Yu Shifu once remarked that the women of her mother's generation were in much better health than the women of her own, even though, as she implied, her mother's generation was often portrayed as more physically constrained by feudal gender ideology. This oldest cohort still retained the socialist state's discourse of labor as providing the essence of meaningful gender identity. In recrafting their identity through that discourse, these women marked the limit of post-Mao visions of modern order through an embodied memory of previous arrangements of space.

The final site of spatial subversions resided in the very sinews of the bodies of the youngest generation, in their gestures and movements around the shop floor. Many of these women, in their late teens and early twenties, were newly arrived from the countryside and had just begun to enter the factories in the previous year. Subject(ed) bodies, they nonetheless refused to remain spatially rooted in one place or to move in the prescribed circuits. In a steady stream, they visited one another, passing back and forth. Their bodily movements did not mimic new standards of rationality. They did not work quickly enough. They made mistakes in the tension of the thread. They did not look carefully to the left or to the right; they did not check, link, or make clear markings. They did not use their hands, eyes, and ears to inspect for quality. The quality of goods produced by this group was well below the standards of the other shifts in the prep shop. Their consciousness did not participate in production problems. They rarely concentrated. Few made a "rational" inspection of their spindles, and none followed the character for "bow" in her movements. After all, as management complained to me, these peasant women could barely read.

Shop managers characterized these women from the countryside as slow and dull-witted. Their comments were an ironic twist on the "nimble fingers, patience" so often ascribed to Asian women as transnational industries have relocated to Asia (see Ong 1987). Managers employed this latter representation of women workers in China as a technique of biopower, part of a reform discourse essentializing women's capabilities. But the "dull-witted and clumsy" peasant women displaced the managers' wish to fix women's bodies in a homogeneous space: they acknowledged their differences from city women while simultaneously continuing to move freely about the shop floor.

These various cohorts' momentary confrontations with post-Mao spatial discipline recall Michel de Certeau's discussion (1984) of poaching on the power of social space. De Certeau suggests that urban citizens poach on urban design by walking through cities in a manner not originally planned by the architects. The problem with his analytical schema, however, is it assumes a fully autonomous consciousness that stands apart from the exercise of spatial power. In contrast, these women workers are, in the moment of displacement, linked with power in the formation of their subjectivities.

ARCHITECTURAL HISTORY

Factories are the sensuous embodiment of productive power, producing both goods and subject positions. Their spatial relations not only provide the setting for disciplinary actions, but themselves form part of the same mode of power and authority. Yet through a seeming paradox, workers' abilities to challenge the reform disciplinary regime were fostered by the factory architecture (see map on pages 272–73).

The architectural paradox begins with the relationship between the offices and the shop floor. Each workshop—prep, weaving, and inspection—is housed in a separate building, each with its own shop office. But the workshop offices are virtually hidden from the shop floor. At Zhenfu, the office stands off to the side in the prep shop, a few floors above the shop floor in the weaving shop, and in a separate building in the case of the inspection shop. The main offices of the party secretary and factory director, in homologous fashion, are located in a separate building well apart from the workshops. Thick concrete walls effect a complete separation between the workshop offices and the shop floor. Office windows look out toward the other buildings but no windows peer into the shops. These offices served as spaces in which managers distanced themselves from the shop floor. The office, then, did not offer a site from which anything even approaching a panoptic gaze could emanate. Equally significant, workers could not observe managers in their exercise of power. They could only imagine their activities. Indeed, it appears that the effect of this spatial relation was not to prevent managers from scrutinizing workers but to keep workers from looking in at them.

This structure has its roots, I believe, in two cultural schemes, one reflecting a prerevolution metaphysics of display and the other developing from recent revolutionary history. These factories, built in the early 1950s, were designed to exemplify displays of hierarchy. Their resemblance to prerevolutionary architecture is striking, specifically to the imperial palace in Beijing, known as the Forbidden City. The Forbidden City's architectural logic, in turn, is echoed in the homes of the former gentry elite, in the dynastic tombs, and in the numerous local official residences known as *yamen*.[12] In nearly identical fashion, contemporary factories, the Forbidden City (now a museum), and old gentry homes are walled off from the rest of the city, though set within its midst, by thick brick walls more than high enough to discourage any outsider's gaze.[13] Each re-creates an entire universe unto itself. For state-run factories, this mimesis often meant a literal attempt to build a self-contained social world; the buildings included a dining hall, nursery, beauty salon, showers, and a small shop selling sundry goods. Workers received everything from food rations to permission to marry from their work units.

The main factory office building, known as the *changbu*, houses the highest level management. It sits, like the emperor's Inner Court, in the center of the factory grounds—well apart from the shop buildings where manual labor occurs. Within this two-story main office, party cadres have offices on the floor above technical managers. As a group, they reside apart from the shop supervisors and, of course, from workers. The shop buildings radiate outward from the *changbu* in linear fashion to the front, back, and to either side. Again, this layout mimics the Outer Audience halls of the Forbidden City and the successive courtyards of wealthier urban homes (Pruitt 1979).

The features of the Imperial Palace embodied the king's power to center the universe. Centering created the boundaries between inner/ outer and upper/lower (Zito 1997). That which was innermost (*nei*) equaled that which was uppermost (*shang*). The architectural design symbolically displayed and enacted imperial power. The display of hi- erarchy was itself a stratagem believed to be sufficiently powerful to impress the imperium's reign over the populace.[14] This cultural scheme was the one I found still embodied in Hangzhou's silk factories. Man- agers, it appeared to me, continued to rely on a metaphysics of display to discipline workers. Public discussion urging factories toward ever more efficient production tellingly focused on the "problem" of factory managers who always sat in their offices and never walked onto the shop floor (e.g., *Baokan Wenzhai*, 19 November 1985, p. 1). Their behavior, I would argue, did not simply demonstrate bureaucratic bumbling and laziness, as the media would have it. Just as important, it revealed chang- ing cultural logics of power—the move from hierarchizing metaphysics into a disciplinary regime.

The second cultural scheme informing factory architecture, which is overdetermined by the first, lies in the more recent history of the socialist revolution. The revolution was waged, after all, in the name of workers

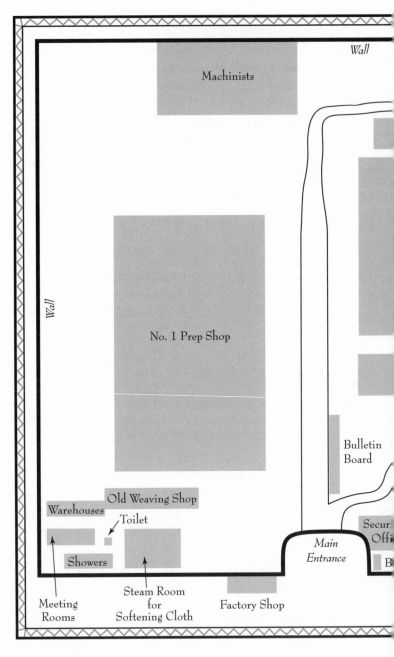

Zhenfu factory

ion Headquarters

Security
Office

Back Gate

Dining
Hall

Women's
Health
Office

No. 3 Weaving
Shop

Medical
Clinic

No. 1 Weaving Shop
and
No. 2 Prep Shop

Hotwater
Taps

Wall

No. 2
Weaving
Shop

dministration
Building

Administration
Building

Beauty
Salon

Transport
and
Warehouse

Inspection Shop

Inspection
Shop Office

Transport

Marketing

Wall

Gate

and peasants. The party-state therefore set about inscribing in space their mythologizing gestures toward the proletariat. Consequently, factory construction of the 1950s mimicked high socialist realism. Inspired by the Soviet example (and by Soviet aid), the state built workshops of massive concrete, with straight lines and a solid utilitarian look. They were modern paeans to proletarian lives.

Yet these factory spaces embodied a contradiction, for the workers did not run them. In the Maoist era, at least, a certain discomfort existed in any brazen display of power over workers. The office–shop floor arrangement enables managers to avoid the discomforting gaze of workers. Equally important, knowledge in the form of state directives, party documents, and personal dossiers (all tellingly referred to as "inside section," or *neibu*), resides in the offices. Those who have access to the knowledge contained in these documents have power because they can interpret the state's will to control the populace.[15] Managers therefore keep workers out of the offices and away from such knowledge.

It is striking, then, that during the Cultural Revolution, workers challenged hierarchical class relations by storming the offices and (after removing the managers) by reading and burning their personal dossiers. They had toppled the old hierarchy, if only for a brief moment. Yet that moment lives on in the memories of workers who have since resumed their place on the shop floor. Their daily displacements, both intentional and inadvertent, indicate that factory architecture, overdetermined by the hierarchy of display and by socialist realism, no longer suffices in itself to discipline workers. But these earlier cultural logics have not disappeared: they have been incorporated into the ongoing search for modernity. At Zhenfu, the local silk bureau financed a new six-story weaving shop at the start of 1985. It stood as a monument to the reformers' calls for higher productivity. The shop towered over the *changbu*, the main office building, directly opposite it. But Zhenfu's party secretary let me know that they planned to erect a new *changbu* that would equal the height of the weaving shop. The logic of display is alive and well in China's search for the modern.

Changing spatial relations, in conjunction with the numerous other practices I have charted in this book, exemplify the repeated disjunctures in culturally specific projects of modernity. The Chinese state aspires to enact a universal modernity—an achievement the West supports in one moment and claims to be impossible in the next. China's silk factories are living shrines to this aspiration. Global transactions fostered by the post-Mao state have placed China squarely within a transnational economy. The silk factory site, though shaped by nationalist ambitions, has become reterritorialized into a transnational landscape. Silk workers literally interweave "western" and "Chinese" desires and tastes into the silk commodities.

Yet the spatial reordering of post-Mao social life presents itself as neither a purely localized matter nor as a mere instantiation of a universal discourse called "modernity." These located—but not just local—practices find the path to modernity strewn with layers of culture, memory, and history. Past colonial exclusions from modernity—exclusions that Europe depended on for its own modern power—continue to have powerful effects in a transnational world. This afterlife of cultural difference signals the cultural mediations of China's deferred desires for a modern disciplinary regime. China's deeply felt need to overcome the "outside" of modernity opens up the imaginary quality of any such quest for modernity. As a phantasmatic project, post-Mao spatial design draws into its folds the specific cultural translations of scientific management. In this process, however, bodies are not turned into Taylorist machines or avatars of postmodern flexibility. Rather, scientific management in Hangzhou's silk factories implies a certain self-consciousness and a need for literacy that echoes both a recent Maoist discourse on consciousness and prerevolutionary beliefs in writing as performance. In architectural reform, a disciplinary regime overlaps and incorporates a metaphysics of display. The Foucauldian panopticon does not capture the relationship between disciplinary gazes and these microtechniques of power, for the search for the modern does not erase history. Managers' interpretations and workers' subversions coalesce in the interstices of specific cultural histories and transglobal borrowings.

These gaps occur in sites and through bodies that hold memories of past spatial relations. Because three cohorts of subalterns coexisted in the silk factories, working side by side, post-Mao modernity could not become a unified project producing a homogeneous form of subjectivity.

The contested memories of older cohorts' challenges to spatial authority and the excessive failures of young peasant women in bodily literacy cast open all the ambivalences, contradictions, and ironies that filled the post-Mao imaginary. The gendering of this terrain was thus fraught with the remnants of the past. To shape women workers' bodies into a disciplined form required layering meanings over other levels of meanings already inscribed in women's sinews, in their bodily performances.

To assert that the order of power in China does not replicate a universal teleology is not to exoticize China. Nor does my assertion place China in a world of essentialized oriental difference. To the contrary, by arguing for the specificities of modern imaginations, I hope to further the critique of the universalizing tendencies of Euro-American social theory. Rather than argue that China has arrived at an originary and singular modernity, I have followed an alternative strategy centered on an anthropology of "other" modernities. There is no singular transnational referent. Indeed, whatever might count as a modern episteme derives from the ways in which China and other formerly colonized countries interpret and enact modernity.

Coda

Since 1992, the "free markets" of capitalism have taken over the dream space of possibility in China. It is the space of global imaginations but it provokes different perspectives. Samuel Huntington (1996), for example, adopts a neo-Weberian point of view but with a lingering cold war twist. He darkly warns Americans to beware of "Confucian culture" and its power to become the dominant force in the new world order. Huntington views Confucian culture neither as a recent reinvention, a dominant ideology, nor a syncretic field of competing interpretations. Rather in the manner of a colonial official, Huntington portrays Confucian culture as ahistorical, essential, enduring. But unlike writers of that earlier colonial period, Huntington speaks to an American audience anxious about the waning ascendancy of the United States. His talk of Confucian culture is intended not merely to reassure American leaders about the goodness and rightness of their world domination but to goad them into viewing China as a world threat. Such racist deployments of "culture" remind anthropologists that culture is a terrain worth fighting over.

In China, capitalists and government leaders invoke "Confucian culture" and "Chinese culture" interchangeably to explain their successes in the pursuit of wealth. Whether these powerful people use these concepts instrumentally or embrace them with conviction, the notion of a culture that has the strength to shape the future is an enticing one. It resonates among a populace eager to step over the ruins of socialism.

From this perspective, "Chinese culture" provides a framework for cultural negotiations. Talk of Chinese culture generates excitement about new possibilities and feeds a nationalist desire to move beyond the humiliations of the semicolonial past. It leads people to believe in the rightness and goodness of new forms of domination. Since the Tiananmen demonstrations of 1989, the Chinese state has fostered a turn away from politics. Any activities that might result in a strong nongovernmental organization have been banned. State-encouraged cultural nationalism fills the resultant void.

A third perspective emerges among those who have developed trenchant and vital critiques of global capitalism (see Dirlik 1994; Harvey 1989; Pred and Watts 1992). Here the notion prevails that worldly capitalists have no cultural commitments.[1] These critiques describe a global phenomenon that is transparent in its goals as if it follows the rational dictates of the pursuit of profit. "Culture" in this view is merely another tool of rationality, or it is the stuff of "local" places that serves as perhaps a weak source of resistance. While Huntington localizes and fixes culture, these critics of the left globalize and erase culture. Ironically, in doing so they agree with capitalists themselves. Global capitalism, from this perspective, homogenizes the world without even the complication of a dialectical struggle.[2] Such theories make it difficult to understand exactly how people get caught up in these fantasies. That they are so widely accepted indicates the need to renew hope in cultural struggles.

As against these notions, I have shown the imaginative dimensions of modernity that infuse postsocialist projects. I have argued that an anthropology of modernity must maneuver between the twin dangers of universalizing and of creating separate, holistic cultures. Each of these tendencies derives from colonial anthropology's attempts to relativize cultures, without attending to the relations of power that conjoin them. Although those in China and elsewhere are not the originating authors of these narratives, though they have been forced to transform themselves in the name of modernity and to adjust to its dominant meanings, their enactments of modernity are by no means merely simulacra of a supposedly pristine form developed in the West.

Instead, I have proposed an anthropology of intersecting global imaginations. The national, regional, and transnational imaginaries of modernity provide frameworks for cultural negotiations in which power relations, gender and cohort identities, and subaltern politics are formulated. I have emphasized this process from heterogeneous subaltern perspectives. Such perspectives illuminate the ways state power is both enacted and challenged. Over time, the state has generated multiple imaginaries of modernity; the conflicts between forgetting and remembering provide salient sites for highlighting the marks of exclusion and the disjunctures that punctuate these deferred aspirations. We have seen how three cohorts of women workers have become subalterns through discursive spaces created by the dreams of socialism, the hopes of ongoing revolution, the politics of memory, international dialogues about feminism, and the aftermath of postsocialism and its new conceptions of nature. These heterogeneous cohorts both embraced state power and maneuvered around it as they pointed to the epistemic violence with which it was administered. By bringing their distinctive cohort agendas to bear on postsocialist imaginings of modernity, women workers confounded the naturalization of power in the name of modernity.

Members of the oldest cohort searched out opportunities within the state's socialist framework of "labor" to create heroic identities not entangled with femininity. Their gendered transgressions ultimately furthered state power, but they also inspired creative performances that exceeded the state's mandates. The Cultural Revolution cohort learned a politics of authority that directly challenged state cadres even as it required an engagement with their power. Both of these cohorts passionately crafted a politics of memory that continued their intimate entanglement with the state. Those in the youngest cohort sought exciting new horizons in postsocialist discussions of nature, feminine bodies, and sexuality. They found the state irrelevant as the source of confirmation for their desires, even as official discourses were directly involved in creating such desires. Each of these cohorts' different identities and relationships to power were formed within overlapping projects of modernity. Each found the others' conception of the world perplexing, sometimes irritating, and occasionally a stumbling block to fulfilling their own. Together, the ways they contended with their subalternity reveal the implicit imaginary quality of modernity and the heterogeneity of power enacted in its name. Through their lives, I have explored how modernity is always a relational signifier whose meanings are contested precisely because the stakes are so high: positions and claims to power and resources in an unequal world.

Feminism has proved to be one of those stakes. China's socialist discourse on women's liberation spoke to a long history of colonial interpretations about Chinese women's oppression. I have shown how U.S. feminists, including myself, took up these matters in a different vein, with the hope of learning from the lives of Chinese women under the socialist regime. Yet our conclusions—that women had not been liberated—inadvertently echoed those reached using earlier interpretive frameworks. In my anthropological fieldwork, I tried to reconsider these matters by taking seriously the insistence of a particular group of women that they had been liberated by the socialist revolution. I argued that liberation had a culturally specific meaning for them; it liberated them not to labor—for they already worked in silk factories—but from a world of sociospatial conceptions of gender. I hope that I have extended these feminist dialogues, for I, like many feminists currently writing in the United States and in China, continue to believe in the possibility of cross-cultural alliances.

Fostering an awareness of global interconnections in conjunction with cultural specificity remains an urgent task. Women's lives in China continue to be the stuff of transnational policy, which is often not informed by feminism. Christian fundamentalists in the United States have been successful in using China's birth policy both to frame American foreign policy and to strengthen a paternalistic state at home. In this kind of world, it is impossible to imagine gender alternatives as if they existed in discrete local cultures. Yet some of the recent work in feminist anthropology on new reproductive technologies, along with their rich insights about nature, power, and kinship, retain this problematic approach: the authors have turned from the study of the other to the study of the West, while maintaining a gulf between the two.[3] In contrast, I have focused on the complexity of cultural production within a transnational world. At the same time, my emphasis on subalternity is meant to highlight positioned knowledges and unexpected challenges to domination.

The experiences of modernity must be seen, then, in their specificity around the globe. Because modernity also derives its power by operating through marks of exclusion, catachreses—paradoxes in the narrations of the nation-state's history—haunt the various strivings for modernity. They are created not by an opposition to modernity but rather, in China, by cultural mediations of various projects of science and management carried out in the name of modernity. Invoking reason, rationality, industrialization, biopower, and the rest are but the first step; discerning how these practices manifest themselves in the specific local/global configurations that inform modernity should be our goal. Only in this way, I believe, can we begin to capture the "other" modernities that have always existed. This anthropological approach to modernity insists on its culturally and historically variable meaning, as those meanings are produced within relations of power. Such an insistence does not naively endorse cultural relativism. Indeed, we must move beyond analyses that privilege discrete cultural modernities—the French modern, the Brazilian modern, and so on—to a more complex specification of practices that neither simply reflect a universal instantiation nor are culturally autonomous.

As we approach the millennium, the allegory of postsocialism has only grown stronger. A conception now prevalent in China—that free-market success requires a hypermasculinity—has found support in a global imagination about the need to rescue, restore, and reinvigorate masculinity.[4] But again, this space of global imaginings provokes different perspectives. From one perspective white men are threatened by Asian men, who take over both white women and the reins of capitalism. Such is the tale of Michael Crichton's orientalist novel *The Rising Sun* (1992),[5] which has been turned into a popular movie. The story counterposes Japanese and American cultures as two separate nations/races, presenting their ways of doing business as unalterably opposed and mutually hostile. One way must, in masculine fashion, conquer the other. The story unfolds in Los Angeles. A white woman has been found dead at a party of Japanese businessmen. The intrigues that follow as a white detective tries to unravel the mystery include "Japanese" business dealings that, by definition, are unsavory but also inscrutable; white businessmen, politicians, and journalists who have sold out their race, country, and manhood by surreptitiously working for Japanese companies; and business contracts whose resolution rest on competition over the woman. In the end, it is immaterial who killed the woman, as the ultimate responsibility lies with Japanese men who have conquered America. Here one finds a telling erasure of Asian and Asian American women and of the importance of their labor to the success of American companies.

One could put in dialogue with this orientalism another popular novel, one written in China by Cao Guilin, called *Beijinger in New York* (1993); it has also been filmed, as a television melodrama viewed in both China and the United States. It, too, tells of the inextricable links between masculinity and transnational capitalism. But from this perspective, the Asian man talks back to the white man: he has the chance to become a success and beat the white man at his own game—this time over the body of a Chinese woman. The story tells of a young man from mainland China, Wang Qiming, who decides to go to America with his wife. Though he had been a musician, racism leaves him little choice of work in New York except being a waiter in a Chinese restaurant. The owner of the restaurant where he finds a job is a Taiwanese woman who has adopted some of the forcefulness and independence of a western woman. She takes a personal interest in the protagonist, but at first he refuses her aggressive advances, remaining with his more traditional wife, Gao Yan. He then begins to think of ways he might succeed in America. His wife works in a garment sweatshop and, together, they begin selling knitwear made from his original designs. In dire financial straits, however, Wang loses his wife to the white American, McCarthy, who owns the garment factory where she works. In scheming both his success and his revenge, Wang takes up with his Taiwanese boss and together they become wealthy enough to buy out the sweatshop owner. Their success is also partially due to Gao Yan, who, out of guilt, reveals the business clientele of her American husband to Wang. In the end,

Wang and McCarthy come to respect one another as worthy competitors who can resolve their differences about race and masculinity in the marketplace.[6]

Such tales alert us to the cultural and political imaginings that permeate transnational capitalism. They are not merely the aftereffects of economic activities; indeed, they provide men around the world with some of the impetus to pursue wealth. In addressing this new world order, then, we might do well to keep in mind the ironies of masculinity as set forth in another fable. In *The Ship of Fools* (1989), a postmodern novel about exile, gender, and writing, Cristina Peri Rossi tells of X, the new man. He is sweet and androgynous and tries to please women. Near the end of the novel, he tells a woman he has met about his recurrent dream. An old king in love with his daughter poses a riddle for her suitors: What is the greatest tribute and homage a man can give to the woman he loves? Suitor after suitor fails to find the right answer; each is beheaded. X explains that in the dream he feels bewildered. Perhaps the question is a trap and he should do nothing. But now, having met the woman to whom he tells the dream, he knows he has finally found the answer and that it has been in him for some time. That night, X again has the same dream. But this time, when the old king asks him the question, he shouts out the answer: virility. Thunder is heard, the earth opens, beasts take refuge in the hills. The old king shrinks into the mud and dies with a whimper.

As I write this conclusion in 1997, I sit in Beijing. While issues of masculinity set the dominant tone for the future, debates abound in China about money, sex, and power. The diversity of identities and politics belies any simple characterization of postsocialism. One feminist I know who wants to protect women from sexual objectification lauds the values of Confucian paternalism. A young woman who tells me she revels in the freedom to have numerous lovers approves of the social order provided by an authoritarian state. Some of the most enthusiastic discussions I have witnessed about the intricacies of making money are held among former Cultural Revolution youths. Avant-garde filmmakers are fascinated with the possibilities that a gay sexuality offers for challenging the official regime. Gay men mock the masculinity of the market while carving out new paths toward a transnational gay imaginary. Liu Nianchun, the well-known labor activist, and Liu Xiaobo, the democracy activist, have been sent back to prison for refusing to remain silent about politics. The debates alert us to the heterogeneity of cultural imaginings. Within such unpredictable cultural politics, forgetting and remembering the past continue to play a critical role in creating a vision of the future, full of unexpected possibilities.

Notes

1. The "Four Modernizations" refer to the modernization of the military, science and technology, industry, and agriculture.

2. I use "imaginary" to suggestively combine Anderson's "imagined communities" (1992), Appadurai's "social imaginaries" (1996), and Lacan's psychoanalytic "imaginary" (J. Mitchell and Rose 1985). Anderson underscores how a collectivity's imagination about its collective self takes hold, Appadurai emphasizes aspirations that make social groups and individual subjects look outside of themselves, and Lacan describes the constant precariousness of human subjectivity that makes the cohesive unity of the subject a fantasy. For Lacan, the imaginary involves a phantasmatic identity because the subject has its identity only in the mirror of the gaze, desires, and language of others, which guarantees its reality but also displaces and refracts it. An inherent instability results from this radical split. Bringing these three usages together allows me to emphasize the powerful hold of modernity, its phantasmic qualities, its displaced desires, and its necessarily dialogical constitution.

3. The term "subaltern," derived from Gramsci's writings attempting to expand Marxist analysis into the realm of culture and civil society, has been most thoroughly theorized by the *Subaltern Studies* collective. Mainly historians, they have combined Marxism and poststructuralism to analyze the discursive traces of subalternity that a motivated historian excavates in the archives. They aim to contest colonial and nationalist histories of India, as well as a reductive Marxism that makes modes of production the agent of history. At this point the literature is voluminous. See, for example, Chakrabarty 1992; Guha and Spivak 1988; Prakash 1990, 1992, 1994; Spivak 1988. These works have influenced my own, particularly in their attention to the way representation mediates what will count as

subaltern experience. In making this theory travel, I heed Gail Hershatter's cogent warning (1997) that the specificity of subalternity in China, including its multiple layerings, necessitates a recognition that the socialist state has blatantly displayed subalterns and brought them to voice. My use of the term reflects this recognition but also signals a challenge to the socialist state's closure on experience. See my discussion later in this chapter.

4.   I am grateful to Angela Zito for suggesting this point. Susan Harding (1987) has inspired many of us to think about the importance of narrative strategies in "convicting" people of their beliefs. Harding focuses on fundamentalist religious beliefs; I borrow from her and move her ideas directly into the realms of the political and the economic.

5.   The distinctive commentaries of these women on post-Mao economic reform also taught me the importance of challenging the assumption that they move through the same life cycle trajectory or experience Chinese politics in the same way. Scholars of China have distinguished in a broad sense between urban and rural Chinese women and between Han and non-Han. But within those respective categories, they assume a homogeneity of subjectivity determined by gender. My emphasis on cohorts formed by political movements is meant to further highlight the nonessential nature of gender differentiation. In this, I join other feminist ethnographers whose recent writings on gender, difference, and culture enlarge an earlier feminist focus on male-female difference that assumed a unity of interests and experiences among women, both within cultures and sometimes across them. See Abu-Lughod 1993; Behar and Gordon 1995; Kondo 1997; Tsing 1993; Visweswaran 1994; Yanagisako and Delaney 1995.

6.   The recent explosion of writing on the anthropology of modernity includes Appadurai 1996; Escobar 1995; Faubion 1993; Holston 1989; Horn 1994; Ivy 1995; Marcus 1992; Ong 1997; Rabinow 1989; Yang 1994. In the wider fields of cultural studies and poststructuralist theory, the list is too large to cite in full. Influential examples include Berman 1988; Foucault 1979, 1980; Habermas 1987; Harvey 1989; Jameson 1991.

7.   It is not my purpose here to delve into the philosophical debates often labeled "Foucault versus Habermas." That disagreement rests on their different assessments of modernity's potential. Habermas (1987) argues that modernity still has liberating and democratic potential, despite its often degrading effects. Most recently he finds that potential in the public sphere. He implicitly assumes that democratic subjects can operate outside of dynamics of power. Foucault criticizes modernity for its peculiarly effective means of domination, weaving power through our very bodies and subjectivity. Although these differences are consequential and I certainly find myself inspired by many of Foucault's insights, I would also underscore that these positions also share certain fundamental assumptions about the "finished" quality of modernity.

8.   For a wonderfully lucid discussion on this point, see W. Brown 1995.

9.   One might note that Foucault addressed himself specifically to the cultural history of Europe. His work, however, has been read as a description of a more general episteme. Gayatri Spivak (1988) has criticized him from another angle, arguing that he presents a self-contained history about the West that ignores, as I also argue here, the necessary imbrications within a wider imperial field. See also Ann Stoler's forceful argument (1995) that successfully extends Foucault's insights about modernity, bourgeois subjectivity, and race into the colonial relationships between Europe and its colonies.

10.   This approach to modernity retains the colonial story of historical stages. See Appadurai 1996, which traces the frustrated aspirations of modernizers to, as he puts it, "synchronize their historical watches" (p. 2). Appadurai prefers the term "alternative modernities," arguing that globalization does not homogenize cultural imaginations.

11.   To clarify matters further, I distinguish my approach to modernity from several other trenchant studies. Paul Rabinow (1989), for example, scrupulously follows Foucault. He assumes the universality of Foucault's version of modernity and the homogeneity of its effects, while ignoring the larger (neo)colonial world and relations of marginalization that might indicate dissident interpretations. In contrast, I argue that modernity at its heart is about cultural difference. Differently located groups of people engage their culturally specific imaginations in conjunction with globally produced cultural differences. Appadurai (1996) develops a transnational version of modernity that highlights certain experiences, especially mass media and diaspora, over others. Appadurai's version has the advantage of indicating a positioned viewpoint—that of the diasporic third world intellectual who, in the past, has felt an imaginative investment in the concept of nationalism. (I am grateful to Anna Tsing for this insight.) Yet despite his explicit statement that globalization does not mean cultural homogeneity, Appadurai's emphasis on ethnoscapes of mass media and diaspora and his idea that imagination has just recently entered ordinary life unwittingly tend to point in that direction. We need instead to leave room for whatever kinds of experiences under the rubric of modernity might be relevant in any given historical context. Ivy's beautifully wrought study (1995) of the phantasms of the modern, national imaginary in Japan tends nonetheless toward an abstract notion of the imaginary that eviscerates any specific history of how "Japan" became and continues to be a meaningful category. Her lack of engagement with the constitution of specific differences that inhabit Japan risks being criticized as a manifestation of the very cultural universalisms she intends to evade.

12.   My argument about modernity resonates with what Lydia Liu (1995) has called "translated modernity," a phrase she uses to indicate that the crosscultural terms of modernity are contingent on a politics of translated knowledge that belies the presumed equivalence of terms. Aihwa Ong (1997) describes modernity as "an evolving process of imagination and practice in particular histor-

ically situated formations" (p. 171). For Ong, distinctive modern practices arise in relation to imagined communities of nation-states and imaginaries of transnational capitalism. These, according to Ong, are metanarratives that operate as knowledge-power systems. My approach differs to the extent that I stress the disjunctures and instabilities one finds in the rhetorical strategies of modern imaginaries.

13.   Moreover, one could make the mistake of assuming these stories follow a western bourgeois mode of life histories that emphasizes the development of the individual. See Gagnier 1991.

14.   It remains to be seen whether or in what fashion the emergence of bourgeois subjects will transform the mode of crafting stories about social life.

15.   James Clifford beautifully renders this point in *The Predicament of Culture* (1988).

16.   Jean Comaroff and John Comaroff (1993) have made this argument, writing that modernity is a malleable sign, attracting different referents and values.

17.   I owe the following to Anna Tsing's insightful critique of an earlier version of this introduction.

18.   For African countries to prove their modernity, they must demonstrate that they can live an ordered, "civilized" life (Comaroff and Comaroff 1991; Shaw 1995). Thus one finds colonial ethnographies that demonstrate support for African peoples by demonstrating the rational and governed nature of their seemingly nonordered, superstitious lives. See, for example, the writings of E. E. Evans-Pritchard, Edward Leach, and Raymond Firth.

19.   Donna Haraway (1997) reminds us, however, that Latour's focus on the startling hybridities lying between nature and culture, while significant, needs to be supplemented with the more consequential questions of for whom and how these hybrids work.

20.   Latour points out that the paradoxical interrelation of these purified realms forces us to see how they serve as counterweights to one another. If nature were not at all made by human beings, its transcendence would make it inaccessible. If society were only the form and matter of human beings, its immanence would destroy it.

21.   In very distinct ways, Lydia Liu's notion of "translated" modernity (1995), Brackette Williams's argument that hybridity, rather than the solution to purified races, coexists with the latter (1995), and Donna Haraway's cyborgs (1985) are exemplary of the networks of mediation to which Latour refers.

22.   In accepting uncritically the division between tradition and modernity, Latour ironically reproduces the very modernist project he eschews. See Appadurai 1996 for a cogent discussion of this point.

23.   As Talal Asad (1993) does beautifully in the realm of religion.

24.   This argument about modernity rehearses a more general rejection of hu-

manist pretensions to universal subjectivity. Those marginalized and excluded from the center have highlighted how their historically produced alterity is itself constitutive of that center. Such critique forms the basis of postcolonial and minority discourse scholarship.

25.   See Frankenberg and Mani 1993; McClintock 1995; Shohat 1992.

26.   I borrow Elizabeth Perry's sense of "proletarian power" (1995), along with her emphasis on how the struggles of the Cultural Revolution were, in part, about the meaning of this term.

27.   Sylvia Yanagisako (1997) has made a compelling critique of the common assumption of a Parsonian model, which holds that discourses of sexuality are only about sexuality and discourses of gender are only about gender.

28.   It should be obvious that I do not assume any essential relationship between female and male bodies and the meanings of femininity and masculinity. These meanings are created through social relations and institutions (Butler 1993; Strathern 1988).

29.   For this reason, I differentiate my study from the critique of Enlightenment phallogocentrism offered in French feminist theory. While recognizing the centrality of sexual difference at the heart of European modernity, this body of theory has inadvertently universalized a particular formation of gender in European bourgeois subjectivity while ignoring the multiplicities of race, class, and culture in that formation. Ann Stoler (1995) has made an important contribution to this discussion with her critique of Foucault's *History of Sexuality*, placing that work on European bourgeois sexuality in a wider colonial theater. She argues that the bourgeois self in Europe was shaped through contrasts forged in the history of empire.

30.   Lata Mani's brilliant work (1987) initially opened up this line of inquiry for many of us.

31.   Meng Yue and Dai Jinhua, prominent Chinese feminists, argue (1990) that women's true history had been obscured by the overweening singularity of the socialist version of women's liberation.

32.   I distinguish these cohorts from biological or social generations, which are often studied by marking decades by age (e.g., 20- to 29-year-olds) or by years (e.g., 1950 to 1960). My concern is with those who found their inspiration, desires, and discontents most fully formed within specific political moments that do not map isomorphically onto discrete decades. They are loosely but not necessarily of similar ages.

33.   "Liberation" was the term commonly used under Maoism to refer to the 1949 revolution.

34.   Some scholars of Chinese history would date modernity in China back to the sixteenth-century Ming dynasty to emphasize the importance of China's internal history (Spence 1990). Others would begin in the nineteenth century, with

China's response to the territorial onslaught of Western imperialism (Hsu 1990). Still others emphasize the early-twentieth-century efforts at nation building (Du-ara 1995). Finally, there are those who would insist on the 1949 socialist revolution as the key turning point of the state's full penetration in the governmentality of everyday life (Yang 1988). Each of these periodizations highlights the ideological interests invested in the term modernity.

35.   Nicholas Dirks's suggestive argument (1992) that the concept of culture was invented with colonialism resonates here.

36.   Hence the numerous discussions in sinology about why China failed to modernize until the West touched it. Answers are sought in the feudal organization of social and economic life, which is said to have stultified change. Arguments against this view have tried to prove that family and lineage in China did not necessarily stymie mobility or initiative.

37.   Ironically, this context continues to reecho today as intellectuals attempt to recapture the spirit of those early cultural movements, now to challenge socialism.

38.   See, e.g., Gilmartin 1995; Spence 1990; their analyses, however, are different from mine. I am reading against the grain of their descriptions.

39.   Hans van de Ven argues that an incongruity exists between communism and nationalism. Although communist regimes claim to be the inevitable and worthy outcomes of national pasts, communist states also portray national pasts as riddled with shameful episodes to be overcome. Overcoming them becomes part of the national essence: "For communists, the dark pages of history remained in the present: the enemy within had to be fought, and bad habits broken" (1995:xx).

40.   Official discourse perseveres in invoking socialism as its governing signifier, even as the state has made capitalism the preeminent means to wealth and power. It is not difficult to argue, however, that especially since the massacres of Tiananmen, China has become a postsocialist country, insofar as "socialism" has been evacuated of any meaningful referent other than the power of the party-state.

41.   To reiterate, the popular approach assumes an always already existent, innate gender arrangement that exists prior to and outside of history and culture, whereas a more critical analysis views gender as always a contingent, socially produced result.

42.   The General Agreement on Tariffs and Trades signals the global shift to a free-market economy. Gordon White (1993) has pointed out that this new emphasis in development economics is a turn away from an earlier insistence on the active intervention of what he calls "development states," which were similar to socialist state economies.

43.   For an incisive critique of leftists' political constitution of knowledge about capitalism, see Gibson-Graham 1996.

44.   See Alexander and Mohanty 1997; Behar and Gordon 1995; Boddy 1989; Kondo 1990, 1997; Tsing 1993; Visweswaran 1994.

CHAPTER 1. LIBERATION STORIES

1.   Numerous recent ethnographies and cultural critiques have addressed this question. The by now classic statement is Clifford and Marcus 1986. See also Behar and Gordon 1995; Clifford 1988; Geertz 1988; Kondo 1990; Rosaldo 1989; Tsing 1993; Visweswaran 1994.

2.   Chiang Kai-shek was the leader of the Guomindang who, with aid from the United States, set up a regime in Taiwan after his defeat by the Chinese Communist Party.

3.   Here I build on Said's critique (1985) of the methodological assumptions in writings about world history that, he argues, assimilate nonsynchronous developments, histories, and cultures to an all-encompassing world historical scheme. Thus an anti-imperialist ideological position in such writings can nonetheless incorporate orientalism. He traces this problematic to the epistemological foundations of historicism that inform the works of Hegel, Marx, and other major philosophers of history. One can find intimations of this problematic in current theories of global capitalism as well.

4.   For the most thoroughly researched of such writings, see Croll 1978 and Davin 1976. These texts, especially Davin's, also weighed the structural and ideological constraints holding Chinese women back from full liberation, even after the socialist revolution. But the optimistic tenor of these and other books was taken up and extended by those of us searching for a universal answer to women's oppression.

5.   For the most influential examples of this argument, see Andors 1983; Johnson 1983; Stacey 1983; Wolf 1985.

6.   See Rey Chow's insightful critique (1995) of Fanon.

7.   I am grateful to the students in my "Feminist Anthropology" class for astutely pointing this out to me.

8.   American scholars often warn about the Chinese government controlling research by showing foreigners only "model" thises and thats—model day-care centers, model factories, model households. They assume that they could find an unmediated voice in China, if only they were given sufficient freedom. By the mid-1980s, the only models on display were walking the fashion runway. But in this case most American scholars were more amused than irritated.

9.   My thinking on the cultural construction of femininity in relation to space has been inspired by Joan Scott (1988c) and Sylvia Yanagisako (1987).

10.   In making this analysis, I eschew ahistorical cultural explanations of "oriental cultures" as "shame cultures." These women's shame was produced out

of a historically specific, gendered configuration of social space that should not be taken as an essential trait of "Chinese culture." Indeed, the socialist revolution's ability to substantially transform the meanings of inside/outside alerts us to the variability of all cultural categories.

11.   Theodore Huters (1996) argues that the recognition that China had been feminized by the West was implicit in scholarly discussions of how China represented the inside, domestic, personal and the West represented the outside, the public.

12.   The importance of inside/outside for defining women's social virtue could be seen as related to analyses of social respectability in terms of social "face" (Kipnis 1995). Lydia Liu (1995) and James Hevia (1995), however, have traced the orientalist preoccupations with "face" by Westerners who use the concept to define an overarching Chinese national/racial character and then authorize their own imperialism. Liu takes this analysis a step further by examining what happened with "translingual practice" when Chinese intellectuals translated orientalist concepts back into Chinese and thus ruptured the original interpretation. Angela Zito (1994) takes a different approach to analyzing the importance of bodily surface for social relationships in prerevolution China, offering a subtle interpretation of Chinese social boundaries of the skin in the eighteenth century.

13.   Footbinding became, in colonial discourse, the epitome of China's backwardness and inability to reach modernity. It thus became symbolic of what the Communist Party needed to overcome in order to reach the same national autonomy as that enjoyed by western imperialists (Zito 1992).

14.   Shaoxing is a small city just south of Hangzhou, famous for its wine and for being the home of one of China's best-known modern writers, Lu Xun.

15.   For interesting analyses that focus instead on the cultural construction of masculinity in relation to space, see Bourdieu 1997; Limón 1994; Rouse 1992.

16.   I should stress that although men dominated women, they did so within this cultural logic rather than by wielding it instrumentally, outside of it.

17.   "Decisions of the Central Committee of the Chinese Communist Party on Woman-Work at Present in the Countryside of the Liberated Areas" (1948), quoted in Davin 1976:201-3.

18.   Strathern (1988) makes a similar argument about the "dividuality" of women in Melanesia who do not always speak or act *as* women. My argument here takes issue with revisionist analyses developed in the post-Mao era, which contend that socialism masculinized women and erased sexual difference. Not only do these points contradict one another, but they both rely on essentialized notions of gender. See M. Yang 1998a for a complex discussion of this position. See chapter 7 for a further elaboration of my critique.

19.   This was a question of liberating women not from male dominance, but from parental authority.

CHAPTER 2. THE POETICS OF PRODUCTIVITY

1. Economic reform had first begun in the countryside in the late 1970s, as communes were broken up and production devolved to the level of the household. See Kelliher 1992; Siu 1989.

2. Jianying Zha (1992) offers an insightful analysis of the dilemmas intellectuals face in relation to the commodification of literature, writing, storytelling, and other cultural productions.

3. Anderson's rethinking (1991) was stimulated by reading Ernest Renan's essay "What Is a Nation?" which had been recently republished (1990).

4. This has parallels with Derrida's discussion (1994) of the specters of Marx haunting Europe.

5. In *The House of Lim*, Margery Wolf writes, "If the guest hall can be considered the symbol of the larger family, the stove is the symbol of the living family. Members of a family are defined as those who share a cooking stove; the colloquial term for the act of family division is literally 'the dividing of the stove.' This identification of stove and family is so important that those who cannot afford to add a room to house the stove of a newly created family unit build a second stove in the same kitchen" (1968:28).

6. The wage system during the Cultural Revolution was actually much more complex. Those who entered the factory during those years received the same wages regardless of task, but those who were already in the factory had their wages frozen at the then-current hierarchical levels.

7. In 1986 weavers earned around ¥100 per month. At that time, they had to save their full salary for five months to buy a bicycle; in terms of food, ¥5 could buy a little over one pound of fish or several pounds of fruit. Five yuan also paid for one month's rent.

8. In this sense, even the oppositional politics of humanism popular among intellectuals share a cultural space with state practices of individuating workers, since both are intended to create a post-Mao nation-state.

9. This preoccupation with the positive qualities of youth recalls the May Fourth Movement—a period, not coincidentally, that inspired many of the current older party leaders (T. Chow 1960).

10. I am grateful to Ann Anagnost for suggesting this point to me.

11. In state-run units, one can only leave the job with the permission of the unit's leaders—unless, that is, one is willing to risk abandoning the state's social security and benefits system. Most women looked for work in other state-run units, which had their own mappings of gender and work.

12. I draw inspiration here from those who have furthered this critique, such as Joan Scott (1988a) and Aihwa Ong (1987, 1991), and also from scholars writing cultural studies of science, who do not deny the reality of scientific objects but

see them nonetheless as constructed through cultural practices. See Haraway 1991; Latour 1993.

13.   For other studies of the historical and cultural variations in the meaning of work and labor, see Gamst 1995; Joyce 1987; Leitch 1996; Miller 1997; Povinelli 1993; Roediger 1991; Joan Scott 1988a.

CHAPTER 3. SOCIALIST NOSTALGIA

1.   Anthropological writings in this vein that have inspired my own include D. Scott's critique (1994) of the anthropology of religion in his study of Sinhalese religious discourses; Steedly's reexamination (1993) of colonial histories; K. Stewart's evocative ethnography (1996) of an "other" America in "Appalachia"; and Taussig's brilliant challenge (1987) to conventional studies of world histories of capitalism.

2.   For an inspiring literary analysis of this nostalgia, which emphasizes its commodification, see Dai 1996, 1997.

3.   A nostalgia for socialism similar to the one I describe, though tellingly not wedded to a particular time or place, can be found in Ahmad 1992.

4.   See Anagnost 1992 for an insightful discussion of speaking bitterness that questions conventional fieldwork assumptions about finding a popular voice in China unmediated by official discourses. My emphasis differs from Anagnost's insofar as I am extending the form of speaking bitterness from the 1950s, the period with which it is conventionally associated, into the contemporary moment.

5.   Hinton's notes were confiscated by the FBI when he returned to the United States. Only after twelve years of legal battles did they give them back—hence the late date of his publication.

6.   It seems probable that the Communist Party did not invent this form of speaking one's grievances but rather adapted an existing local form to political purposes.

7.   One ironic fallout of workers learning to speak bitterness in Hangzhou, as Yu Shifu's description makes clear, is that they quickly turned this tool against the state in the early 1950s, when they protested against the government's continuing support for their previous capitalist bosses. They also protested that the new state was not stabilizing and sufficiently improving the material conditions of their lives. Local officials in Hangzhou told workers they were speaking their complaints inappropriately.

8.   Rey Chow (1991a) has traced a related aesthetic formation of national culture in the literature of the 1920s and 1930s, prior to the communist revolution.

There, the conception of national culture took the form of a literary preoccupation with various figures that connoted powerlessness.

9.   It might be useful to remember that feminist consciousness-raising was explicitly inspired by and styled after Chinese speaking bitterness as it was then understood in the United States.

10.   Cf. Faye Ginsburg's insightful analysis (1989) of life stories among anti-abortion activists and their importance in moving others to take up political action.

11.   This term is derived from a story of the same name, one of the first in this genre, by Lu Xinhua (translated in Barme and Lee 1979).

12.   See Barlow 1991 for a provocative genealogy of the constitution of "intellectual" as a state category under socialism.

13.   As I have been arguing here, narrative performances of speaking bitterness turn people into subjects of the socialist state. The real break that the post-Mao generation has made is not simply in refusing to make socialist politics a matter of their concern but in refusing to narrate their lives within the limits of this genre. Their discussions of pleasure, desire, and sexuality are far removed from tales of suffering.

14.   I thank both Kathleen Biddick and Stephen Collier for insightful discussions of Spivak on this point.

INTERLUDE

1.   Lisa Yoneyama (1994) deftly argues, in regard to memories of the war and atom bomb in Hiroshima, that one must question even the most accepted notions of life and death as well as categories of emotion to discern how they are shaped by the production of discourses on Hiroshima.

2.   Against the background of another socialist milieu, Milan Kundera (1985) wrote of the "unbearable lightness of being" induced by efforts to forget the past while at the same time the burden of that past continues to carry significance. Edward Casey (1987:307–15) carries this insight further in his explication of Nietzsche's notion of "active forgetfulness." Nietzsche stressed the virtues of willed forgetting as the counterpart of the enforced remembering he detected in societies to ensure rigid conformity, and Casey uses Nietzsche as a counterpoint to Casey's own phenomenological study of memory. He assumes a universal need to bring memory back to our active consideration as residing at the heart of most human experience. But Casey's phenomenology remains on the level of the individual consciousness; he does not consider the culture and politics of memory tied to various forms of power.

CHAPTER 4. SHE

1.   The issues of confidentiality have also shifted for me in the interim. She will have long retired from Zhenfu by now, and Zhenfu's leaders can thus no longer touch her in any meaningful way. The enormous transitions in China since this incident have also attenuated the power of those in the state-run sector of the economy. While Zhenfu's cadres may take issue with my portrayal of them, I have waited long enough that I believe she will not suffer the consequences.

CHAPTER 5. THE POLITICS OF AUTHORITY

1.   For critiques of theories of resistance, see Abu-Lughod 1990; T. Mitchell 1990; Starn 1995.
2.   Katherine Verdery (1996) explains such phenomena in Eastern Europe as the result of a socialist economy built on the scarcity of resources. Such scarcity, she argues, meant that the chief problem was how to procure things. In this system, the locus of competition is not for customers but for connections with other buyers. Thus the procurers and customers must ingratiate themselves with suppliers rather than the other way around, as in capitalism.
3.   Markers of femininity such as dresses were attacked as exemplifications of bourgeois culture. Sexuality was also fraught with problems of bourgeois immorality. For example, young women who spent time with men inappropriately could be thrown into labor camps.
4.   It might be more accurate to state that no one who continued to believe in Cultural Revolution politics spoke with me. I eventually realized who these people were, both from the expression of barely suppressed contempt they exhibited toward me and from the way that management kept a close watch on them.
5.   Marshall Sahlins (1976) argued long ago that the division between culture and materiality resulted from the very system of capitalism.
6.   I am grateful to Jacqueline Brown for encouraging this line of analysis.
7.   Here one can see how gendered representations of embodied skill arbitrarily divide not just women from men but certain categories of women, in this case "peasant," from other categories, such as "urban."
8.   Since the early 1990s, the government has basically abandoned any effort to keep people from the countryside out of the major cities.
9.   See, for example, Judith Butler (1993), who argues that heterosexual regimes produce the abject "queers" who unsettle the norms of heterosexuality, or Homi Bhabha (1994a), who contends that colonial discourses produce mimetic

colonial subjects who create a third space of ambivalence because of the impossibility within a colonial regime that the colonized other would ever become a perfect imitation of the colonial self.

CHAPTER 6. YEARNINGS

1.   For a more detailed discussion of *Yearnings*, see Zha 1992 and Rofel 1994.

2.   See also McClintock 1995 for a discussion of abjection that creatively moves it into the realm of colonialism and capitalism.

3.   As with the woman whose story was the focus of chapter 4, I spent many years pondering the issues of confidentiality before deciding to write down the story of SJX. In retrospect, I believe the romantic view of politics we shared exaggerated our need for secrecy, though the state's Fellini-esque interpretations of public security might have reached down into my notes. At this point, however, SJX has left his original work unit, has cultivated an excellent relationship with the police in the aftermath of the 1989 Tiananmen demonstrations, and has not, to my knowledge, been involved in any political trouble. This story, I hope, could only provide him with pleasurable memories.

4.   This statement of desire reflects a pervasive poetics of narrating success in everyday talk as well as in mass media in post-Mao China.

5.   For examples of this kind of literature, see X. Zhang 1986; C. Zhang 1990; Zhu 1988.

6.   Hong Kong writer Sun Longji, in his popular and widely read study titled *The Deep Structure of Chinese Culture* (1983), borrows from Lévi-Strauss to attribute this problem of what he labels the "eunuchization" of Chinese men to Chinese culture *tout court*.

7.   Though not explicitly noted in either sympathetic or critical analyses of these works, it is evident that the masculinity being created is imagined in the context of a global cultural economy in which China, and Chinese men, have been feminized in relation to the masculine West. R. Chow (1991b) theorizes this issue more generally.

8.   For example, Zhang Xianliang's *Half of Man Is Woman* (1986) was an enormously popular and controversial novel and then play about one man's political suffering at the hands of the state. Zhong Xueping (1994) has argued that the story equates male suffering—the main character's inability to possess a woman and therefore his inability to possess the body politic—with the suffering of the entire nation. Zhong Xueping herself has been attacked by Chinese male intellectuals who have accused her of inserting divisive gender politics into what they argue is a unified political critique.

CHAPTER 7. ALLEGORIES OF POSTSOCIALISM

1.   See Honig and Hershatter 1988 for a discussion of gender in Chinese popular culture in the early years of economic reform.

2.   Freudian theory, which has become increasingly pervasive in China, provides a discursive framework about sexual repression that reinforces this allegory of political repression.

3.   Rey Chow (1991b) addresses this issue by arguing that Chinese people have always had an interior psyche that bespeaks their sexual desires and sexual identities as modern subjects. I take the invention of the psyche to be one of the more compelling means of asserting a modern subjectivity.

4.   Women writers have similarly created a space for difference in their writings (Li Ziyun 1992). See also Barlow 1994.

5.   Zhu Di, "Liangci Liyihoude chuangtong yü Sisuo" (The traumas and reflection after two divorces), Zhiyin (An understanding friend) 3 (1986): 12–13.

6.   Much of the controversy over maternity leave in China is over the way many workplaces have pushed women out by pressuring them to take extended leave. But the silk industry, because it is both short of labor and a "women's" industry, cannot afford this strategy.

7.   One finds direct discussion of socialist labor along these lines in the writings of sociologist Michael Burawoy (1985). The more general political economic approach, which separates materiality from culture, once invigorated important anthropological discussions of world systems. I find it reincarnated in analyses of global capitalism.

8.   Aihwa Ong (1997) terms the use of family in Asian capitalist networks a form of "family governmentality."

9.   Xin Guancha (New outlook), no. 7, 10 April 1986, p. 22.

10.   "Cosmetics Beautify and Benefit Beijing," China Daily, 11 March 1986, p. 8.

11.   The government established Television University in the early 1980s, encouraging those who had received no formal education during the Cultural Revolution to study courses offered for credit through the television bureau.

12.   Wang Anyi, Love in a Small Town (1988:19–20, 37). Wang Anyi is a well-known and controversial Shanghai writer.

13.   Wang Mingzhen, "Re'aide Youli" (Love's travels), Qingnian Yidai (The young generation), no. 6 (1990): 28–29.

14.   By the late 1980s and certainly the early 1990s, a popular critique of state corruption linked to the corrupting influence of money and the marketplace had spawned nostalgia for the virtues of the Maoist era that have been lost in the present. See Dai 1996, 1997.

15.   I follow Foucault (1980) in this regard.

16.   Yang Li, ed., *A Comprehensive Overview of Pregnancy and Maternal and Baby Hygiene* (1997: 3, 7-8).

17.   We should also note that the increased "floating" of people from the countryside into cities has created a significant segment of the population for whom it has become difficult for the government to regulate birth.

18.   By using the term "cultural citizenship," I mean to highlight how citizenship, or belonging to a nation-state, is not merely a political attribute but also a process in which culture becomes a relevant category of affinity.

19.   Sherry Ortner opened the way for these analyses in her classic anthropological essay "Is Female to Male as Nature Is to Culture?" (1974). Judith Butler (1993) makes this point in the language of philosophy. She deconstructs the foundationalism of gender by arguing that rather than providing the underlying basis or surface upon which gender is placed, the materiality of the "sex" of bodies is produced by highly gendered regulatory schemas.

20.   It is interesting to note that the abortion rate in the United States is virtually the same: 26.4 abortions for every 1,000 women of childbearing age (see *Abortion Policies* 1992-95). I am grateful to Tyrene White for providing this source.

21.   For an exception, see McClintock 1995.

CHAPTER 8. RETHINKING MODERNITY

1.   As will become evident later in this chapter, I mean "panopticon" metaphorically. Those who have contributed to the reassertion of a spatial perspective in contemporary social theory include Bourdieu 1977; Davis 1990; de Certeau 1984; Harvey 1989; Holston 1989; Jameson 1984; Moore 1986; Rabinow 1989; Soja 1989.

2.   The paraphrase of Kant is found in Foucault's 1961 doctoral thesis, "Introduction à l'anthropologie de Kant," as cited in Rabinow 1988:355.

3.   In this respect, it is critical to note the argument put forth by Timothy Mitchell (1988). While agreeing with Foucault on the function of the panopticon, Mitchell has argued that it was first invented by colonial regimes in colonial theaters such as the Ottoman Empire and then exported back to Europe. In colonial contexts, it created both modern western and nonmodern, non-western subjects, as it differentiated the populace into rulers and ruled.

4.   After the initial battles, many workers would come to work and then leave because lack of supplies left them with virtually nothing to do. These actions have also been reinterpreted as signifying laziness.

5.   Ann Anagnost (1989) has written of the analogous program in the countryside to individuate peasant households.

6.   In his otherwise excellent discussion of bourgeois distinctions in taste,

Pierre Bourdieu (1984) pays little attention to the decisive role of neocolonial hegemonies in the construction of European tastes.

7.   Taylorism, derived from F. W. Taylor's *Principles of Scientific Management* (1911), attempts to increase labor productivity by breaking down each labor process into component motions and organizing fragmented work tasks according to rigorous standards of time and motion study (see Noble 1977).

8.   This invocation of the character for "bow" recalls an earlier historical context, where the proper shape of the bound foot is compared to a bow. As with these factory techniques, footbinding, too, has a long history in colonial dialogues about China's fitness for modernity. See Gao Hongxing's *Canzu Shi* (History of footbinding) (1995:22). I am grateful to Angela Zito for this citation.

9.   Yet I would maintain that this form of disciplining is distinct from other forms found in the Maoist era. To lump them together as China's singular project of modernity would, I think, miss the specificities shaped by history. With the economic reform regime, for example, party cadres have turned to "psychology" as a repository of truths to be mined for thought work.

10.   A simultaneous western intellectual tradition of questioning the transparency of signs begins with Saussure (1986 [1916]) and continues through Derrida (1974). But the point of these authors is to question the correspondence between signifier and signified. They do not theorize about how writing might bring into existence the world. See Zito 1997 for an excellent discussion of these issues.

11.   This quip refers to inner-party struggles at the highest levels that became increasingly common knowledge near the end of the Cultural Revolution and led many people to feel manipulated by the very leaders whom they had followed—especially Mao Zedong.

12.   I am grateful to David Keightley for pointing this out to me. See Chang 1977; Pruitt 1979.

13.   Ida Pruitt writes of a Beijing gentry home: "There was, I knew, endless variety within the pattern in those compounds guarded by the great gates and by the spirit screens inside the gates and shielding them. Credited with keeping ghosts and demons from entering the compounds and wandering through the courtyards and house, the spirit screens effectively kept out the peering eyes of those who passed on the streets" (1979:10)

14.   One could contrast the metaphysics of display with Foucault's discussion of the visibility and invisibility of power (1979). Foucault used visibility/invisibility as yet another trope to capture the disjuncture between the sovereign state and the modern disciplinary state. In China, the same trope seems to apply, yet with the opposite associations.

15.   In the possession of *neibu* knowledge, the workings of a panoptic procedure begin to be discernible.

CODA

1.   For an important exception, see Ong 1998 on Chinese capitalists.

2.   Overlooked in the haste to capture the essence of this new world order is what the term "global capitalism" implies. Progressive critics have "forgotten" that capitalism has always been "global." This phrase, in contrast with the term "transnational capitalism," indicates not that capitalism has reached for the first time beyond its "original" boundaries but that its center of impetus has shifted— to Asia. Thus the politics of the term itself occlude the cultural and racial politics of capitalism.

3.   For some exceptions, see several of the essays in Ginsburg and Rapp 1995.

4.   See Katherine Verdery's description (1996) of gender politics in Eastern Europe for another compelling perspective on this phenomenon of hypermasculinity in the free market.

5.   See Dorinne Kondo's excellent critique (1997) of the novel and of Crichton's misuse of anthropology. Her criticisms are all the more compelling because of Crichton's misuse of her own work on Japanese culture.

6.   Lydia Liu's fascinating deconstruction of the television serial (1998) argues that it simultaneously produces transnationalism and postsocialism. Mayfair Yang (1997) reminds us that the melodrama was received in complex ways by television viewers in China, who interpreted the story as being about the possibilities of transnational mobility and the depiction of capitalism as war.

Bibliography

Abortion Policies: A Global Review. 1992–95. 3 vols. New York: United Nations.

Abu-Lughod, Lila. 1990. "The Romance of Resistance: Tracing Transformations of Power through Bedouin Women." *American Ethnologist* 17: 41–56.

———. 1993. *Writing Women's Worlds: Bedouin Stories.* Berkeley: University of California Press.

Ahmad, Aijaz. 1992. *In Theory: Classes, Nations, Literatures.* New York: Verso.

Alexander, Jacqui, and Chandra Talpade Mohanty, eds. 1997. *Feminist Genealogies, Colonial Legacies, Democratic Futures.* New York: Routledge.

Althusser, Louis. 1971. "Ideology and Ideological State Apparatuses (Notes towards an Investigation)." In *Lenin and Philosophy and Other Essays,* translated by Ben Brewster, 127–86. New York: Monthly Review Press.

Anagnost, Ann. 1989. "Prosperity and Counterprosperity: The Moral Discourse on Wealth in Post-Mao China." In *Marxism and the Chinese Experience,* edited by Arif Dirlik and Maurice Meisner, 210–34. Armonk, N.Y.: M. E. Sharpe.

———. 1992. "Who Is Speaking Here? Discursive Boundaries and Representation in Post-Mao China." Department of Anthropology, University of Washington. Photocopy.

———. 1995. "A Surfeit of Bodies: Population and the Rationality of the State in Post-Mao China." In *Conceiving the New World Order: The Global Politics of Reproduction,* edited by Faye D. Ginsburg and Rayna Rapp, 22–41. Berkeley: University of California Press.

———. 1997. *National Past-Times: Narrative, Representation, and Power in Modern China.* Durham, N.C.: Duke University Press.

Anderson, Benedict. 1991. *Imagined Communities.* Rev. ed. New York: Verso.

Andors, Phyllis. 1983. *The Unfinished Liberation of Chinese Women: 1949–1980.* Bloomington: Indiana University Press.

Anzaldúa, Gloria. 1987. *Borderlands/La Frontera: The New Mestiza.* San Francisco: Spinsters/Aunt Lute.

Appadurai, Arjun. 1996. *Modernity at Large: Cultural Dimensions of Globalization.* Minneapolis: University of Minnesota Press.

Apter, David. 1995. "Discourse as Power: Yan'an and the Chinese Revolution." In *New Perspectives on the Chinese Communist Revolution,* edited by Tony Saich and Hans van de Ven, 193–234. Armonk, N.Y.: M. E. Sharpe.

Asad, Talal. 1993. *Genealogies of Religion: Discipline and Reasons of Power in Christianity and Islam.* Baltimore: Johns Hopkins University Press.

Barlow, Tani. 1991a. "Theorizing Woman: *Funü, Guojia, Jiating* [Chinese Women, Chinese State, Chinese Family]." *Genders,* no. 10 (spring): 132–60.

———. 1991b. "Zhishifenzi (Chinese Intellectuals) and Power." *Dialectical Anthropology* 16: 209–32.

———. 1994. "Politics and Protocols of Funü: (Un)Making National Woman." In Gilmartin et al. 1994:339–59.

———. 1997. "Woman at the Close of the Maoist Era in the Polemics of Li Xiaojiang and Her Associates." In *The Politics of Culture in the Shadow of Capital,* edited by Lisa Lowe and David Lloyd, 506–43. Durham, N.C.: Duke University Press.

Barme, Geremie, and Bennett Lee, eds. 1979. *The Wounded: New Stories of the Cultural Revolution, 77–78.* Hong Kong: Joint Publishing.

Behar, Ruth, and Deborah A. Gordon, eds. 1995. *Women Writing Culture.* Berkeley: University of California Press.

Belden, Jack. 1949. *China Shakes the World.* New York: Monthly Review.

Benjamin, Walter. 1968. "Theses on the Philosophy of History." In *Illuminations,* edited by Hannah Arendt, translated by Harry Zohn, 153–64. New York: Schocken Books.

———. 1977. *The Origin of German Tragic Drama,* translated by John Osborne. London: Verso. (Originally published in German in 1963.)

Berlant, Lauren. 1997. *The Queen of America Goes to Washington City: Essays on Sex and Citizenship.* Durham, N.C.: Duke University Press.

Berman, Marshall. 1988. *All That Is Solid Melts Into Air: The Experience of Modernity.* New York: Penguin.

Bhabha, Homi. 1994a. "Conclusion: 'Race,' Time, and the Revision of Modernity." In *The Location of Culture,* 236–56. London: Routledge.

———. 1994b. "Of Mimicry and Man: The Ambivalence of Colonial Discourse." In *The Location of Culture,* 85–92. London: Routledge.

Billeter, Jean-Francois. 1985. "The System of 'Class Status.' " In *The Scope of State Power in China,* edited by Stuart R. Schram, 127–69. New York: St. Martin's Press.

Boddy, Janice. 1989. *Wombs and Alien Spirits: Women, Men, and the ZAR Cult in Northern Sudan.* Madison: University of Wisconsin Press.

Bourdieu, Pierre. 1977. *Outline of a Theory of Practice*, translated by Richard Nice. Cambridge: Cambridge University Press.

———. 1984. *Distinction: A Social Critique of the Judgement of Taste*, translated by Richard Nice. Cambridge, Mass.: Harvard University Press.

———. 1997. "Masculine Domination Revisited." *Berkeley Journal of Sociology* 41: 189–203.

Braverman, Harry. 1974. *Labor and Monopoly Capital*. New York: Monthly Review Press.

Briggs, Jean L. 1970. *Never in Anger: Portrait of an Eskimo Family*. Cambridge, Mass.: Harvard University Press.

Brown, Jacqueline. Forthcoming. "Black America, Black Liverpool and the Gendering of Diasporic Space." *Cultural Anthropology*.

Brown, Wendy. 1995. *States of Injury: Power and Freedom in Late Modernity*. Princeton: Princeton University Press.

Burawoy, Michael. 1985. *The Politics of Production: Factory Regimes under Capitalism and Socialism*. London: Verso.

Butler, Judith. 1989. *Gender Trouble: Feminism and the Subversion of Identity*. New York: Routledge.

———. 1993. *Bodies That Matter: On the Discursive Limits of "Sex."* New York: Routledge.

Butler, Judith, and Joan W. Scott, eds. 1992. *Feminists Theorize the Political*. New York: Routledge.

Cao Guilin. 1993. *Beijinger in New York*. San Francisco: Cypress Book Co.

Casey, Edward S. 1987. *Remembering: A Phenomenological Study*. Bloomington: Indiana University Press.

Caton, Steven. 1990. *"Peaks of Yemen I Summon": Poetry as Cultural Practice in a North Yemeni Tribe*. Berkeley: University of California Press.

Chakrabarty, Dipesh. 1989. *Rethinking Working-Class History: Bengal, 1890–1940*. Princeton: Princeton University Press.

———. 1992. "Postcoloniality and the Artifice of History: Who Speaks for 'Indian' Pasts?" *Representations*, no. 37 (winter): 1–26.

Chambers, Ross. 1991. *Room for Maneuver: Reading Oppositional Narrative*. Chicago: University of Chicago Press.

Chan, Anita, Richard Madsen, and Jonathan Unger. 1992. *Chen Village under Mao and Deng*. Berkeley: University of California Press.

Chang, K. C. 1977. *The Archaeology of Ancient China*. New Haven: Yale University Press.

Chatterjee, Partha. 1990. "A Response to Taylor's 'Modes of Civil Society.'" *Public Culture* 3(1): 119–32.

———. 1993. *The Nation and Its Fragments: Colonial and Postcolonial Histories*. Princeton: Princeton University Press.

Chow, Rey. 1991a. "Male Narcissism and National Culture: Subjectivity in

Chen Kaige's *King of the Children.*" *Camera Obscura,* no. 25/26 (January–May): 9–39.

———. 1991b. *Woman and Chinese Modernity: The Politics of Reading between West and East.* Minneapolis: University of Minnesota Press.

———. 1995. "The Politics of Admittance: Female Sexual Agency, Miscegenation, and the Formation of Community in Frantz Fanon." *The UTS Review* 1(1): 5–29.

Chow, Tse-tsung. 1960. *The May Fourth Movement: Intellectual Revolution in Modern China.* Cambridge, Mass.: Harvard University Press.

Chun, Allen. 1985. "Land Is to Live: A Study of the Concept of Tsu in a Hakka Village, New Territories, Hong Kong." Ph.D. diss., University of Chicago.

———. 1996. "The Lineage-village Complex in Southeastern China: A Long Footnote in the Anthropology of Kinship." *Current Anthropology* 37: 429–50.

Clayton, Cathryn. 1995. "Nationalism and Tradition in China." Anthropology Department, University of California, Santa Cruz. Photocopy.

Clifford, James. 1988. *The Predicament of Culture: Twentieth-Century Ethnography, Literature, and Art.* Cambridge, Mass.: Harvard University Press.

Clifford, James, and George Marcus, eds. 1986. *Writing Culture.* Berkeley: University of California Press.

Comaroff, Jean, and John Comaroff. 1991. *Of Revelation and Revolution: Christianity, Colonialism, and Consciousness in South Africa.* Chicago: University of Chicago Press.

———. 1993. Introduction to *Modernity and Its Discontents: Ritual and Power in Postcolonial Africa,* edited by Jean and John Comaroff, xi–xxxi. Chicago: University of Chicago Press.

Crichton, Michael. 1992. *The Rising Sun.* New York: Knopf.

Croll, Elisabeth. 1978. *Feminism and Socialism in China.* New York: Schocken Books.

Dai Jinhua. 1995. "Invisible Women: Contemporary Chinese Cinema and Women's Film." *positions: east asia cultures critique* 3: 255–80.

———. 1996. "Redemption and Consumption: Depicting Culture in the 1990s." *positions: east asia cultures critique* 4: 126–43.

———. 1997. "Imagined Nostalgia." In *Postmodernism and China,* edited by Arif Dirlik and Zhang Xudong. A special issue of *boundary 2* 24(3): 143–61.

Davin, Delia. 1976. *Woman-Work: Women and the Party in Revolutionary China.* Oxford: Clarendon Press.

Davis, Mike. 1990. *City of Quartz: Excavating the Future in Los Angeles.* London: Verso.

de Certeau, Michel. 1984. *The Practice of Everyday Life,* translated by Steven Rendall. Berkeley: University of California Press.

de Lauretis, Teresa. 1984. *Alice Doesn't: Feminism, Semiotics, Cinema.* Bloomington: Indiana University Press.

Derrida, Jacques. 1974. *Of Grammatology*, translated by Gayatri Chakravorty Spivak. Baltimore: Johns Hopkins University Press.

———. 1994. *Specters of Marx: The State of the Debt, the Work of Mourning, and the New International*, translated by Peggy Kamuf. New York: Routledge.

Dirks, Nicholas B. 1990. "History as a Sign of the Modern." *Public Culture* 2(2): 25–32.

———. 1992. Introduction to *Colonialism and Culture*, edited by Nicholas B. Dirks, 1–25. Ann Arbor: University of Michigan Press.

Dirlik, Arif. 1989. *The Origins of Chinese Communism*. New York: Oxford University Press.

———. 1994. *After the Revolution: Awakening to Global Capitalism*. Hanover, N.H.: Wesleyan University Press.

Donham, Donald. 1990. *History, Power, Ideology: Central Issues in Marxism and Anthropology*. Cambridge: Cambridge University Press.

Dreyfus, Hubert L., and Paul Rabinow. 1982. *Michel Foucault: Beyond Structuralism and Hermeneutics*. Chicago: University of Chicago Press.

Duara, Prasenjit. 1995. *Rescuing History from the Nation*. Chicago: University of Chicago Press.

Dutton, Michael. 1995. "Dreaming of Better Times: 'Repetition with a Difference' and Community Policing in China." *positions: east asia cultures critique* 3: 415–47.

Ebron, Paulla. 1997. "Traffic in Men: Gendered Encounters." In *Gendered Encounters and Sexual Hierarchies in Africa*, edited by Maria Grosz-Ngate and Omari Kokole, 223–44. New York: Routledge.

Escobar, Arturo. 1995. *Encountering Development: The Making and Unmaking of the Third World*. Princeton: Princeton University Press.

Evans-Pritchard, E. E. 1937. *Witchcraft, Oracles, and Magic among the Azande*. Oxford: Clarendon Press.

Fabian, Johannes. 1983. *Time and the Other: How Anthropology Makes Its Object*. New York: Columbia University Press.

Faubion, James. 1993. *Modern Greek Lessons: A Primer in Historical Constructivism*. Princeton: Princeton University Press.

Foucault, Michel. 1961. "Introduction à l'anthropologie de Kant." Thèse complementaire pour le Doctorat des Lettres, Université de Paris.

———. 1973. *The Order of Things: The Archaeology of the Human Sciences*. New York: Vintage.

———. 1975. *The Birth of the Clinic: An Archaeology of Medical Perception*, translated by A. M. Sheridan Smith. New York: Vintage.

———. 1979. *Discipline and Punish: The Birth of the Prison*, translated by Alan Sheridan. New York: Vintage.

———. 1980. *The History of Sexuality*. Vol. 1, *An Introduction*, translated by Robert Hurley. New York: Vintage.

Frankenberg, Ruth, and Mani Lata. 1993. "Crosscurrents, Crosstalk—Race, Postcoloniality, and the Politics of Location." *Cultural Studies* 7: 292–310.

Friedman, Edward. 1994. "Reconstructing China's National Identity: A Southern Alternative to Mao-Era Anti-Imperialist Nationalism." *Journal of Asian Studies* 53: 67–91.

Gagnier, Regenia. 1991. *Subjectivities: A History of Self-Representation in Britain, 1832–1920.* New York: Oxford University Press.

Gamst, F. G., ed. 1995. *The Meanings of Work.* New York: State University of New York Press.

Gao Hongxing. 1995. *Chanzu Shi* (The history of footbinding). Shanghai: Wenyi chubanshe.

Gee, James P., Glynda Hull, and Colin Lankshear. 1996. *The New Work Order: Behind the Language of the New Capitalism.* Boulder, Colo.: Westview Press.

Geertz, Clifford. 1988. *Works and Lives: The Anthropologist as Author.* Stanford: Stanford University Press.

Ghosh, Amitav. 1988. *The Shadow Lines.* New York: Penguin Books.

Gibson-Graham, J. K. 1996. *The End of Capitalism (as We Knew It): A Feminist Critique of Political Economy.* Cambridge, Mass.: Blackwell.

Gilmartin, Christina. 1995. *Engendering the Chinese Revolution: Radical Women, Communist Politics, and Mass Movements in the 1920s.* Berkeley: University of California Press.

Gilmartin, Christina K., Gail Hershatter, Lisa Rofel, and Tyrene White, eds. 1994. *Engendering China: Women, Culture, and the State.* Cambridge, Mass.: Harvard University Press.

Gilroy, Paul. 1993. *The Black Atlantic: Modernity and Double Consciousness.* Cambridge, Mass.: Harvard University Press.

Ginsburg, Faye D. 1989. *Contested Lives: The Abortion Debate in an American Community.* Berkeley: University of California Press.

Ginsburg, Faye D., and Rayna Rapp, eds. 1995. *Conceiving the New World Order: The Global Politics of Reproduction.* Berkeley: University of California Press.

Gramsci, Antonio. 1971. *Selections from the Prison Notebooks,* edited and translated by Quiton Hoare and Geoffrey Nowell Smith. New York: International Publishers.

Grewal, Inderpal, and Caren Kaplan, eds. 1994. *Scattered Hegemonies: Postmodernity and Transnational Feminist Practices.* Minneapolis: University of Minnesota Press.

Grieder, Jerome. 1981. *Intellectuals and the State in Modern China.* New York: Free Press.

Guha, Ranajit, and Gayatri Chakravorty Spivak, eds. 1988. *Selected Subaltern Studies.* New York: Oxford University Press.

Habermas, Jurgen. 1987. *The Philosophical Discourse of Modernity: Twelve Lectures,* translated by Frederick G. Lawrence. Oxford: Oxford University Press.

Hacking, Ian. 1991. "How Should We Do the History of Statistics?" In *The Foucault Effect: Studies in Governmentality*, edited by Graham Burchell, Colin Gordon, and Peter Miller, 181–96. Chicago: University of Chicago Press.

Hannerz, Ulf. 1989. "Notes on the Global Ecumene." *Public Culture* 1(2): 66–75.

Haraway, Donna J. 1985. "A Manifesto for Cyborgs: Science, Technology, and Socialist Feminism in the 1980s." *Socialist Review* 15(2): 65–107.

———. 1989. *Primate Visions: Gender, Race, and Nature in the World of Modern Science*. New York: Routledge.

———. 1991. *Simians, Cyborgs, and Women: The Reinvention of Nature*. New York: Routledge.

———. 1997. *Modest_Witness@Second_Millenium.FemaleMan_Meets_OncoMouse: Feminism and Technoscience*. New York: Routledge.

Harding, Harry. 1987. *China's Second Revolution: Reform after Mao*. Washington, D.C.: Brookings Institution.

Harding, Susan. 1987. "Convicted by the Holy Spirit: The Rhetoric of Fundamental Baptist Conversion." *American Ethnologist* 14(1): 167–81.

———. 1990. "If I Should Die Before I Wake: Jerry Falwell's Pro-Life Gospel." In *Uncertain Terms: Negotiating Gender in American Culture*, edited by Faye Ginsburg and Anna Lowenhaupt Tsing, 76–97. Boston: Beacon Press.

Harvey, David. 1989. *The Condition of Postmodernity*. London: Basil Blackwell.

Hershatter, Gail. 1986. *The Workers of Tianjin, 1900–1949*. Stanford: Stanford University Press.

———. 1995. "The Subaltern Talks Back: Reflections on Subaltern Theory and Chinese History." *positions: east asia cultures critique* 1: 103–30.

———. 1997. *Dangerous Pleasures: Prostitution and Modernity in Twentieth-Century Shanghai*. Berkeley: University of California Press.

Hevia, James. 1995. "The Scandal of Inequality: Koutou as Signifier." *Positions: East Asia Cultures Critique* 3: 97–118.

Hinton, William. 1966. *Fanshen: A Documentary of Revolution in a Chinese Village*. New York: Vintage.

Holston, James. 1989. *The Modernist City: An Anthropological Critique of Brasilia*. Chicago: University of Chicago Press.

Honig, Emily. 1984. "Private Issues, Public Discourse: The Life and Times of Yu Luojin." *Pacific Affairs* 57: 252–65.

———. 1986. *Sisters and Strangers: Women in the Shanghai Cotton Mills, 1919–1949*. Stanford: Stanford University Press.

Honig, Emily, and Gail Hershatter. 1988. *Personal Voices: Chinese Women in the 1980s*. Stanford: Stanford University Press.

Horn, David G. 1994. *Social Bodies: Science, Reproduction, and Italian Modernity*. Princeton: Princeton University Press.

Hoston, Germaine A. 1994. *The State, Identity, and the National Question in China and Japan.* Princeton: Princeton University Press.

Hsu, Immanuel. 1990. *The Rise of Modern China.* 4th ed. Oxford: Oxford University Press.

Hu, Ying. Forthcoming. *Tales of Translation: Composing the New Woman in China, 1898–1918.* Stanford: Stanford University Press.

Huntington, Samuel P. 1996. *The Clash of Civilizations and the Remaking of World Order.* New York: Simon and Schuster.

Huters, Theodore. 1996. "Appropriations: Another Look at Yan Fu and Western Ideas." *Xueren* (The scholar), no. 9 (April): 296–355.

Ivy, Marilyn. 1995. *Discourses of the Vanishing: Modernity, Phantasm, Japan.* Chicago: University of Chicago Press.

Jameson, Fredric. 1991. *Postmodernism, Or, the Cultural Logic of Late Capitalism.* Durham, N.C.: Duke University Press.

Jeffery, Lyn. 1995. "Qian/Quan: Money and Power among China's Nouveaux Riches." Ph.D. qualifying examination paper, University of California, Santa Cruz.

John, Mary E. 1996. *Discrepant Dislocations: Feminism, Theory, and Postcolonial Histories.* Berkeley: University of California Press.

Johnson, Kay Ann. 1983. *Women, the Family, and Peasant Revolution in China.* Chicago: University of Chicago Press.

Joyce, Patrick. 1987. *Historical Meanings of Work.* New York: Cambridge University Press.

Judd, Ellen. 1989. "Niangjia: Chinese Women and Their Natal Families." *Journal of Asian Studies* 48: 525–44.

Kelliher, Daniel Roy. 1992. *Peasant Power in China: The Era of Rural Reform, 1979–1987.* New Haven: Yale University Press.

Kingsolver, Anna. 1992. "Contested Livelihoods: Placing One Another in Cedar, Kentucky." *Anthropological Quarterly* 65(3): 128–36.

Kipnis, Andrew. 1995. " 'Face': An Adaptable Discourse of Social Surfaces." *positions: east asia cultures critique* 3: 119–48.

Kondo, Dorinne. 1990. *Crafting Selves: Power, Gender, and Discourses of Identity in a Japanese Workplace.* Chicago: University of Chicago Press.

———. 1997. *About Face: Performing Race in Fashion and Theater.* New York: Routledge.

Kraus, Richard. 1981. *Class Conflict in Chinese Socialism.* New York: Columbia University Press.

Kristeva, Julia. 1974. *Des Chinoises.* Paris: Des Femmes.

Kundera, Milan. 1985. *The Unbearable Lightness of Being,* translated by M. H. Heim. New York: Harper and Row.

Latour, Bruno. 1993. *We Have Never Been Modern,* translated by Catherine Porter. Cambridge, Mass.: Harvard University Press.

Lavie, Smadar. 1990. *The Poetics of Military Occupation: Mzeina Allegories of Bedouin Identity under Israeli and Egyptian Rule.* Berkeley: University of California Press.

Leach, Edmund Ronald. 1964. *Political Systems of Highland Burma: A Study of Kachin Social Structure.* London: Athlone Press.

Leitch, Alison. 1996. "The Life of Marble: The Experience and Meaning of Work in the Marble Quarries of Carrara (Italy)." *Australian Journal of Anthropology* 7(3): 235–57.

Li Xiaojiang. 1990. "Zouxiang nüren" (Toward woman). In *Du Yanling, Cong "ren" dao "nüren"* (From person to woman). Nüxing/Ren 4(9): 255–66.

———. 1994. "Economic Reform and the Awakening of Chinese Women's Collective Consciousness." In Gilmartin et al. 1994:360–84.

Li Ziyun. 1994. "Women's Consciousness and Women's Writing." In Gilmartin et al. 1994:299–317.

Liang, Heng, and Judith Shapiro. 1983. *Son of the Revolution.* New York: Random House.

Limón, José. 1994. *Dancing with the Devil: Society and Cultural Poetics in Mexican-American South Texas.* Madison: University of Wisconsin Press.

Lin, Yü-sheng. 1979. *The Crisis of Chinese Consciousness: Radical Anti-traditionalism in the May Fourth Era.* Madison: University of Wisconsin Press.

Liu, Kang, and Tang Xiaobing, eds. 1993. *Politics, Ideology, and Literary Discourse in Modern China.* Durham, N.C.: Duke University Press.

Liu, Lydia. 1991. "The Female Tradition in Modern Chinese Literature: Negotiating Feminisms across East/West Boundaries." *Genders,* no. 12 (winter): 22–44.

———. 1993. "Invention and Intervention: The Female Tradition in Modern Chinese Literature." In *Gender Politics in Modern China: Writing and Feminism,* edited by Tani E. Barlow, 33–57. Durham, N.C.: Duke University Press.

———. 1995. *Translingual Practice: Literature, National Culture, and Translated Modernity—China, 1900–1937.* Stanford: Stanford University Press.

———. 1998. *What's Happened to Ideology? Transnationalism, Postsocialism, and the Study of Global Media Culture.* Working Papers in Asian/Pacific Studies. Durham, N.C.: Duke University.

Lorde, Audre. 1986. "On my way out I passed over you and the Verrazano bridge." In *Our Dead behind Us.* New York: Norton.

Louie, Kam. 1991. "The Macho Eunuch: The Politics of Masculinity in Jia Pingwa's 'Human Extremities.' " *Modern China* 17(2): 163–87.

Lukács, Georg. 1971. "Reification and the Consciousness of the Proletariat." In *History and Class Consciousness: Studies in Marxist Dialectics,* translated by Rodney Livingstone, 83–222. Cambridge, Mass.: MIT Press.

Luo, Zi-ping. 1990. *A Generation Lost: China under the Cultural Revolution.* New York: Avon Books.

Mani, Lata. 1987. "Contentious Traditions: The Debate on SATI in Colonial India." *Cultural Critique,* no. 7 (fall): 119–56.

————. 1990. "Multiple Mediations: Feminist Scholarship in the Age of Multinational Reception." *Feminist Review* 35: 24–42.

Mann, Susan. 1994. "Learned Women in the Eighteenth Century." In Gilmartin et al. 1994:27–46.

Marcus, George. 1992. "Past, Present, and Emergent Identities: Requirements for Ethnographies of Late-Twentieth-Century Modernity Worldwide." In *Modernity and Identity,* edited by Scott Lash and Jonathan Friedman, 309–30. Cambridge, Mass.: Blackwell.

Martin, Emily. 1994. *Flexible Bodies: The Role of Immunity in American Culture from the Days of Polio to the Age of AIDS.* Boston: Beacon Press.

Marx, Karl. 1967. *Capital: A Critique of Political Economy.* 3 vols. New York: International Publishers. (First published in German in 1867, 1885, 1894.)

McClintock, Anne. 1995. *Imperial Leather: Race, Gender, and Sexuality in the Colonial Contest.* New York: Routledge.

Meng Yue and Dai Jinhua. 1990. *Fuchu Lishi Dibiao* (Floating up from the surface of history). Zhengzhou: Henan People's Press.

Miller, Daniel. 1997. *Capitalism: An Ethnographic Approach.* Oxford: Berg.

Mitchell, Juliet, and Jacqueline Rose, eds. 1985. *Feminine Sexuality: Jacques Lacan and the école freudienne,* translated by Jacqueline Rose. New York: Pantheon.

Mitchell, Timothy. 1990. "Everyday Metaphors of Power." *Theory and Society* 19: 545–77.

————. 1991. *Colonising Egypt.* Berkeley: University of California Press.

Miyazaki, Ichisada. 1976. *China's Examination Hell: The Civil Service Examinations of Imperial China,* translated by Conrad Schirokauer. New York: Weatherhill.

Mohanty, Chandra Talpade. 1991. "Under Western Eyes." In *Third World Women and the Politics of Feminism,* edited by Chandra Talpada Mohanty, Ann Russo, and Lourdes Torres, 51–80. Bloomington: Indiana University Press.

Mohanty, Chandra Talpade, Ann Russo, and Lourdes Torres, eds. 1991. *Third World Women and the Politics of Feminism.* Bloomington: Indiana University Press.

Moore, Henrietta. 1986. *Space, Text, and Gender: An Anthropological Study of the Marakwet of Kenya.* Cambridge: Cambridge University Press.

Noble, David F. 1977. *America by Design: Science, Technology, and the Rise of Corporate Capitalism.* New York: Knopf.

O'Hanlon, Rosalind. 1988. "Recovering the Subject: Subaltern Studies and Histories of Resistance in Colonial South Asia." *Modern Asian Studies* 22: 189–224.

Ong, Aihwa. 1987. *Spirits of Resistance and Capitalist Discipline*. Albany: State University of New York Press.

———. 1991. "The Gender and Labor Politics of Postmodernity." *Annual Review of Anthropology* 20: 279–309.

———. 1997. "Chinese Modernities: Narratives of Nation and Capitalism." In *The Cultural Politics of Modern Chinese Transnationalism*, edited by Aihwa Ong and Donald Nonini, 171–202. New York: Routledge.

———. 1998. *Flexible Citizenship: The Cultural Logics of Transnationality*. Durham, N.C.: Duke University Press.

Ortner, Sherry B. 1974. "Is Female to Male as Nature Is to Culture?" In *Woman, Culture, and Society*, edited by Michelle Rosaldo and Louise Lamphere, 67–87. Stanford: Stanford University Press.

Peña, Devon. 1997. *The Terror of the Machine: Technology, Work, Gender, and Ecology on the US-Mexico Border*. Austin: University of Texas Press.

Peri Rossi, Cristina. 1989. *The Ship of Fools*, translated by Psiche Hughes. New York/London: Reader's International.

Perry, Elizabeth. 1993. *Shanghai on Strike: The Politics of Chinese Labor*. Stanford: Stanford University Press.

———. 1995. "Working at Cross-Purposes: Shanghai Labor in the Cultural Revolution." Harvard University. Photocopy.

Porter, Theodore. 1986. *The Rise of Statistical Thinking, 1820–1900*. Princeton: Princeton University Press.

Povinelli, Elizabeth. 1993. *Labor's Lot: The Power, History, and Culture of Aboriginal Action*. Chicago: University of Chicago Press.

Prakash, Gyan. 1990. "Writing Post-Orientalist Histories of the Third World: Perspectives from Indian Historiography." *Comparative Studies in Society and History* 32: 383–408.

———. 1992. "Can the 'Subaltern' Ride? A Reply to O'Hanlon and Washbrook." *Comparative Studies in Society and History* 34: 168–84.

———. 1994. "Subaltern Studies as Postcolonial Criticism." *American Historical Review* 99: 1475–90.

Pred, Allan, and Michael John Watts. 1992. *Reworking Modernity: Capitalisms and Symbolic Discontent*. New Brunswick, N.J.: Rutgers University Press.

Price, Richard. 1983. *First Time: The Historical Vision of an Afro-American People*. Baltimore: Johns Hopkins University Press.

Pruitt, Ida. 1979. *Madame Yin: A Memoir of Peking Life*. Stanford: Stanford University Press.

Rabinow, Paul. 1988. "Beyond Ethnography: Anthropology as Nominalism." *Cultural Anthropology* 3: 355–63.

————. 1989. *French Modern: Norms and Forms of the Social Environment.* Cambridge, Mass.: MIT Press.

Renan, Ernest. 1990. "What Is a Nation?" In *Nation and Narration,* edited by Homi K. Bhabha, 8–22. New York: Routledge.

Roediger, David R. 1991. *The Wages of Whiteness: Race and the Making of the American Working Class.* New York: Verso.

Rofel, Lisa B. 1994. " 'Yearnings': Televisual Love and Melodramatic Politics in Contemporary China." *American Ethnologist* 21: 700–722.

Rosaldo, Renato. 1980. *Ilongot Headhunting, 1883–1974: A Study in Society and History.* Stanford: Stanford University Press.

————. 1989. *Culture and Truth: The Remaking of Social Analysis.* Boston: Beacon Press.

Rouse, Roger. 1992. "Making Sense of Settlement: Class Transformation, Cultural Struggle, and Transnationalism among Mexican Migrants in the United States." In *Towards a Transnational Perspective on Migration,* edited by Nina Glick Schiller, Linda Basch, and Cristina Blanc-Szanton, 25–52. Annals of the New York Academy of Sciences 645. New York: New York Academy of Science.

Sahlins, Marshall. 1976. *Culture and Practical Reason.* Chicago: University of Chicago Press.

————. 1985. *Islands of History.* Chicago: University of Chicago Press.

Saich, Tony, and Hans van de Ven, eds. 1995. *New Perspectives on the Chinese Communist Revolution.* Armonk, N.Y.: M. E. Sharpe.

Said, Edward. 1983. *The World, the Text, and the Critic.* Cambridge, Mass.: Harvard University Press.

————. 1985. "Orientalism Reconsidered." *Cultural Critique,* no. 1 (fall): 89–108.

Sakai, Naoki. 1988. "Modernity and Its Critique: The Problem of Universalism and Particularism." *South Atlantic Quarterly* 87: 475–504.

Saussure, Ferdinand de. 1986. *Course in General Linguistics,* edited by Charles Bally and Albert Sechehaye, translated by Roy Harris. LaSalle, Ill.: Open Court. (First published in French in 1916.)

Scott, David. 1994. *Formations of Ritual: Colonial and Anthropological Discourses on the Sinhala Yaktovil.* Minneapolis: University of Minnesota Press.

Scott, James. 1985. *Weapons of the Weak: Everyday Forms of Peasant Resistance.* New Haven: Yale University Press.

Scott, Joan Wallach. 1988a. *Gender and the Politics of History.* New York: Columbia University Press.

————. 1988b. "A Statistical Representation of Work: *La Statistique de l'industrie à Paris, 1847–1848.*" In Joan Scott 1988a:113–38.

————. 1988c. "Work Identities for Men and Women: The Politics of Work and Family in the Parisian Garment Trades in 1848." In Joan Scott 1988a:93–112.

———. 1992. "Experience." In *Feminists Theorize the Political*, edited by Judith Butler and Joan W. Scott, 22–40. New York: Routledge.

Shaw, Carolyn Martin. 1995. *Colonial Inscriptions: Race, Sex, and Class in Kenya.* Minneapolis: University of Minnesota Press.

Shih, Shu-mei. 1998. "The Lure of the Modern: Writing Modernism in Semicolonial China." East Asian Languages and Literature, UCLA. Photocopy.

Shohat, Ella. 1992. "Notes on the Post-Colonial." *Social Text*, nos. 31/32: 99–113.

Silber, Cathy. 1994. "From Daughter to Daughter-in-Law in the Women's Script of Southern Hunan." In Gilmartin et al. 1994:47–68.

Siu, Helen. 1989. *Agents and Victims in South China: Accomplices in Rural Revolution.* New Haven: Yale University Press.

Siu, Helen F., and Zelda Stern. 1983. *Mao's Harvest: Voices from China's New Generation.* Oxford: Oxford University Press.

Soja, Edward W. 1989. *Postmodern Geographies.* New York: Verso.

Spence, Jonathan D. 1990. *The Search for Modern China.* New York: Norton.

Spivak, Gayatri Chakravorty. 1987. *In Other Worlds: Essays in Cultural Politics.* New York: Routledge.

———. 1988. "Can the Subaltern Speak?" In *Marxism and the Interpretation of Culture*, edited by Cary Nelson and Lawrence Grossberg, 271–313. Chicago: University of Illinois Press.

———. 1990. *The Post-Colonial Critic: Interviews, Strategies, Dialogues*, edited by Sarah Harasym. New York: Routledge.

———. 1991. "Feminism in Decolonization." *differences* 3(3): 139–70.

Stacey, Judith. 1983. *Patriarchy and Socialist Revolution in China.* Berkeley: University of California Press.

Starn, Orin. 1995. "To Revolt against the Revolution: War and Resistance in Peru's Andes." *Cultural Anthropology* 10: 547–80.

Steedly, Mary. 1993. *Hanging without a Rope: Narrative Experience in Colonial and Postcolonial Karoland.* Princeton: Princeton University Press.

Steedman, Carolyn. 1986. *Landscape for a Good Woman: A Story of Two Lives.* London: Virago.

Stewart, Kathleen. 1988. "Nostalgia—A Polemic." *Cultural Anthropology* 3: 227–41.

———. 1996. *A Space on the Side of the Road: Cultural Poetics in an "Other" America.* Princeton: Princeton University Press.

Stewart, Susan. 1993. *On Longing: Narratives of the Miniature, the Gigantic, the Souvenir, the Collection.* Durham, N.C.: Duke University Press.

Stoler, Ann Laura. 1995. *Race and the Education of Desire: Foucault's "History of Sexuality" and the Colonial Order of Things.* Durham, N.C.: Duke University Press.

Strathern, Marilyn. 1988. *The Gender of the Gift*. Berkeley: University of California Press.

———. 1992. *After Nature: English Kinship in the Late Twentieth Century*. Cambridge: Cambridge University Press.

Su Xiaokang and Wang Luxiang. 1991. *Deathsong of the River*, translated by Richard W. Bodman and Pin P. Wan. Cornell East Asia Series. Ithaca: East Asia Program, Cornell University.

Sun Longji. 1983. *Zhongguo Wenhuade Shengceng Jiegou* (The deep structure of Chinese culture). Hong Kong: Jixianshe.

Taussig, Michael. 1987. *Shamanism, Colonialism, and the Wild Man: A Study in Terror and Healing*. Chicago: University of Chicago Press.

———. 1992. "Maleficium: State Fetishism." In *The Nervous System*, 111–40. New York: Routledge.

———. 1997. *The Magic of the State*. New York: Routledge.

Thompson, E. P. 1963. *The Making of the English Working Class*. London: Gollancz.

Trinh, T. Minh-ha. 1989. *Woman, Native, Other: Writing Postcoloniality and Feminism*. Bloomington: Indiana University Press.

Tsing, Anna Lowenhaupt. 1990. "Monster Stories: Women Charged with Perinatal Endangerment." In *Uncertain Terms: Negotiating Gender in American Culture*, edited by Faye Ginsburg and Anna Lowenhaupt Tsing, 282–99. Boston: Beacon Press.

———. 1993. *In the Realm of the Diamond Queen: Marginality in an Out-of-the-Way Place*. Princeton: Princeton University Press.

Van de Ven, Hans. 1995. Introduction to *New Perspectives on the Chinese Communist Revolution*, edited by Tony Saich and Hans Van de Ven, xiii–xxii. Armonk, N.Y.: M. E. Sharpe.

Verdery, Katherine. 1996. *What Was Socialism, and What Comes Next?* Princeton: Princeton University Press.

Visweswaran, Kamala. 1994. *Fictions of Feminist Ethnography*. Minneapolis: University of Minnesota Press.

Walder, Andrew G. 1987. "Wage Reform and the Web of Factory Interests." *China Quarterly*, no. 109 (March): 22–42.

———. 1991. "Workers, Managers, and the State: The Reform Era and the Political Crisis of 1989." *China Quarterly*, no. 127 (September): 467–92.

Wang Anyi. 1988. *Love in a Small Town*, translated by Eva Hung. Hong Kong: Renditions.

Wang, Yuejin. 1989. "Mixing Memory and Desire: *Red Sorghum*—A Chinese Version of Masculinity and Femininity." *Public Culture* 2(1): 31–53.

Watson, James L., ed. 1984. *Class and Social Stratification in Post-Revolution China*. Cambridge: Cambridge University Press.

Watson, Rubie. 1985. *Inequality among Brothers: Class and Kinship in South China.* New York: Cambridge University Press.

Watson, Rubie, and Patricia Buckley Ebrey, eds. 1991. *Marriage and Inequality in Chinese Society.* Berkeley: University of California Press.

Weber, Max. 1968. *Economy and Society: An Outline of Interpretive Sociology,* edited by Guenther Ross and Claus Wittich, translated by Ephraim Fischoff et al. New York: Bedminster Press. (First published in German in 1922.)

White, E. Frances. 1990. "Africa on My Mind: Gender, Counter-Discourse, and African-American Nationalism." *Journal of Women's History* 2: 73–97.

White, Gordon. 1976. *The Politics of Class and Class Origin: The Case of the Cultural Revolution.* Canberra: Australian National University Press.

———. 1993. *Riding the Tiger: The Politics of Economic Reform in Post-Mao China.* Stanford: Stanford University Press.

White, Hayden. 1987. *The Content of the Form: Narrative Discourse and Historical Representation.* Baltimore: Johns Hopkins University Press.

White, Tyrene. 1992. *Family Planning in China.* Armonk, N.Y.: M. E. Sharpe.

Williams, Brackette. 1995. "Classification Systems Revisited: Kinship, Caste, Race, and Nationality as the Flow of Blood and the Spread of Rights." In *Naturalizing Power: Essays in Feminist Cultural Analysis,* edited by Sylvia Yanagisako and Carol Delaney, 201–36. New York: Routledge.

Williams, Raymond. 1977. *Marxism and Literature.* Oxford: Oxford University Press.

Wolf, Arthur, and Chieh-Shan Huang. 1980. *Marriage and Adoption in China, 1845–1945.* Stanford: Stanford University Press.

Wolf, Eric. 1982. *Europe and the People without History.* Berkeley: University of California Press.

Wolf, Margery. 1968. *The House of Lim: A Study of a Chinese Farm Family.* Englewood Cliffs, N.J.: Prentice-Hall.

———. 1972. *Women and the Family in Rural Taiwan.* Stanford: Stanford University Press.

———. 1985. *Revolution Postponed: Women in Contemporary China.* Stanford: Stanford University Press.

Yanagisako, Sylvia. 1985. *Transforming the Past: Tradition and Kinship among Japanese Americans.* Stanford: Stanford University Press.

———. 1987. "Mixed Metaphors: Native and Anthropological Models of Gender and Kinship Domains." In *Gender and Kinship: Essays toward a Unified Analysis,* edited by Jane Fishburne Collier and Sylvia Junko Yanagisako, 86–118. Stanford: Stanford University Press.

———. 1997. "Sexuality and Gender and Other Intersections." In *Das Dreifach Dilemma der Differenz,* edited by Sabine Strasser. Vienna: Winere Frauenverlag.

Yanagisako, Sylvia, and Carol Delaney, eds. 1995. *Naturalizing Power: Essays in Feminist Cultural Analysis.* New York: Routledge.

Yang Li, ed. 1997. *A Comprehensive Overview of Pregnancy and Maternal and Baby Hygiene.* Tianjin: Tianjin Science and Technology Translation Company.

Yang, Mayfair Mei-hui. 1988. "The Modernity of Power in the Chinese Socialist Order." *Cultural Anthropology* 3: 408–27.

————. 1994. *Gifts, Favors, and Banquets: The Art of Social Relationships in China.* Ithaca: Cornell University Press.

————. 1997. "Mass Media and Transnational Subjectivity in Shanghai: Notes on (Re)Cosmopolitanism in a Chinese Metropolis." In *The Cultural Politics of Modern Chinese Transnationalism,* edited by Aihwa Ong and Donald Nonini, 287–319. New York: Routledge.

————. 1998a. "From Gender Erasure to Gender Difference: State Feminism, Consumer Sexuality, and a Women's Public Sphere in China." In *Spaces of Their Own: Women's Public Sphere in Transnational China,* edited by Mayfair Yang. Minneapolis: University of Minnesota Press.

————. 1998b. Introduction to *Spaces of Their Own: Women's Public Sphere in Transnational China,* edited by Mayfair Yang. Minneapolis: University of Minnesota Press.

Yoneyama, Lisa. 1994. "Taming the Memoryscape: Hiroshima's Urban Renewal." In *Remapping Memory: The Politics of Timespace,* edited by Jonathan Boyarin, 99–135. Minneapolis: University of Minnesota Press.

Young, Robert. 1990. *White Mythologies: Writing History and the West.* New York: Routledge.

Zha, Jianying. 1992. "*Yearnings: Public Culture in a Post-Tiananmen Era.*" *Transition* 57: 26–51.

Zhang Chengzhi. 1990. *The Black Steed,* translated by Stephen Fleming. Beijing: Chinese Literature Press.

Zhang Xianliang. 1986. *Half of Man Is Woman,* translated by Martha Avery. New York: Norton.

Zhong, Xueping. 1994. "Male Suffering and Male Desire: Politics of Reading *Half of Man Is Woman* by Zhang Xianliang." In Gilmartin et al. 1994:175–94.

Zhu, Hong. 1988. *The Chinese Western.* New York: Ballantine Books.

Zito, Angela. 1992. "Bound to be Represented: Fetishizing Footbinding." Paper presented at American Anthropological Association meeting, San Francisco (November).

————. 1994. "Silk and Skin: Significant Boundaries." In *Body, Subject, and Power in China,* edited by Angela Zito and Tani E. Barlow, 103–30. Chicago: University of Chicago Press.

————. 1997. *Of Body and Brush: Grand Sacrifice as Text/Performance in Eighteenth-Century China.* Chicago: University of Chicago Press.

Index

Index: Margie Towery
Maps: Deborah Reade
Composition: Binghamton Valley Composition
Text: 10/14 Palatino
Display: Snell Roundhand Script and Bauer Bodoni
Printing and binding: Maple-Vail Book Manufacturing Group